HOLMES' OWN STORY
Confessed 27 Murders - Lied then Died

HOLMES' OWN STORY

Confessed 27 Murders - Lied then Died

JD Crighton and
Herman W. Mudgett, M. D.

Eighty-Seven (87) Rare Historical
Illustrations and Photos with Sources

Copyright © 2016 JD Crighton. All rights reserved.
www.jdcrighton.com
Cover design by Kristin N. Spencer

Eighty-Seven (87) Rare Historical Illustrations and Photos restored and sourced. To the Reader, Lied then Died, Bibliography, Notes, and Index by JD Crighton. *Holmes' Own Story*, by Herman W. Mudgett, M. D., *alias* H. H. Holmes, first published in 1895 by Burke & McFetridge Co. Confessed 27 Murders, by H. H. Holmes, first published in 1896 by *Philadelphia Inquirer*.

Published by Aerobear Classics
Murrieta, CA USA

PUBLISHER'S CATALOGING-IN-PUBLICATION DATA:

Names: Crighton, JD, author. | Mudgett, Herman W., 1861-1896, author.
Title: Holmes' own story : confessed 27 murders, lied then died / JD Crighton ; Herman W. Mudgett, M. D.
Description: Murrieta, CA : Aerobear Classics, 2016. | Includes bibliographical references and index.
Identifiers: LCCN 2016959542 | ISBN 978-1-946100-01-6 (pbk.) | ISBN 978-1-946100-00-9 (ebook) | 978-1-946100-06-1 (lrg prnt pbk.)
Subjects: LCSH: Mudgett, Herman W., 1861-1896. | Geyer, Frank P. | Serial murderers--Illinois--Chicago. | Chicago (Ill.)--History--1875- | Biographical sources. | BISAC: TRUE CRIME / Murder / Serial Killers. | HISTORY / United States / State & Local / Midwest (IA, IL, IN, KS, MI, MN, MO, ND, NE, OH, SD, WI) | HISTORY / United States / 19th Century.
Classification: LCC HV6248.M8 C751 2016 (print) | LCC HV6248.M8 (ebook) | DDC 364.152/32--dc23.

Contents

List of Illustrations	vii
TO THE READER	2
HOLMES' OWN STORY	6
Handwritten Statement	7
Holmes' Preface	8
Holmes' Own Story	11
Moyamensing Prison Diary Appendix	158
CONFESSED 27 MURDERS	190
The Tale of the Greatest Criminal in History	195
Murder 1: Dr. Robert Leacock	199
Murder 2: Dr. Russell	203
Murders 3, 4: Mrs. Julia L. Connor, Daughter Pearl	204
Murder 5: Rogers	207
Murder 6: Charles Cole	208
Murder 7: Lizzie	209
Murders 8, 9, 10: Mrs. Sarah Cook, Baby, Niece	210
Murder 11: Miss Emeline Cigrand	211
Three Unsuccessful Attempts of Triple Murder	217
Murder 12: Miss Rosine Van Jassand	218
Murder 13: Robert Latimer	220
Murder 14: Miss Anna Betts	221
Murder 15: Miss Gertrude Conner	222
Murder 16: Miss Kate Durkee	223
Murder 17: Mr. Warner	224
Murder 18: Rogers, A Young Englishman	226
Murder 19: A Female Boarder	228
Murders 20, 21: Minnie and Nannie Williams	229
Murder 22: Unknown Chicago Man	234
Murder 23: Baldwin Williams	235
Murder 24: Benjamin F. Pitezel	236

Murder 25: Howard Pitezel	244
Murders 26, 27: Alice and Nellie Pitezel	249
Attempted Murder of Mrs. Pitezel, Two Children	255
Conclusion of Confession	257
Statement from Detective Geyer	272
LIED THEN DIED	275
Judgment Day - Thursday, May 7, 1896	277
Concrete Burial - Friday, May 8, 1896	282
Holmes' Reincarnation?	286
Illustration Credits	288
Bibliography	293
Notes	296
Index	303
Other Books by This Author	321

List of Illustrations

Fig. 1. Handwritten Statement by Holmes	7
Fig. 2. H. H. Holmes Portrait	9
Fig. 3. Various Illustrations of Holmes	10
Fig. 4. Herman Mudgett Birth Certificate	17
Fig. 5. Gilmanton Academy, New Hampshire	18
Fig. 6. Degrees, University of Michigan	20
Fig. 7. Benjamin F. Pitezel	27
Fig. 8. Benjamin F. Pitezel, c1888	28
Fig. 9. Benjamin Pitezel's Patent	33
Fig. 10. Emeline Cigrand	37
Fig. 11. ABC Copier Company Listing	38
Fig. 12. Nannie Williams	45
Fig. 13. Floor Plan, Nannie Williams	48
Fig. 14. Mrs. Pitezel	67
Fig. 15. Benjamin Pitezel Arrested, Newsclip	69
Fig. 16. A Smiling Marion Hedgepeth	82
Fig. 17. Marion Hedgepeth, No. 11,205	83
Fig. 18. Jeptha D. Howe, St. Louis Attorney	84
Fig. 19. Holmes Burning Pitezel's Clothing	94
Fig. 20. Mercantile Library, Philadelphia	95
Fig. 21. Callowhill Street House in Philadelphia	102
Fig. 22. Callowhill Street House Photo, 1894	103
Fig. 23. News clip of B. F. Perry Found Dead	103
Fig. 24. Holmes' Castle	106
Fig. 25. Holmes' Castle, 1896	107
Fig. 26. Holmes' Castle, 1937	108
Fig. 27. Alice Pitezel	115
Fig. 28. Alice Pitezel Photo	116
Fig. 29. Howard Pitezel	128
Fig. 30. Howard Pitezel Photo	129

Fig. 31. Nellie Pitezel	134
Fig. 32. Nellie Pitezel Photo	135
Fig. 33. Minnie R. Williams	136
Fig. 34. Albion Hotel in Toronto, Canada	138
Fig. 35. Ophir La Forrest Perry, Fidelity Mutual	156
Fig. 36. William B. Watts, Pinkerton Agency	157
Fig. 37. Moyamensing Prison	159
Fig. 38. Philadelphia City Hall, 1884	160
Fig. 39. William A. Shoemaker, Attorney	161
Fig. 40. Mrs. Pitezel and Children in Jail	163
Fig. 41. Georgiana Yoke, Holmes' Third Wife	188
Fig. 42. Samuel P. Rotan, Attorney	189
Fig. 43. Confession, *Philadelphia Inquirer*	191
Fig. 44. Holmes' Denial, *Philadelphia Inquirer*	192
Fig. 45. Herman Mudgett, *alias* H. H. Holmes	193
Fig. 46. Holmes Writes Confession	194
Fig. 47. Dr. Robert Leacock	201
Fig. 48. Dr. Robert Leacock Death	202
Fig. 49. Mrs. Julia Connor	205
Fig. 50. Pearl Connor	206
Fig. 51. Emeline Cigrand Illustration	215
Fig. 52. Campbell-Yates Company	216
Fig. 53. Emily Van Tassel	219
Fig. 54. Holmes Murders Mr. Warner	225
Fig. 55. Minnie Williams	232
Fig. 56. Nannie Williams	233
Fig. 57. Benjamin F. Pitezel	241
Fig. 58. Callowhill Street House	242
Fig. 59. Room, Pitezel's Body Found	243
Fig. 60. Howard Pitezel	247
Fig. 61. The Irvington Cottage	248
Fig. 62. Alice Pitezel	251

Fig. 63. Nellie Pitezel	252
Fig. 64. Holmes Murders Pitezel Girls	253
Fig. 65. The Vincent Street House	254
Fig. 66. Mrs. Pitezel	256
Fig. 67. Holmes' Signature	257
Fig. 68. Holmes' Castle	258
Fig. 69. Plan of Holmes' Castle	259
Fig. 70. Stove and False Safe in the Castle	260
Fig. 71. Gas Oven in the Castle	261
Fig. 72. Trap Door in the Castle	262
Fig. 73. Gas Tank in the Castle	263
Fig. 74. M. G. Chappell, Articulator	264
Fig. 75. Assistant District Attorney Barlow	265
Fig. 76. District Attorney George S. Graham	266
Fig. 77. Miss Yoke, Holmes' Third Wife	267
Fig. 78. Pat Quinlan, Holmes' Janitor at the Castle	268
Fig. 79. A Young Patrick Quinlan	269
Fig. 80. President Fouse, Fidelity Mutual	270
Fig. 81. Detective Frank P. Geyer	273
Fig. 82. Detective Frank P. Geyer Photo	274
Fig. 83. Holmes March to the Scaffold	278
Fig. 84. Holmes' Final Address Before Execution	279
Fig. 85. Holmes at the Scaffold	280
Fig. 86. Mudgett/Holmes' Death Certificate	284
Fig. 87. Mudgett/Holmes' Registration of Death	285

TO THE READER

This book is a fascinating look into the mind of one of America's first serial killers, H. H. Holmes, featured in Erik Larson's popular book, *The Devil in the White City*. Holmes built a three story 'Murder Castle' with secret rooms, vaults, furnaces, and dissection tables to kill unsuspecting men, women and children. He tortured and gassed victims and used chloroform and powerful acids. Holmes took advantage of the Chicago World's Columbian Exposition in 1893 by advertising rooms and offering employment opportunities to lure his victims.

After authorities indicted Holmes for the murder of his friend and business partner, Benjamin Pitezel, Chicago police searched the Castle and found disturbing evidence of murder. According to Robert Corbitt, a reporter allowed in the Castle during the investigation, police found human ribs in a fire clay stove, a metallic bar of a woman's hand satchel, and a woman's shoe. They also found a bottle of carbolic acid, pearl buttons, an ink bottle thought to be that of Minnie R. Williams, dress fragments stuck to the inside of the stove, and hair in the hole of the stove pipe.[1]

News agencies reported seeing blood on Castle walls, woodwork, and clothing. Police confirmed they found blood leading across the floor of Minnie R. Williams room to the bathroom. From there, the trail led to the secret trap in the bathroom and down the stairs to the basement. In Mrs. Connor's dining room, police found bloody fingerprints.[2]

No doubt about it, Holmes earned despicable nicknames such as Arch Fiend, Butcher, Modern Bluebeard, Swindler, and Moral Degenerate. Holmes was a monster in disguise as a doctor, a perfect ruse to lure his victims. After all, who would not trust a doctor?

This project came about while I researched Holmes for several nonfiction books. A few documents related to him were difficult to read, especially his memoir, *Holmes' Own Story* and his *Philadelphia Inquirer* confession of 27 murders. Both original documents had long paragraphs and low quality photos and illustrations. While I found some online books recreated the two documents, I also found text, illustrations, and photos added without their associated sources, which made it difficult to determine what the original was and what was added, without comparing the original works side-by-side. This compelled me to write a sourced book related to H. H. Holmes.

In the following pages, you will find three parts to Holmes' complicated story: *Holmes' Own Story, Confessed 27 Murders,* and *Lied then Died.*

Eighty-seven rare historical illustrations and photographs are in the book, which include Holmes birth and death certificates, Benjamin Pitezel's patent, and more. I restored all illustrations and photographs to remove debris and artifacts and identified a source for each. All that were not in the original *Holmes' Own Story* and *Confessed 27 Murders* text will be easy to spot as they include their sources.

For Parts One and Two, I left long sentences intact to preserve original text and meaning. I apologize in advance if those two parts make a difficult read for you. Holmes had a tendency to write sentences the length of a paragraph. To make for an easier read, I shortened paragraphs but under no circumstances did I change or delete original text. Words common for the 1800's were left as is. Obvious misspellings will have [sic] after the misspelled word or the correct word inside brackets. For example: "I were [sic] born in Gilmanton, New Hampshire," or "Benjamin Pitzel [Pitezel] was dead."

Part One: *Holmes' Own Story* is a memoir penned while Holmes awaited trial for the murder of Benjamin Pitezel. Holmes wrote his memoir to exonerate himself from Benjamin's murder and do away with suspicion of others. In the memoir, Holmes encouraged detectives to use the chronological account of his life as an investigation tool. But, there were three major issues. First, in typical Holmes style, some of his confession included outright lies and half-truths. Second, Holmes avoided discussion of his only legal wife, Clara, and their son, Robert Lovering Mudgett. Third, Holmes left out information about his bigamous marriage to Myrta Z. Belknap, and their beautiful daughter Lucy Theodate Holmes. Like other aspects of his life, the exclusions of his wives and children were strategic and purposeful. It was to substantiate his marriage to his third wife, Georgiana Yoke, to prevent her from testifying against him at trial.

Holmes wrote about an elaborate scheme to fake Benjamin Pitezel's death and his extensive movement across the United States and Canada with three separate groups of people. Holmes and his new wife, Georgiana, traveled in one group. Holmes and the three Pitezel children, Alice, Nellie, and Howard traveled in a second group. And Mrs. Pitezel and her two remaining children, Nellie and baby Horton, traveled in the third group. Holmes controlled all three groups, who were completely unaware of the nearby presence of each other. For example, Holmes would register himself and the three children at one hotel, then register himself and his wife at another, while Mrs. Pitezel and her remaining two children registered at still another.

To divert authorities away from himself as a suspect, Holmes introduced a man named Hatch. He claimed Hatch took charge of the Pitezel children at times when the children went missing. He also hinted Hatch may have had a motive, for Holmes said he gave Alice $500 and told her to hide it in her dress.

At the end of his memoir, you will find Holmes' Moyamensing Prison diary. In it, Holmes wrote about daily prison life and his reaction to the discovery of the three missing Pitezel children. He also wrote about lack of motives and why he didn't murder the children or anyone else. To drive home his key points, he wrote about issues with photographic identification.

Part Two: *Confessed 27 Murders* is the complete confession written by Holmes and published in *Philadelphia Inquirer* two weeks before his execution. William Randolph Hearst, owner of the *New York Morning Journal*, teamed up with James Elverson, Jr., General Manager of the *Philadelphia Inquirer* to copyright Holmes' confession. They placed a notice in the *Inquirer*, April 11, 1896, announcing the confession would appear the next day. The notice stated the following:

"The Inquirer has gone to great trouble and expense to lay before its readers the story, in fact, the autobiography of the greatest criminal perhaps that the world has produced. The confession is copyrighted, and The Inquirer hereby gives notice that it will prosecute any newspaper attempting to infringe on its rights in any way."[3]

Superintendent Perkins verified the *Philadelphia Inquirer* confession was the only valid confession, "We have a full knowledge of all communications which are sent out of the prison by inmates, and The Inquirer has the only genuine Holmes confession."[4]

Hearst, Elverson, or both paid Holmes a handsome fee, reportedly between $5,000 and $7,500, which was said to have been for his eighteen-year-old son, Robert Lovering Mudgett. A version of the confession was printed in Hearst's paper, the *New York Morning Journal* and reprinted in several other papers.[5]

To further confuse matters, after the *Philadelphia Inquirer* printed their notice, the *Daily Inter Ocean* printed their own version of a notice:

"This remarkable statement was secured from the condemned criminal by the New York Journal, and by special arrangement with that paper is published simultaneously in The Inter Ocean." It goes on to say, "This article was copyrighted April 10, 1896, by the *Morning Journal Association* of New York. Any unauthorized publication of the whole or part of this matter will be made the subject of vigorous legal prosecution."[6]

Regardless of newspaper in-fighting and competing versions of confessions, the *Philadelphia Inquirer* version is authentic. As such, I have used that version in part two.

On a side note, it appears Holmes enjoyed toying with officials. Investigators determined some victims he confessed to killing were alive and well.

Part Three: *Lied then Died* includes information, illustrations, and photographs about Holmes death and unusual burial. It also includes an odd story Holmes told about his reincarnation.

JD CRIGHTON

PART ONE
HOLMES' OWN STORY

Handwritten Statement

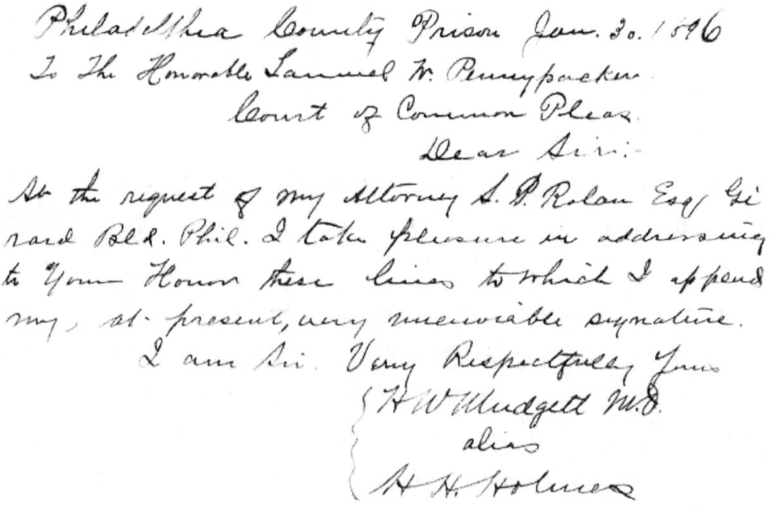

Philadelphia County Prison Jan. 30. 1896
To The Honorable Samuel W. Pennypacker
Court of Common Pleas.
Dear Sir:-
At the request of my Attorney S. P. Rolan Esq, Girard Bld. Phil. I take pleasure in addressing to Your Honor these lines to which I append my, at present, very unenviable signature.
I am Sir. Very Respectfully Yours
H W Mudgett M.D.
alias
H. H. Holmes

Fig. 1. Handwritten Statement from Herman Webster Mudgett for *Holmes' Own Story*
Source: Herman W. Mudgett, *Holmes' Own Story*, 1895.

Holmes' Preface

The following pages are written under peculiar circumstances, perhaps the most peculiar that ever attended the birth of a literary work. Incarcerated in prison and awaiting trial for the most serious offense known to the law, it has been written only after mature deliberation, against the advice of my friends, and in direct opposition to the positive instructions of my counsel, who have attempted in every way to dissuade me from its publication; but the circumstances under which I am placed, in my judgment, make it imperative that I should disregard all of these considerations.

For months I have been vilified by the public press, held up to the world as the most atrocious criminal of the age, directly and indirectly accused of the murder of at least a score of victims, many of whom have been my closest personal friends.

The object of this extended and continuous enumeration of alleged crimes has been apparently to create a public sentiment so prejudiced against me as to make a fair and impartial trial impossible. My friends have been alienated, my nearest kindred plunged in grief, and the world horrified by the bloody recital of imaginary crimes.

I feel therefore justified in the course I am now pursuing, and am impelled by an imperative sense of duty to publicly deny these atrocious calumnies.

The following pages will therefore be found to contain a simple and complete narrative of my entire life, and a full history of my associations and dealings with Mr. and Mrs. B. F. Pitezel and their children, the alleged disappearance of Minnie Williams and the tragic death of her sister Nannie.

My sole object in this publication is to vindicate my name from the horrible aspersions cast upon it, and to appeal to a fair-minded American public for a suspension of judgment, and for that free and fair trial which is the birthright of every American citizen, and the pride and bulwark of our American Constitution. H. H. M.[7]

Fig. 2. Herman Webster Mudgett *alias* H. H. Holmes
Source: Frank P. Geyer. *The Holmes-Pitezel Case*. 1896.

Fig. 3. Various Illustrations of H. H. Holmes
Source: "Various Types of that Many-Sided Individual, H. H. Holmes," *Chicago Tribune*, November 25, 1894.

Holmes' Own Story

COME with me, if you will, to a tiny, quiet New England village, nestling among the picturesquely rugged hills of New Hampshire. This little hamlet has for over a century been known as Gilmanton Academy. So called in honor of an institution of learning of that name, founded there by a few sturdy, self-denying and God-fearing men, over a hundred years ago, who, could they now leave their silent resting places in the church-yard near by, and again wander for an hour through these quiet streets, would, with the exception of new faces, see little change.

Here, in the year 1861, I, Herman W. Mudgett, the author of these pages, was born. That the first years of my life were different from those of any other ordinary country-bred boy, I have no reason to think.

That I was well trained by loving and religious parents, I know, and any deviations in my after life from the straight and narrow way of rectitude are not attributable to the want of a tender mother's prayers or a father's control, emphasized, when necessary, by the liberal use of the rod wielded by no sparing hand.

On my fifth birthday I was given my first suit of boy's clothing, and soon after was sent to the village school-house where the school was "kept."

I had daily to pass the office of one village doctor, the door of which was seldom if ever barred. Partly from its being associated in my mind as the source of all the nauseous mixtures that had been my childish terror (for this was before the day of children's medicines), and partly because of vague rumors I had heard regarding its contents, this place was one of peculiar abhorrence to me, and this becoming known to two of my older schoolmates, they one day bore me struggling and shrieking beyond its awful portals; nor did they desist until I had been brought face to face with one of its grinning skeletons, which, with arms outstretched, seemed ready in its turn to seize me.

It was a wicked and dangerous thing to do to a child of tender years and health, but it proved an heroic method of treatment, destined ultimately to cure me of my fears, and to inculcate in me, first, a strong feeling of curiosity, and, later, a desire to learn, which resulted years afterwards in my adopting medicine as a profession.

When I was about eight years old, an unusual occurrence took place in our village—the arrival of an itinerant photographer. He was a man apparently suffering from some slight lameness, and gladly accepted my offer to act as his errand boy, and in payment for my services he was to execute for me a likeness of myself.

One morning upon going to his office I found the door still locked. It was immediately opened, however, by the artist, sufficiently for him to hand to me a small wooden block broken in two pieces.

He instructed me to take them to our village wagon maker and have him make a new one, which I was to return to him. I did this, and upon entering the office again, I found the artist partially clothed and sitting near the door, which he at once locked.

He then proceeded to remove the greater portion of one of his legs, and not having known until then what was the cause of his lameness, in fact, not ever having seen or even known that such a thing as artificial limbs existed, my consternation can better be imagined than described. Had he next proceeded to remove his head in the same mysterious way I should not have been further surprised.

He must have noticed my discomfiture, for as soon his mending process had sufficiently progressed, he quickly placed me in a dim light, and standing upon his whole leg, and meantime waving the other at me, he took my picture, which in a few days he gave to me.

I kept it for many years, and the thin terror-stricken face of that bare footed, home-spun clad boy I can yet see.

In those days in our quiet village, so remote from the outside world, that even a locomotive whistle could scarcely be heard, daily newspapers were rare and almost unknown, our usual source of information being the weekly papers and a few periodicals; and in one of these I saw a glowing offer, emphasized by a fine illustration of a gold watch and chain, a few of which would be sold at a comparatively trifling sum.

Surely this was for me the one opportunity of my life, and although my entire wealth at that time consisted mostly of pennies and other small coins, almost every one having for me its own peculiar history, all of which I converted into more transferable shape by exchanging them with our shoemaker, who was also my confidant in the matter, was hardly more than sufficient to buy the watch.

I was far more concerned lest, before my order should reach the distant city, all would be sold, than troubled over the depleted condition of my purse.

Then came anxious days of waiting and later the arrival of the watch, and after going alone to my room to wind it and deciding which pocket was most suitable for its reception, and still later going to the several stores and some houses, bargaining beforehand with a little friend that, in consideration of his accompanying me and at each place asking in an unconcerned manner what time it was, that he should wear it the greater part of the day, although I was to be present that no harm befell my treasure; but before it came time for him to wear it the wheels had ceased to turn, the gold had lost is lustre, and the whole affair had turned into an occasion of ridicule for my companions and of self-reproach to myself.

My first falsehood and my first imprisonment occurred synchronously, and were occasioned as follows:—

One morning as I was driving our small herd of cows, which had a few days previously been increased by the addition of several others belonging to a neighbor, to their usual feeding ground, outside the limits of the village, an inquisitive neighbor met me and asked, "Whose be they?"

I replied very proudly, "Ours."

"What, all of them?"

"Yes, *all*, everyone [sic], and that best one is mine, my own."

An hour later upon returning to my home I found father waiting to receive me. He demanded why I had told Richard the lie about the cows, but before I could answer him my mind was most effectually taken up by the production of an implement, to which I was no stranger, and by its vigorous use.

After this I was consigned to an upper room and strictly enjoined to speak to no one, and for the ensuing day I should have no food.

My absence was soon noticed by my playmates and the cause ascertained, and not long after upon looking out of the window I saw my little friend perched upon the fence nearby, looking almost as disconsolate as I, and later in the day, after sundry pantomime communications he came with liberal supply of food, which, with the aid of the ever present ball of cord, which you can find in almost every boy's pocket, I was soon enjoying.

Accompanying the food was a note written in his scrawly hand encouraging me "never mind," and that upon the following Saturday we would go down and let Richard's cows into his cornfield.

But this was not done, for late at night when the shadows in my room had assumed strange and fearful shapes, my mother came and taking me into her own room, knelt down and earnestly plead with me and for me, and it was many days before I forgot that lesson.

This little note, however, with two others form a unique collection.

The second was a joint production of my friend and myself, addressed to an unpopular school teacher one vacation upon our hearing that some slight financial calamity had overtaken him.

This was done with the belief that a new teacher was to take his place during the coming year, but in this we were mistaken.

I had abundant evidence during the first day of the following term that he had received our letter, when he changed my seat from one I had long occupied, and which was very favorably located for looking into the street, to the opposite side of the room. My seatmate was a very disagreeable and unpopular girl.

The third note was also a joint production, written upon brown paper and tacked upon the barn door of a village farmer, who had, as we thought, misused us.

It was not a lengthy note, the words being "Who will pull your weeds next year?"

This note was occasioned by the farmer engaging us for a stipulated price to rid a field of a large weed that is common there, and a great hindrance to the healthy growth of other products. The weeds were tall and strong, and the pittance we were to receive was ridiculously small for the amount of work. But when we had finished and held out our tiny, blistered hands for our pay, it was not forthcoming.

We went again and again for it, and being convinced it was useless to go more, we returned quietly with two large baskets to where we had piled the weeds, to be dried preparatory to their being burned, and very soon thereafter the seeds from all that we had pulled were sown broadcast over the field again.

It is, perhaps, a small matter to speak of here, but it so well illustrates the principle that many times in my after life influenced me to make my conscience become blind, that I thought well to write of it.

My first business ventures consisted of a pair of twin calves that I raised, and later to bring home, on a stormy winter day, a tiny lamb given to me by a farmer, which, in time, together with a few others purchased later, expanded into a flock of about forty sheep.

Both ventures were failures, however, from a financial point of view, but the failures were nothing compared with the collapse of the innumerable air castles which had depended upon the result of these speculations.

One day I found a purse containing about $40; an immense sum at that time to me. In the purse were other papers showing me plainly who the owner was. I know that I hesitated, but only for a moment; and having made up my mind could not too soon return it to its owner, and because I had hesitated was adverse to receiving the reward offered me.

When I was about nineteen years of age (the preceding years having been filled in for the most part with six to nine months each year of preparatory studies and the balance of the time devoted to work and teaching) I was prepared to enter the Dartmouth College, but instead of doing so, I decided to commence a medical course at once, and, with this object in view, I matriculated at the University of Vermont, at Burlington, where I remained one college year, deciding, before it had expired, to complete my course at some larger college, and the following September found me at Ann Arbor, Mich.

After having paid my college fees, bought my books and other articles necessary for my second year in college, I found myself hundreds of miles away from friends and relatives, and with about $60 in money with nine months of hard study before me, allowing but little time for outside work if I wished to keep up in my studies with the other members of my class.

About this time I first became acquainted with a Canadian, a fellow-student, and from then until the time of his death he was one of the very few intimate friends I have ever allowed myself.

Child's Name	Mudgett
Date of Birth	May 16, 1861
Place of Birth	Gilmanton
Sex	Male Color White
Living or Stillborn	Living
No. of Children, 1st, 2d, etc.	3d
Father's Name	Levi H. Mudgett
" Birthplace	Gilmanton
" Color	White Age
" Residence	Gilmanton
" Occupation	Merchant
Mother's Maiden Name	Theodate P. Mudgett
" Birthplace	Gilmanton
" Color	White Age
" Occupation	

THE STATE OF NEW HAMPSHIRE.

OFFICE OF REGISTRAR OF VITAL STATISTICS.

I hereby certify that the above birth record is an exact copy of the return made to the State according to law.

Irving A. Watson
Registrar of Vital Statistics.

Fig. 4. Herman Webster Mudgett Birth Certificate
Source: State of New Hampshire, Office of Registrar of Vital Statistics.

Fig. 5. Historic Gilmanton Academy, New Hampshire, where Holmes lived and went to school

Source: The Miriam and Ira D. Wallach Division of Art, Prints and Photographs: Photography Collection, The New York Public Library, Gilmanton Academy, Gilmanton, N.H., circa 1869.

THE UNIVERSITY OF MICHIGAN.

Charles Jacob Scroggs,
Marcellus John Thompson, A.B.,
Helen S. Wyllis, A. B.,
Edward Reed Wagner,
Frank Caspar Wagner,

DOCTOR OF PHILOSOPHY.

George Wells Knight, A. M., Charles Emmet Lowrey, A. M.

DOCTOR OF MEDICINE.

[DEPARTMENT OF MEDICINE AND SURGERY].

Edwin X. Amoss,
Belle Evans Anderson,
Zachary Taylor Arnold,
James Anthony Bach,
Judson Henry Bennett,
Harvy Ervin Blacksten,
Asa Prior Booth,
Ida Rebecca Brigham,
Benjamin Isaac Coman Buckland,
Almond Eugene Calkins,
Hugh Cary,
Calvin Survill Case,
Albert Eugene Coy,
Marion Craig,
Sara Craig,
Minnie A. G. Crawford,
George Willis Crosby,
Austin P. Culbertson,
Sidney Hollister Culver,
Henry Clay Doan,
Charles Wilcox Dodd,
William Milan Edwards,
Ferdinand Thomas Field,
Frank Marion Foote,
John Willis Fowler,
Albert Theodore Getchell,
Frank Mortimer Gier.
George Albert Haynes,
Lucy May Heath,
Lydia Higgins,
Wilbert Arthur Hobbs,
Edward Hofma,
William Bailey Hunter,
Woods Hutchinson,
Thompson Linn Iddings,
William Warren Johnson,
John Kelly, Jr.,
James Asahel King,
Richard Willis Kitchen,
William Whiting Lathrop,
Robert Charles Leacock,
Laura L. Liebhardt,
Clyde Clark Lovin,
Stephen Ludlum,
Frederick George Lundy,
James Henry Lyons,
John Madden,
Frederick Williams Main,
James Wesley McGregor,
Andrew Barclay Mercer,
Emma Wilson Mooers,
Albert Irvin Moore,
Herman Webster Mudgett,
William George Muir.

Fig. 6. List of degrees conferred at University of Michigan to include Herman Webster Mudgett and his Canadian friend, Robert Leacock
Source: *Calendar of the University of Michigan.* Ann Arbor, Michigan: Courier Printing House, 1885, p. 148.

The limits of this book will not allow me to write the many quaint and some ghastly experiences of our medical education where I otherwise disposed to do so. Suffice it to say, that they stopped far short of desecration of country graveyards, as has been repeatedly charged, as it is a well-known fact that in the State of Michigan all the material necessary for dissection work is legitimately supplied by the State. At the end of my junior year I entered into an agreement with a fluent representative of a Chicago firm to spend my vacation in the northwest portion of Illinois representing his firm as a book agent. In this venture I committed the first really dishonest act of my life.

The firm as well as the book itself, from the sale of which I had been assured I could earn hundreds of dollars during my vacation, was a fraud, and after the most strenuous efforts, having succeeding in selling a sufficient number to defray my expenses and pay my return fare to Ann Arbor, I came back without making a settlement with the firm there, and for the remainder of my vacation earned what money I could in and about the college city.

I could hardly count my Western trip a failure, however, for I had seen Chicago.

The remainder of my medical course differed very little from the first two years; filled perhaps more completely with hard work and study, and almost wholly devoid of pleasure and recreation. At last, however, in June, 1884, our examinations were passed, our suspense was ended and I left Ann Arbor with my diploma, a good theoretical knowledge of medicine, but with no practical knowledge of life and of business. After taking a vacation of less than one week in my old New Hampshire home, I went to Portland, Maine, and engaged with a large business firm of that city to represent them in Northern New York in the sale of their products; my prime object being to find some favorable location in this way where I could become a practitioner. Such an opening was not easily found, however, and I accepted a winter school to teach at Mooers Forks, N. J., and later opened an office in that village. Here I stayed for one year doing good and conscientious work, for which I receive plenty of gratitude but little or no money, and in the fall of 1885 starvation was staring me in the face, and finally I was forced to sell one and then the last of my two horses, and having done this I resolved to go elsewhere before all my needs were again exhausted.

During my long years there in New York I had abundant time to work out the details of a scheme that my University friend, before referred to, and myself have talked over during our hungry college days as a possible last resort in case our medical practice proved a failure; and from certain letters I had received from him, I judge that he, too, had not found all his hardships at an end upon receiving his diploma. I therefore went to where he was located, and found that though his experience had been less disheartening than my own, it had from a pecuniary standpoint been far from successful. During this visit we carefully planned the following method of obtaining money:—

At some future date a man who my friend new [knew] and could trust, who then carried considerable life insurance, was to increase the same so that the total amount carried should be $40,000; and as he was a man of moderate circumstances he was to have it understood that some sudden danger he had escaped (a runaway accident) had impelled him to more fully protect his family in the future. Later he should become addicted to drink, and while temporarily insane from its use should, as it would appear afterwards, kill his wife and child.

In reality they were to go to the extreme West and await his arrival there at a later date. Suddenly the husband was to disappear, and some months later a body badly decomposed and dressed in the clothing he was known to wear was to be found, and with it a statement to the effect that while in a drunken rage he had killed his family and had shipped their dismembered bodies to two separate and distant warehouses to conceal the crime, first having partially preserved remains by placing them in strong brine. That he did not care to live longer, and that his property insurance should pass to a relative whom he was to designate in this letter.

At the proper time he was to join his family in the West, and remain there permanently, the relative collecting the insurance, a part of which was to be sent to him, a part to be retained by the relative, and the remainder to be divided between us. This scheme called for a considerable amount of material, no less than three bodies in fact. This difficulty was easily overcome, however, so long as it was supposed that they were needed for experimental purposes, but no doctor could call for three bodies at one time without exciting suspicion, and so it was arranged that I was to go to Chicago for the winter, and some time during the intervening months we should both contribute towards the necessary supply. I reached Chicago in November, 1885, but finding it difficult to obtain satisfactory employment, I went to Minneapolis, where I spent the winter in a drug store as a clerk.

Meantime, my friend had promptly obtained his portion and placed it in the storage in Delaware, from which place it was shipped to me later in Chicago. I remained in Minneapolis until May, 1886, when I returned to Chicago. My own life I had insured meantime for $20,000, which, at a later date, I intended to realize upon. I had prior to this time made arrangements to furnish my portion of the material. After reaching Chicago, certain sudden changes in my plans called me hastily to New York City, and I decided to take a part of the material there and leave the balance in a Chicago warehouse. This necessitated the repacking of the same, and to accomplish this I went to a hotel (May, 1886), where I registered under an assumed name, and occupied a room and had the package, which had been shipped from Detroit, taken there, and carefully removing the carpet from one portion of the room I divided the material into two packages. In doing this the floor became discolored.

Later, one of these packages was placed in the Fidelity Storage Warehouse in Chicago, and the other I took with me to New York and placed it in a safe place. Upon my trip from Chicago to New York I read two accounts of the detection of crime connected with this class of work, and for the first time I realized how well organized and well prepared the leading insurance companies were to detect and punish this kind of fraud, and this, together with a letter I received upon reaching my destination, and the sudden death of my friend, caused all to be abandoned.

Soon after leaving New York I came to Philadelphia, where I sought employment in some drug store where I could hope to become either a partner or an owner. Not finding such an opportunity at once I took a situation as a keeper in the Norristown Asylum. This was my first experience with insane persons, and so terrible was it that for years afterwards, even now sometimes, I see their faces in my sleep. Fortunately within a few days after entering the Asylum I received word that I could obtain different employment in a drug store on Columbia Avenue, which I at once accepted.

About July 1st, one afternoon, a child entered the store and exclaimed, "I want a doctor! The medicine we got here this morning has killed my brother (or sister)." I could remember of no sale that morning corresponding to the one she hastily described, but I made sure that a physician was at once sent to the house, and having done this I hastily wrote a note to my employer, stating the nature of the trouble, and left the city immediately for Chicago, and it was not until nine years later that I knew the result of the case.

Later, when it became necessary to disprove the alarming statements that were made relative to various persons having been killed at 701 Sixty-third street, I placed in the proper authorities' hands a full collection of documentary evidence, consisting of railroad and storage warehouse receipts, letters, references and dates sufficient to show the truthfulness of my statements.

Upon reaching Chicago I found I could obtain no employment as a druggist until I had passed an examination at Springfield, Ill., and when I went there for that purpose I gave my name as H. H. Holmes, and under this name I have since done most of my business. Later, in July, 1886, I went to 701 Sixty-third street, Chicago, where I found a small store owned by a physician, who, owing to ill-health, wished to sell badly. A little later I bought it, paying for it for the most part with money secured by mortgaging the stock and fixtures, agreeing to repay this loan at the rate of $100 dollars per month. My trade was good, and for the first time in my life I was established in a business that was satisfactory to me.

But very soon my landlord, seeing that I was prospering well, made me aware that my rent would be increased, and to protect myself I was forced to purchase at a great expense the vacant property opposite the location I then occupied, and to erect a building thereon. Here my real troubles commenced. The expense incurred was wholly beyond the earning capacity of my business, and for the next few years I was obligated to plunge deeply in debt in every direction; and worse than this, when these debts became due, if unable to meet them to resort to all means of procuring a stay or evading them altogether. At last there came a day when Thomas Fallon, a constable, together with a lawyer named Sanforth, both of Chicago, came to my store to attach the same to satisfy the claim of some inpatient creditor. And during the appraisal of the goods they came and asked me the contents of two small barrels.

I gave them some misleading answer, and bringing out other goods to attract their attention, they were passed for the time being. They were the two packages I arranged more than a year before at a certain hotel, and which had been removed from the storehouses in Chicago and New York, first to my former store, and later to the new one.

A [sic] soon as possible after this attachment took place, I resolved to permanently dispose of both these packages, and to do so, I open the smaller of them and commenced its destruction by burning in a large furnace, then in the basement. The experience was so unpleasant, owing to the terrible odor produced, that I did not think it safe to destroy more of it in the same way, and therefore buried the remainder of that package, as well as the fragments that were partially burned, in the places where they have lately been found.

The other package was removed, unopened, from the building, and so disposed of that it is hardly probable it will ever be found, and I do not feel called upon to bring it forth, as it would only serve to add more newspaper notoriety to the case.

If, however, my life is ever jeopardized, or my other statements discredited owing to want of additional proof in this matter, I shall at once cause it to be produced, and my so doing will result in showing that the portions therein contained are parts of the two bodies already found, and more important still that the package thus brought to light has necessarily occupied its present location for nearly seven years.

This will be corroborated by documentary evidence, freight, express and warehouse receipts, letters, etc., already in the hands of the authorities, together with evidence from workmen, if still alive and to be found.

Early in 1888, needing some extra carpenters, there came to me, in response to an advertisement, a tall, thin, muscular man, whom, at the time, I took to be a farmer from the Western plains.

Fig. 7. Benjamin F. Pitezel
Source: Herman W. Mudgett, *Holmes' Own Story*, 1895, p. 26.

Fig. 8. Benjamin F. Pitezel, c1888
Source: Miller Images

He assured me, however, that he was a carpenter, able to do as much and as good work as anyone else, that his name was Benjamin F. Pitezel, that he had a large family, was badly in need of work for their support and begged me to give him a trial. This I did, but soon found him to be a dreamer.

Coming to him at his work I would find him with a set of figures and perhaps a diagram illustrative of their use, or busy making a model of some complicated contrivance. This proceeded so far that for my own protection I had to cause him to work by contract instead of by the day, although I found him fully as improvident of his own time as he had been of mine. Little by little I grew to like his quiet ways, and to depend upon him to take charge of the work at times when I was obliged to be absent, and one day I said to him, "Ben, with all your mechanical ingenuity you should have been a rich man before now. How is it?" His answer was that heretofore the world had not seemed to be inclined to be kind to him. This seemed so aptly to describe my own case, that I talked with him further from time to time, and a summary of what I learned was as follows:—

He, like myself, had been a country-bred boy, knowing few pleasures, but, unfortunately, receiving few school advantage. At a comparatively early age he had married and commenced life as a farmer in Illinois or Indiana. Later he had moved to Kansas, and, later still, had been forced to leave that State owing to some legal trouble with a bank there, to which he had given a worthless mortgage to secure a loan in money. After leaving Kansas he had wandered through the Western States, principally in the gold regions, and finally had settled in Chicago with his family, which, while he traveled, had remained in Kansas. Very soon after reaching Chicago he had commenced working for me, and from that time until September 2, 1894, when he died, he was continually in my employ, working as a carpenter and builder, and as a real estate dealer and as a wholesale lumber merchant, buying and shipping lumber from the South and West to Chicago and St. Louis, where I also sold the same products.

I think it was in 1889 that I was one day waited upon by two gentlemen who wished to sell me a gas machine, by using which I could be forever independent of the regular city gas company. So great were the inducements held out that I later met them at their office in La Salle street, and before leaving them had bought one of the machines, which a few days later was arranged in the basement of my building, and I had notified the city company that thereafter I should cease to be one of their patrons. For two days the new machine performed wonders, and I recommended it to many of my customers and friends. The third evening when I was very busy my store was suddenly enveloped in darkness. I was obliged to turn away my customers and close for the want of light, and from then until morning I wrestled with my gas machine; and when Pitezel came to his day's work he found me still perspiring, and, I fear, swearing over it.

The machine was to him as a new toy to a child, although he soon assured me that as a gas producer it was an absolute failure. That afternoon I instructed him to temporarily connect it with the city gas to provide light for the evening, and the next day I would go to the company and make a new application to again become a permanent customer. As he finished making the connection he remarked that he thought that it would be a good permanent arrangement without going to the gas company. His quiet remark resulted in my having him, next day, lead the gas from the city main to the machine underground in such a way that it would not be known without a close inspection, and this I did, not to defraud the city, but "to get even" with the company who had defrauded me. A few evenings thereafter the president of this company called upon me, and, after quietly studying my new light for a time, spoke to me of it.

I then told him that I bought this machine for the purpose of trying a new gas that for years I had been experimenting with. Several other visits followed, and although I was apparently averse to disposing of my new discovery, I finally did so, taking in return first a contract so skillfully worded that there could later be no claims brought against me, and, second, a check for a large sum of money. Had matters stopped here as I had at first intended, all would have been well, but I neglected disconnecting from the city supply from day to day, until finally an inspector, more energetic than his fellow-workers, became aware of it, and this resulted in my very willingly choosing to pay a five hundred dollar gas bill in preference to being openly written up and perhaps prosecuted.

There have occurred other deals of somewhat similar nature, and generally inspired by the same motive, but this one suffices as an example of those that occurred later. Sometime previous to this I had had occasion to employ an attorney to transact some business in which certain papers had to be signed in my New Hampshire name [Mudgett], and to do this work I employed one I did not know in order that my real name should not be confounded with the name of Holmes, under which I have been known and had done all my work since commencing business in Chicago.

About a year after consulting this attorney, I was called into court as a witness on some trivial case, and while giving my testimony under the name of Holmes, I saw him sitting in the court room apparently much mystified. Instead of denouncing me to the court, as he might easily have done, he spoke to me alone, and, later, feeling he had done me a most kind favor I gave to him the greater part of my legal work; but though he attended to this conscientiously for me as an attorney, he at no time encouraged me to acts that were wrong, nor was he a party to them, and the late newspaper comments reflecting upon his integrity are most unjust and uncalled for.

Aside from this one incident I know of no time during the nine years prior to my arrest that my two names conflicted the one with the other, or caused me trouble or annoyance.

In 1890 I added a jewelry store to my business, and placed Julius L. Connor in charge of that and my drug business, his wife, Julia Connor, assisting him as cashier for a time, who, after the sale of the store, lived in the building and supported herself and child by taking boarders. That she is a woman of quick temper and perhaps not always of a good disposition may be true, but that any of her friends and relatives will believe her to be an immoral woman, or one who would be a party to a criminal act, I do not think. She lived for her child, and her one fear was that she should lose her, and as soon as the daughter is of sufficient age to protect herself, I feel that her whereabouts will be made known. I last saw her about January 1, 1892, when the settlement of her rent was made. At this time she had announced not only to me, but to her neighbors and friends, that she was going away.

At this interview she told me that, while she had given her destination as Iowa, she was going elsewhere to avoid the chance of her daughter being taken from her, giving the Iowa destination to mislead her husband. I corresponded with her upon business matters later, and the so-called secreted letters lately found could only have been obtained from my Chicago letter files, in which hundreds of my business letters were stored away in alphabetical order.

In 1890 I opened an office on Dearborn street, Chicago, and organized "The Warner Glass-Bending Co.," the principal value of which consisted in certain not very clearly-defined ideas I possessed upon the subject of bending glass for mechanical purposes. This was a stock company, in which I had interested, among others, Osmer W. Fay, a most reputable and honest man (a retired minister), of whom I will speak later in this history. Suffice it say here that, when I found that he had invested the principal part of his savings in my company, knowing that it would not be a successful business venture to others, save myself, I returned to him his investment with interest. At this time Pitezel was in the same office with me, selling an invention he had lately patented, known as "Pitezel's Automatic Coal Bin." I later established him in an office by himself, where he opened a patent exchange similar to the one he was conducting in Philadelphia at the time of his death.

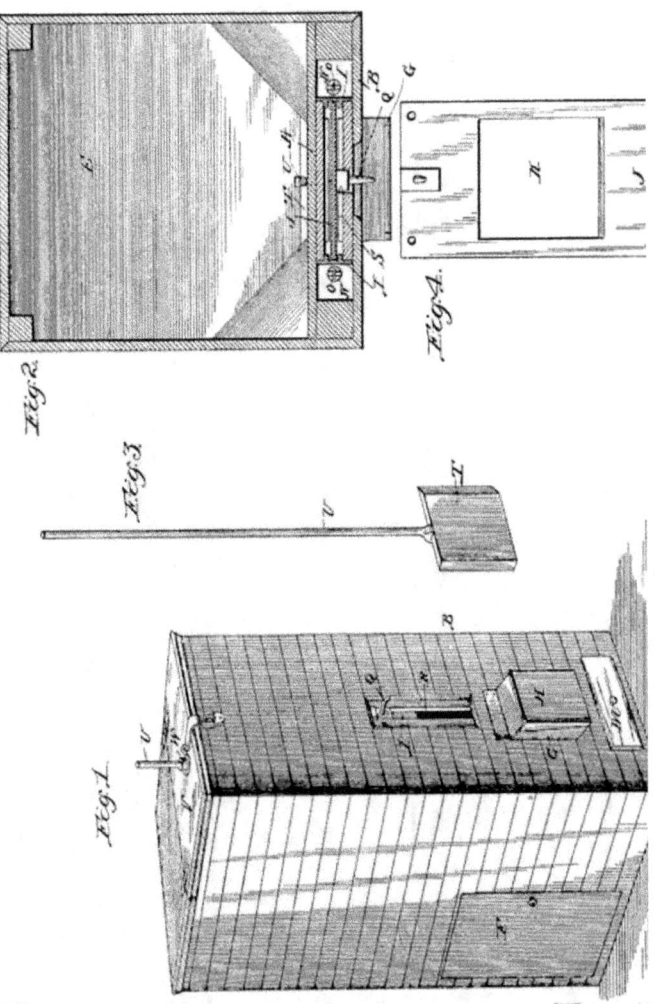

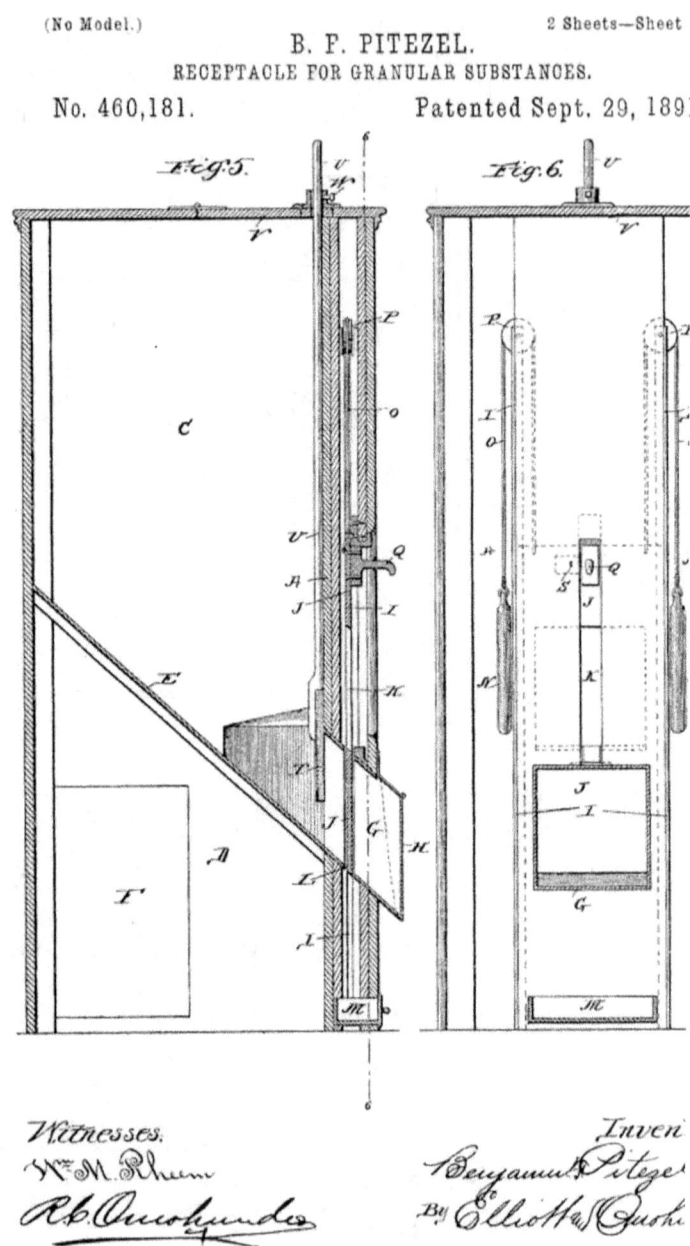

Fig. 9. Benjamin Pitezel Patent No. US 000460181
Source: United States Patent and Trademark Office, September 29, 1891.

At about this time, Patrick Quinlan, a whole-souled Irishman, had left his farm in Michigan to come to the city to work during the winter months, and commenced his service with me. He soon became almost indispensable, owing to his careful management and supervision of help and general faithfulness, and for several years he worked for me continually, though during that time he did no illegal act nor committed any wrong so far as I know.

Early in 1891 I became interested in one of the most seductive and misleading inventions that has ever been placed before the American public; a device known as the "A B C Copier," which had been brought to this country from Europe by a prominent official of the World's Fair.

He had been swindled in its purchase, and, knowing this, was very willing to dispose of one-half interest in the invention to me for $9,000 worth of "securities." A company was immediately formed, and by using his name freely as the president of same, we were able to make over $50,000 worth of contracts for future delivery before our offices had been open sixty days, numbering among our customers many large insurance companies and prominent wholesale houses.

However, I was glad to sell my interests, clearing about $22,000 in cash upon the entire deal. It was at this time, while employing quite a large office force, that Mr. J. L. Connor [Julius] asked me to give his sister Gertrude some work to do. Instead of doing so at once I told him I would aid him in furnishing her with the means to take a short course in a business college, and if later she proved proficient, I would give her employment.

Shortly after her commencing to attend this business college, she received an offer of marriage from a young clerk in Chicago. She spoke to us of it, and asked us to learn, if we could, of the antecedents of the young man and of his prospects. Our investigation resulted in learning that he had a wife living in Chicago. Gertrude was inclined to disbelieve this statement, and not expressing herself as being willing to break the engagement, Mr. Connor thought best to send her to her home in Iowa. A statement from the physician who attended her at the time of her death, long after this, speaks for itself, effectually disproving one of the most persistent and disagreeable charges that have been brought against me. I have had many young ladies in my employ, most of whom are still living in and about Chicago, whose parents and friends know only too well that far from being their seducer I have done much to materially help them in their narrow lives, owing to the enormous competitions in Chicago for positions.

At about this time I sent Pitezel South upon an extended lumber purchasing trip, and upon his return to Chicago he encountered some severe domestic troubles, the full details of which he did not tell me until long afterwards. But at the time they resulted in a neighborhood quarrel and some arrests, and thereafter he grew more morose, and drank more freely than he had done heretofore, but managed to do so during my absence or after working hours, as he knew me to be wholly intolerant of drunkenness in my employees.

It was about January 1, 1893, when I first met Minnie R. Williams at the intelligence office of Mr. William Campbell on Dearborn street, Chicago, whom she had engaged to provide her with a position as stenographer.

Fig. 10. Miss Emeline (Emily, Emma) G. Cigrand
Source: Herman W. Mudgett, *Holmes' Own Story,* 1895, p. 38.
Note: No mention of Emeline Cigrand appeared in this section. Perhaps Holmes meant for Minnie Williams photo to appear here to correspond to his mention of Minnie.

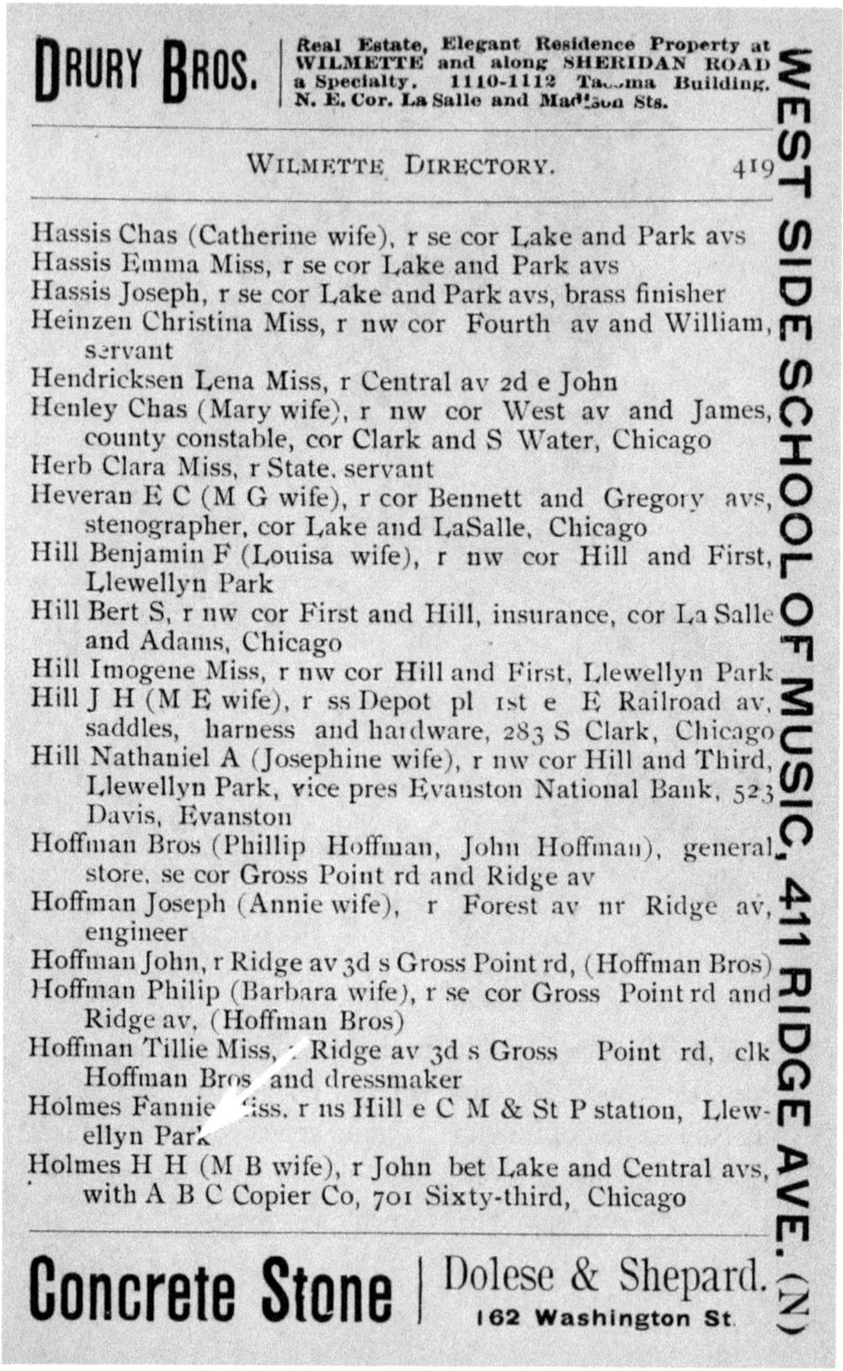

DRURY BROS. | Real Estate, Elegant Residence Property at WILMETTE and along SHERIDAN ROAD a Specialty. 1110-1112 Tacoma Building. N. E. Cor. La Salle and Madison Sts.

WILMETTE DIRECTORY. 419

Hassis Chas (Catherine wife), r se cor Lake and Park avs
Hassis Emma Miss, r se cor Lake and Park avs
Hassis Joseph, r se cor Lake and Park avs, brass finisher
Heinzen Christina Miss, r nw cor Fourth av and William, servant
Hendricksen Lena Miss, r Central av 2d e John
Henley Chas (Mary wife), r nw cor West av and James, county constable, cor Clark and S Water, Chicago
Herb Clara Miss, r State. servant
Heveran E C (M G wife), r cor Bennett and Gregory avs, stenographer, cor Lake and LaSalle, Chicago
Hill Benjamin F (Louisa wife), r nw cor Hill and First, Llewellyn Park
Hill Bert S, r nw cor First and Hill, insurance, cor La Salle and Adams, Chicago
Hill Imogene Miss, r nw cor Hill and First, Llewellyn Park
Hill J H (M E wife), r ss Depot pl 1st e E Railroad av, saddles, harness and hardware, 283 S Clark, Chicago
Hill Nathaniel A (Josephine wife), r nw cor Hill and Third, Llewellyn Park, vice pres Evanston National Bank, 523 Davis, Evanston
Hoffman Bros (Phillip Hoffman, John Hoffman), general store, se cor Gross Point rd and Ridge av
Hoffman Joseph (Annie wife), r Forest av nr Ridge av, engineer
Hoffman John, r Ridge av 3d s Gross Point rd, (Hoffman Bros)
Hoffman Philip (Barbara wife), r se cor Gross Point rd and Ridge av, (Hoffman Bros)
Hoffman Tillie Miss, r Ridge av 3d s Gross Point rd, clk Hoffman Bros and dressmaker
Holmes Fannie Miss, r ns Hill e C M & St P station, Llewellyn Park
Holmes H H (M B wife), r John bet Lake and Central avs, with A B C Copier Co, 701 Sixty-third, Chicago

Concrete Stone | Dolese & Shepard. 162 Washington St.

WEST SIDE SCHOOL OF MUSIC, 411 RIDGE AVE. (N)

Fig. 11. A B C Copier Company listing in The Evanston Rogers

Park & Wilmette Directory in 1892. His wife was listed as M B, which was most likely Myrta Belknap
Source: *The Evanston Rogers Park & Wilmette Directory.* Evanston: Evanston Press Co., 1892, p. 419.

I found her to be a bright, intelligent woman, an interesting conversationalist and one who I could see had seen much of the world. When she had been working in my office for a few weeks, knowing that she had a history, I asked her one stormy winter afternoon to tell it to me. After considerable hesitation she did so, in nearly the following words:—

"My earliest remembrance is of a poor home in the South. My father was a drunkard and my poor mother was not strong. One terrible day my father was brought to us dead, and very soon after this mother's strength seemed to leave her utterly, and she soon followed him, leaving me, a tiny child, together with a still younger sister and a baby brother, to the tender mercies of the world. An aunt in Mississippi took my sister to live with her, and another relative cared for brother, and an uncle, a physician, adopted me.

"During the short time he lived he was a loving and tender father to me, and at his death willed to me all of his possessions. A guardian was appointed to care for me, but I was not again happy until years later, when Mr. Massie was appointed to take his place, and since then I have looked upon him and his wife as my parents.

"When I was 17 years old I was sent to Boston to finish my education at the Conservatory of Music. At first, after leaving my warm Southern home, I nearly died from homesickness, and you will not wonder that having met at some place of entertainment in Boston a young gentleman, and having found that he was an honest clerk, occupying a position where he could hope for advancement, I allowed him to address me, and later became engaged to him.

"Soon after the engagement he introduced me to a gentleman who is prominently known throughout the New England States. He is much older than myself.

"From the first time I met him he seemed to exert a powerful influence over me. I loved his wife, and my visits to her made a pleasant break in the tedium of my school work, but as soon as he came home, or I was in his company, I was ill at ease, my mind being filled with an indefinable presentiment of evil. I avoided meeting him alone upon all occasions when it was possible for me to do so, but he would often insist upon accompanying me to my home, and this, owing to their continued courtesies to me, I could not well refuse.

All too soon there came a day when I could no longer look into the eyes of either my lover or of those of my betrayer, and for more than a year thereafter I was wholly under the influence of my seducer; so much so, that any and all good resolutions I would make during his absence would vanish upon meeting him again, and my life became one of mental torture to me, for by nature I was a pure-minded girl.

"Our meetings for the most part took place at a hotel near his place of business, a portion of which was available for meetings of this kind, so long as the parties were known to the manager.

"During the year I broke my engagement with my lover, and by so doing apparently deserved his reproaches for heartlessness, although if he could have known it my motive was of an entirely different nature. As though my burden had not at this time been sufficiently heavy for me to bear, about the end of this year I became aware that another and still more terrible calamity was in store for me.

"For days I sat in my room until it seemed I should go mad, and fearing lest I should utterly lose my reason I decided to kill myself, but no one realizes how dear life is until, thinking it worthless, they have tried to destroy it.

"I could not do it, and there was nothing left for me to do but to go quietly away in a strange place, under a different name, and bear my shame.

"I went to New York, engaged board under the name of Adele Covell, in a quiet portion of the city.

"Physically, I had never been strong, and now followed days and weeks of serious illness until, to save my reason, the life of my unborn child was sacrificed. As soon as I was able I returned to my Texas home, accounting as best I could for my terribly haggard appearance.

"Later, feeling that there was left little that I could do, and being wholly reckless of my future, I prepared for the stage, and for three years I was almost continually before the public. Becoming somewhat ambitious I organized a company, and for a time traveled through the New England towns and small cities under the name of Geraldine Wande.

"This venture cost me between five and ten thousand dollars, and in 1891 I went to Denver, Colorado, as a member of a theatrical company then playing a prominent engagement. There I staid [sic] until the burning of the theatre, which caused my engagement to end, and not being able to find another suitable opening, I decided to prepare myself for office work.

"Unfortunately, while in Denver, I attracted the attention of a young man engaged to be married to a lady whom I knew and liked, and rather than to cause them trouble I decided to go elsewhere, though against the wishes of the young man, who, if I had allowed it, would have married me. At about this time my brother, whom I had never seen much of, was killed, or rather died, as the result of a railroad accident at Leadville, Colorado, leaving sister Nannie, who is now teaching in Nudlothean, Texas, and to me, about $400 each, payable about one year after his death.

"I went to Leadville to attend his funeral, and later came here to Chicago, where, until I obtained my position with you, I have been at times really in need of money, as owing to my unfortunate theatrical venture all my ready money has been used, and I now have left only one piece of good real estate in Fort Worth, Texas, valued at $6,000 but encumbered for $1,700.

"A piece of land adjoining my property, of which Mr. Massey has recently written me, can be sold by him for $2,500, besides paying a heavy mortgage standing against it.

"I have also one small, unimproved lot near Dallas, Texas, worth about $200."

During the spring of 1893 I was, if possible, more busy than ever before.

Among other work, preparing my building to rent to a prospective tenant, who would use the entire five stories and forty rooms, at a good rental, if I could get it completed in time for World's Fair purposes.

This left me with little time to attend to my office duties, which gradually Miss Williams took more and more into her own hands, showing a remarkable aptitude for the work. During the first weeks she boarded at a distance, but later, from about the 1st of March until the 15th of May, 1893, she occupied rooms in the same building and adjoining my offices.

Here occasionally meals were served from the restaurant near at hand, and if any bones have really been found in the stove there I think it will later be learned, by microscopical examination, that they are the remnants of such meals. Certain it is that no human being was ever cremated there during my occupancy of the room, my own experience years ago being quite sufficient to show me the danger of such proceedings on account of the awful odor, if I had no other motive to deter me from such a course.

About the first of April I dictated quite a number of urgent letters to parties who were owing me, requesting them to make immediate settlement of their accounts, as I was much in need of the money at this time. Some days later Minnie brought me a draft for about $2,500 and asked me to use it until she should need it, explaining that this was the proceeds of the Texas sale she had previously spoken to me about. I could make good use of the money at that time, but declined to take it until I had explained to her, at some length, more of my business affairs than she had before known. And, finally, I caused to be transferred to her, by warranty deed, a house and lot at Wilmette, Ill., valued at about $7,500, in order that she should be well protected against loss in case of my death.

This money was returned to her about May 10, 1893, from money obtained for this purpose from Isaac R. Hitt & Co., Chicago, who paid it to Miss Williams personally. At about this time she expressed a wish that I should aid her in converting her remaining Southern property into either cash or improved Northern property. This was hard to do, and I finally advised her to execute a worthless deed (by having some one other than herself sign same) to a fictitious person and offer the property for sale at a very low cash figure, and years later, if she chose to do so, to demand additional sum in exchange for the good deed.

This was done, forging the name upon the deed so made, which deeds are still in existence. When matters had progressed thus far in our various transactions, Miss Williams was taken seriously ill for several days at the house where we were stopping at the time. She suffered from the same form of acute mania that she had been troubled with in New York years before. She was under restraint at this hotel a few days about May 22d, but owing to careful nursing and good medical attendance, she soon became so much better that she could plan intelligently with me what steps were best to be taken for her safety.

It was decided that she should go to the Presbyterian Hospital, near the Clybourne avenue car limits in Chicago, to stay until I could determine if she were in further danger. She entered this institution about May 23, 1893, as a private patient, and her ailment being such that it was prudent for her to pass for a married woman, she was enrolled upon the records there as Mrs. Williams.

The greatest drawback to her improvement here was the fact

that she knew she was in an asylum with other insane persons, and she soon begged me to take her to some private apartments where she could receive special attention. To accomplish this, I hired a house at 1220 Wrightwood avenue, and early in June accompanied Miss Williams there, and during my absences she was in care of a young woman hired for this purpose.

Here she rapidly improved, and during the following months exhibited only once any maniacal symptoms, when, owing to some trivial disagreement with her attendants, she so frightened her that she left at once. At this time Miss Williams first spoke of inviting her sister to spend the summer and fall months with us, and in response to a letter Nannie came from Texas.

Fig. 12. Nannie [Anna] Williams
Source: Mudgett, Herman W. *Holmes' Own Story*, 1895, p. 49.

I met her at the train and found her to be a remarkably quiet and gentle woman—apparently not very strong—certainly of a most kindly disposition. The sisters had never lived together for any considerable length of time, and they anticipated much pleasure in the society of each other. Minnie had asked that it should appear to her sister that we were married, and also that nothing should be said of her recent illness, which she now, day by day, seemed to be overcoming.

I cannot imagine a happier, quieter life than they passed there during the month of June and the first part of July 1893. I was extremely busy in the city, but was at the house whenever I could conveniently arrange it. Minnie had so far recovered as to attend to several business matters and to aid me in my writing. Among other things, arrangements were made to convert her own and her sister's interests in her brother's estate into money, and to commence certain preliminary proceedings that would ultimately cause her betrayer in Boston to pay her a considerable sum, and, to make this easier, it was thought wise that she obtain some evidence in support of her claim by wiring to him for a small amount of money.

This was done, and to this telegram he promptly responded by sending to her, by wire, $100. At the time it came to the Western Union office she was not feeling well enough to go there for it, and I executed the proper papers, signing her name in her stead, and next day, to more fully protect her attorney in the matter, she executed a supplementary receipt in her own name.

Later in the year it was her intention to return to Boston and go further with the matter. Late in June, upon returning one day from my business in the city, I met and was introduced by Miss Williams to a Mr. Edward Hatch, whom she had formerly known during her theatrical life (he was at the time attending the Columbian Exposition at Chicago). A few evenings later he accompanied Minnie, Nannie and myself to the Exposition.

Early in July it became necessary for Miss Williams to leave the city for a day, and before doing so she asked that I come home early and not allow Nannie to remain alone during the evening and night. I went with Miss Williams to the cars, and later accompanied her sister as far as the business portion of the city, upon her way to spend the day at the Exposition. That evening I returned to the house at about 6 o'clock, and soon after Nannie also returned.

During the previous weeks of Miss Williams' illness, I had been unable to be away from the house at night, and wishing to go out that evening I asked Nannie if she would mind staying in the rooms alone, explaining to her that there were two other families in the house. She replied that she would have no fear, and that being so tired from her day's exertions among the crowds, she felt sure that she would sleep all night.

This being arranged I went away, agreeing to call on my way to the city next morning, and asking her if her sister returned before I did to refrain from telling her I had staid [sic] elsewhere, giving to Nannie as my reason for this that her sister would feel annoyed at my leaving her alone. Next morning I reached the house at about 8:30 o'clock, and shortly before Miss Williams returned.

Being in haste to reach the city I welcomed her, and almost immediately bade them both goodbye, and taking my bicycle from the hall started down the street. At this time both sisters were standing within the doorway of the house.

Quite early in the afternoon, upon returning, I was surprised to notice the shades at the windows closely drawn. Entering the hall and passing from thence into the parlor, I was greeted by Miss Williams screaming to me:—

"Is that you? My God! I thought you would never come. Nannie is dead!"

She was seated upon the floor holding her sister's head in her arms rocking back and forth and moaning, much as a mother would over a child that was dying or dead. I did not believe it at first—I made no effort to do so—looking upon it as one of the jokes which, when well, she so liked to indulge in, but a moment later I noticed the disordered condition of the room, and as my eyes became accustomed to the darkness, Miss Williams' terrified face, which good actress though she was, I knew she could not so successfully counterfeit.

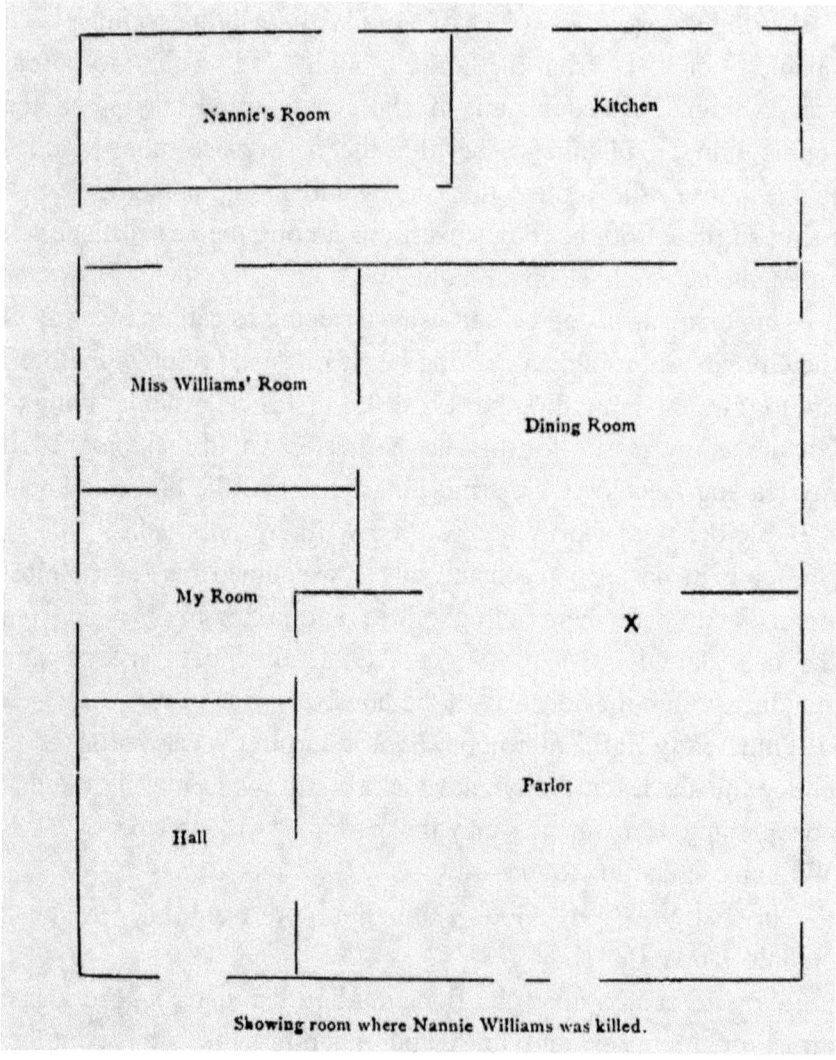

Fig. 13. Room where Nannie Williams was Killed
Source: Herman W. Mudgett, *Holmes' Own Story*, 1895, p. 51.

I was alarmed and instantly was upon my knees beside them, to find to my horror that Nannie had probably been dead for hours. By this time Miss Williams seemed almost as lifeless as her sister, and half leading, half carrying her, I took her to her room and did all I could to restore her, but it was hours before she was in a condition that would allow of her giving me an intelligent account of what had taken place during my absence.

In the meantime I had carried Nannie to my own room, where she lay, looking more like one asleep than dead. The only mark of violence discernable being a slight discoloration upon one of her temples, from which a small quantity of blood had apparently flowed.

Later, in answer to my questions, I gained the following knowledge:—

Upon my leaving the house in the morning, Miss Williams had seized her sister by the arm and ran romping with her through the rooms to the dining room, and without waiting to remove her hat had sat down at the table and drank some coffee, talking to Nannie the while. She had asked her what time I had reached the house the preceding evening, to which question Nannie answered that she did not know, as I was at home when she had herself returned, thus giving the impression that I had been there during the night.

After finishing her lunch, Minnie had passed into her own room, had exchanged her street costume for a house dress, and then, in going to the front portion of the house, had passed through my room, and in doing so had noticed that it had not been occupied during the night.

With this one thought in her disordered mind she had rushed into the adjoining room where her sister then sat, and in a voice, which only the very few who have been intimately acquainted with Miss Williams can appreciate and understand the tragedy of, had said:

"You devil! You have stolen my husband from me."

At the same time she had struck her sister with a small footstool, causing her to fall to the floor, where, with hardly a struggle, she had ceased to breathe.

Miss Williams had, at the first moment, run to the lower portion of the house for assistance, but the people being absent for the time being, she had returned, and at first thinking her sister had only fainted, had resorted to all the means of which she knew to resuscitate her. She soon found her efforts useless, and from then until I had arrived, had remained in the position in which I found her.

After this came the terrible question of what steps should be taken. It is useless for me to speak now of what should have been done. What was finally decided upon is as follows:—

I first wished to call in the authorities and explain fully, and also have it known that at the moment the act was committed Miss Williams was not accountable for what she had done. She would not listen to this. Next, I suggested that it should appear that death had resulted from an accidental fall, but to any and all propositions that necessitated a court investigation she would hear nothing, begging me to go to Englewood, and with Patrick Quinlan's aid take the body to some quiet place and bury it.

Finding that the discussion was worrying her into another serious condition, I gave her some medicine, and as soon as I could do so safely, I left her, intending to go to Englewood, and did go as far as Twenty-second street.

There were some reasons why this last mentioned course would have been advantageous, as it was not generally known that I was living with Miss Williams as her husband; and those who did know of it did not know my identity, and to have this matter known, as well as the death of her sister under such distressing circumstances, would have occasioned an amount of notoriety that would have been ruinous to me.

But as I rode towards Englewood, I could see good reasons for not using Quinlan in the matter. His loyalty to me was such that I should not have feared his making it public, but I did not think I had a right to burden him with so terrible a secret.

In fact, it was by never asking him to do any act that he could be held accountable for or that would jeopardize his property that the loyal feeling had been caused to exist.

Leaving the cars at Twenty-second street, I returned to the house, finding Miss Williams still asleep; later we clothed her sister in a light dress she had liked to wear, and taking the large trunk she had brought with her from Texas, I placed her therein as carefully as I could.

No funeral rites were observed; no prayers were said, for I felt that from either of us such would have been a mockery. I also took her small, well-worn Bible (this without Miss Williams' knowledge) and later consigned it with her to her last resting place, which was all I felt at liberty to do. I then went to a livery stable and obtained a covered conveyance, stopping upon my return at the car barns near by, where there were many workmen waiting to take the cars. I engaged one of them to accompany me to the house and help me place the trunk in the carriage.

I then drove to the lake-side, and waited until night had fallen, making it appear to parties noticing me, if any, that I was awaiting the return of some belated boating party. Afterwards, I procured a boat at some distance, and took it near my waiting place, and still later, with considerable difficulty, I placed the trunk in it, and proceeded about one mile from the shore.

There in the darkness, passed beyond the sight of this world, into the ever grasping depths of Lake Michigan, all that was mortal of this beautiful Christian girl; but from my sight it has never passed, nor has there been a day, an hour, since that awful night that I would not have given my life if by doing so that of Nannie Williams could have been returned.

Upon coming towards the shore I thought it wise to deposit the trunk upon another and more remote portion of the beach. I did this, and, after returning the boat, drove away, and later came back for the trunk.

Upon reaching the house I found Miss Williams more at ease. She had occupied her mind during my absence by collecting and placing in Nannie's room all of her belongings, even those of her own things that her sister had used. She was inclined to talk to me and plan for the future, but for this I had no heart, and little by little, as often as I could do so without exciting her again, I told her that our life together was ended.

I did not do this with anger, and agreed to guard her secret so long as it did not place my own life in danger. The housekeeping was broken up, and very shortly thereafter Mr. Hatch took her to Milwaukee, where she remained in a private institution until later in the summer. The cause that had produced her unsound mental condition had been removed.

Hatch did not know of her sister's death for months afterward, and then against my advice was it told to him, he supposing she had returned to her Texas friends. All of the things that Minnie had separated from her own were packed and taken to Englewood and were placed in a room in the second story, where they were kept for several weeks until I could obtain time to dispose of them, when I assorted some of them and gave them to Pitezel, telling him that they were some that Miss Williams had sent to his children. All the others were burned in the large stove in the third-story office, and this I plainly told the Philadelphia authorities in the fall of 1894, and all the subsequent excitement occurred as a direct result of a visit made there by their representative in verification of my statement.

Another trunk, containing pictures and books, was not taken from the express company owing to a mistake in charges, though Miss Williams supposed this had also been disposed of, and this was the one later returned to Fort Worth. Before going to Milwaukee, Miss Williams was in such a nervous condition that only one important step was taken, which was that her people in the South should suppose that she, together with her husband and sister, had gone to Europe or elsewhere, this being made easier inasmuch as some talk had been had earlier of a short fall trip abroad if money matters would allow it.

At about this time there occurred a very severe lake storm, July 18, 1893, doing much damage and it was hoped they would conclude that all had perished during this storm. Certain it is that Miss Williams wrote no more letters to her friends and did not appear publicly in Chicago, if possible to avoid it, in order to carry out this idea, but fortunately for my (our) present safety there are, as I shall show later, several instances when she did appear and in my company.

While she was in Milwaukee, I did what I could to arrange our business affairs so that neither she nor myself should suffer loss, it being impossible for her to make new transfers of a later date or to go to Texas without abandoning the idea of deceiving her friends there regarding her existence.

I was determined, too, as soon as possible, to sever all my relations with her, deeming it unsafe to continue them, and from time to time I encouraged Hatch in his attentions to her, which he was more willing to bestow than she to accept.

Just here it would not be amiss to return to an exciting incident, which lasted some days, in connection with one of my insurance cases.

It happened shortly after the death of my medical friend and former college chum.

The sad announcement of his death—for to me it was a sad one—set me to thinking. I began to seriously consider the chances of my carrying out the plans which my old friend and I had spent so many anxious days and nights in perfecting.

The prospect was a good one, and I desired, and finally determined, to carry at least one of them to a conclusion, single-handed and alone. No person was to be in my confidence, and I set to work getting my scheme in order.

Some time previous to this I had, while in Minneapolis, insured my life for $20,000 in favor of my wife. Failure in this one instance, where my friend was concerned, made a desperate man of me. I determined to succeed at any cost. The prospective profits in the work were most alluring. The chance for detection, of course, must be guarded against, and the contingencies of all other serious accidents which might arise, and make exposure certain, had to be taken into consideration.

Upon figuring up what the gross proceeds had been in similar operations, the result showed me that, with the very modest outlay of $3,950, they aggregated $68,700. This work one can easily see was profitable beyond any legitimate work that might be entered into.

The assessments having been paid up on my recent $20,000 policy to and including the month of June, 1887, I thought that it was time to bring this case to a close.

In order to realize the $20,000 before September 1st, I accordingly went to Chicago and had a long conversation with an acquaintance of a year before, who was an assistant at —— [Holmes omitted the name] Medical College, over certain details of my proposed work.

However, I found it more difficult to obtain a body that would prove a substitute for my own. I had a "cow-lick" which could not be imitated by artificial means, and it was absolutely necessary to get a subject so favored by nature, and I had a most gloomy wait, lasting about two weeks, going to the dead room of the college each morning to inspect the "arrivals," which had come in during the preceding twenty-four hours.

Finally, my patience was rewarded, about May 20th, when I was informed that a man had been killed accidentally falling from a freight car. The body in due time arrived, and after making a most minute and critical examination of it, I determined that it was just what I required for my purpose. Satisfactory arrangements having been made with the hospital for my possession of the subject, I started out to ascertain the best way to have it moved.

It was here that a chain of most extraordinary and gruesomely interesting circumstances began. All the precautions that the mind can conceive and the body execute had to be brought into execution. No chance for detection now could be entertained. No loophole for surprise and discomfiture was to be left uncovered; and I had to do all that was vitally necessary to this end alone.

Knowing that I had a most trustworthy friend in a certain expressman, I at once repaired to his abode. My surprise and discomfiture were great. He was dead. He had died some time previously. All hope for assistance in that quarter, naturally, had to be given up.

From inquiries I made of the janitor of the college, I learned that a certain expressman in the neighborhood could be employed for the purpose I desired, as he had on former occasions been hired for "outside work" by some of the men in the institution, I called at this man's address, and after seeing him I stated my business. "How much will you charge me for taking a body from — [Holmes omitted the name] College to Polk Street Station?" I asked.

"Five dollars," was the reply this man gave me.

This price being satisfactory to me, we started for the place where I had ordered a trunk to be made according to a special design. This trunk was one of more than ordinary large size, and externally it resembled one of those iron-bound, burglar-proof arrangements jewelry salesmen call sample cases. Inside, the construction was of a very elaborate nature.

The greater portion of it being occupied by a large zinc box of sufficient dimensions to allow a man to occupy it by doubling his joints, where doubling was necessary. This was fitted by a lid of wood to deaden any sound that might be caused through the possible rattling of the ice, which was to surround the inner box. The entire trunk was made water-proof, but who knows how it could travel on a railroad train without undergoing severe usage, and possible demolition?

The trunk was taken to the college, the body placed in it with the aid of the expressman, who did not seem to relish that sort of work. He seemed to weaken at times, and once or twice I noticed him grow pale. After the trunk was carefully packed and ready for conveyance to the station, we found that it was almost too early to remove it.

After standing about for some time, the Jehu grew more courageous, inasmuch as he gazed through a few inverted liquor glasses when their contents were amber-lined. He said: —

"I can't do this job for $5."

"Why not?" I asked, very much surprised.

"Because, if I make a hearse of my wagon and personally act as combination driver, undertaker and pall-bearer, I must have $35. If I don't get that sum, I shall inform the police that all is not right."

Of course I expostulated with the man, and resorting, as often before, to my sugar-and-fly policy, I placated him, gave him $5 in cash and promised the other $30 when we reached the station.

This was all right, for he said if I did not pay he would have me arrested instantly.

In due course of time the trunk was carted to the Illinois Central Station, and, after having it placed on the platform, the driver turned to me and demanded the $30 forthwith.

This was the chance I had been waiting for.

"I shall not give you another cent," said I.

"Oh, yes, you will!"

"Besides, I have a mind to demand the return of the $5 from you for attempting to extort money from me."

"You would stand a great chance of getting it, too. Now, give me $30 or to the 'cops' I go."

"You may go, but first listen to me and answer my questions. Did you not, in the presence of the janitor and myself, help place the corpse in the trunk? Did you not haul it here? Have you not assisted me in all this work?"

"Yes, I have."

"That man was murdered. Speak a word about it to any one,

and I will have you arrested as an accessory to his murder."

The driver was evidently very much frightened, as his eyes widened and bulged, and his hair began to assume a perpendicular position.

"The body must go in the lake," I continued, "and let the waves bury it forever from human sight. I hope you understand me."

Then he told me that he did not want any more money, and as I knew his address, he would always be at my service at any future time.

Having purchased my ticket for the timber lands of Michigan, I checked my trunk, and it began its adventurous trip North.

Everything had gone along as well as I could have wished until our train was nearing Grand Rapids. My attention was attracted to a group of trainmen standing about a trunk in the baggage section which occupied the forward part of the smoker in which I was traveling.

I got up and looked closer, and was almost stricken dumb with horror when I saw that it was my trunk, and that the men were talking as though they suspected something wrong with it.

I immediately changed my plans about going North directly, and was in a feverish state of excitement when we reached Grand Rapids. As soon as the trunk was deposited in the baggage room, I went in as though to claim it. As I did so, I noticed a stranger looking at me and on the trunk in a manner which made me feel quite uncomfortable. I pretended not to notice him, and thereby got a better chance to study him. I soon concluded that he was a Secret Service man, and that I had been "spotted."

Realizing that some decisive and telling action was necessary at this time I stepped to the telegraph office and wired myself at the hotel, as follows: —

"Holmes. Look after my trunk, which left Chicago this morning.

(Signed) HARVEY."

The initial "H" was the same as that on my trunk, and when I got to the hotel, I showed the clerk the telegram, which he held for me, and engaged communicating rooms for Harvey and myself, with a bath attachment, I sent a porter for the trunk, and after seeing it in the rooms, I then learned the cause which attracted the attention of the trainmen to it. My suspicions had been confirmed, for an awful odor emanated from the trunk, and I then knew that the man had been dead longer than the college attendants stated, and, also, that I had been imposed upon.

Fearing that such a contingency might arise, I formulated a plan while on the smoking car of transferring the body from the Chicago trunk to another, which I should purchase.

After locking my room carefully, I started out to look for a suitable trunk, but stopped long enough to tell the clerk that my baggage would be on hand in the course of an hour or so. It was growing toward evening, and I had but little time to spare.

After looking about for a short while, I soon got a used trunk that suited my purpose quite well. I ordered the lock to be changed on it, and while this was being done I made several trips to a couple of plumbing shops and bought a considerable quantity of old lead pipe. I had this cut up into suitable lengths, and made into packages. I made several trips to the trunk store, and each time I placed a package of the heavy material in the new trunk, after which I had it sent to my room at the hotel. This was done to make it appear that it was filled with my effects.

The day had been warm, and the night also promised to be sultry. No time was to be lost in getting things in order and to guard against surprises.

During my several trips to the trunk store I noticed the man I first saw at the Grand Rapids Station was looking after me, and I was placed on my guard.

As I said, the night was going to be warm; I knew that it would be but a short time until all the floor I occupied would be permeated with the odor from my friend in the trunk.

I went out again and secured a water-proof hunting bag, and

carried a considerable amount of ice to the room, which I placed in the bath tub.

I then took the lead pipe from my new trunk and laid it beside the first one in the adjoining room.

While doing this work the atmosphere became so stifling that I had to hoist the window. This window opened out on the roof of a porch, and by the time that was done it had grown quite dark.

I decided to defer further work until after I had eaten.

As I entered the dining room I could see the eye of that mysterious stranger watching me in the reflection of the mirror from the bar.

I was somewhat troubled at this, and I did not enjoy my dinner very well.

After my repast, I lounged out to the office and then went to my room.

I went to the bath room first, drained the water from the ice, and prepared a place for the dead man to lie in. When this was done to my satisfaction, I went to the trunk my supposed friend was to occupy and opened it. The usual balancing and cording precautions which I had taken were all right, but the face that met my gaze was drawn, colored and hideous, yet it somewhat resembled the outlines of my own when I first secured the body.

The sight was disgusting, yet when I looked upon it, and realized that at least $20,000 would come to me after a little further trouble, I gazed on it as a very good investment which was about to mature.

The monetary possibilities of this work set me thinking, and yet I knew I had in this instance to work rapidly. I loosed the cords, raised the body, and carried it to the bath tub, where I sought to freeze it hard enough for another day's transportation.

There, in the twinkling light of a solitary gas jet, lay all that was mortal of—I knew not whom.

I claimed him as my own, and as I studied the now rigid form, strange questions arose and floated across my mind.

Who was he? What had he been? Was he a father, a lover, or brother? Was his absence from home noted? Was he cared for? Or, was he, like myself, a wayward son? Such thoughts troubled me but little before, and yet, as he lay there on his frozen bed, I, seemingly fascinated by the awful solemnity of death, did not seem able to tear myself away.

The gas flickered, a door slowly opened, and before I knew what had transpired, I was given the opportunity of looking straight into the eyes of the mysterious stranger—the Secret Service man—over the glittering barrel of a death-dealing weapon.

Not a word was spoken, but our eyes instinctively turned towards the object in the bath tub.

"Consider yourself under arrest, sir," said the nocturnal intruder.

"I am at your service," I replied, knowing that it would be useless to try conclusions with that man in such a small room.

While he was getting some iron bracelets out of his pocket, I mentally determined to have him in the street, glad enough to get away from me and my rooms.

I was ready for him when he walked out into the next room; he keeping his pistol leveled at me with one hand, and trying to get his handcuffs out with the other.

By the merry little twinkle in his eye I read his character as though it lay printed before me on an open page. It was part of my game, and I intended to play my hand as well as I knew how. He seemed to hold a good one, too, but as I had the greatest bower—money—I knew that it was worth the while to play it as best I could.

Desperate, indeed, did my situation become when I saw that he had a companion awaiting us in the room, and a glance at the window explained how their entrance had been effected.

As we got into the chamber the man with the pistol, who was much larger than his associate, looked at me and winked.

"John, go to the station house, and wait until I send for you; but do not say anything until you get word," my captor said to the other.

No sooner had the man called "John" gotten out on the porch roof than the other turned to me with: —

"This is a nice sort of a business, and I have entrapped you neatly in it. It looks very much like the rope for you."

"My dear sir, you will let me explain, I hope. This man was my brother. He has just died of a malignant and very contagious disease. He had been sent to a medical college for dissection, and when I learned of it, I determined to save the body from the demonstrator's knife. Come, look again, and see if you cannot discern a family resemblance?"

As I was talking, the man drew back, and, at my invitation, turned an ashen color. His hands trembled, and as they dropped listlessly the pistol fell to the floor and exploded with a loud report.

Critical as the moment was, it was time for me to act, and I made a successful effort to get the weapon, and as I did so, I ordered him to go to the window and save his life if it was of any value to him.

He lost no time, and as his form disappeared over the ledge of the porch I fired a shot into the air.

This of course brought the landlord and several guests to my door, which I opened in response to repeated knockings.

I was very much excited, apparently, and called out, "There, see, there he goes." The crowd of half-dressed men and women rushed to the window and gave me a chance to close the bathroom door. Heavens, but I did breathe more easily! The escape was a narrow one, but I succeeded in allaying suspicion by saying that the man had attempted burglary, and as I shot he jumped from the roof.

The figure of a running man was discernible in the darkness when they were at the window, which had the effect of verifying my explanations.

After they had gone the landlord offered me the use of another room, which I, of course, declined.

Now my real hard work was to begin. The man was apparently satisfied that I had told the truth, yet he had a suspicious look which I did not like.

As early as possible in the morning, I packed my own trunk with the lead pipe, and to leave that of the fictitious Harvey, while I took my dead friend from his frigid resting place, and repacked him in the new trunk. Upon going to breakfast, I explained that I must go to a place which was somewhat distant, on the early train; but would leave my friend's trunk in the room, as he was expected at any time.

Therefore I had the porter take the newly-packed trunk to the station, where he brought me a ticket and had the trunk checked to my pretended destination.

I timed myself to get to the station just as the train was going out, and as the coast seemed clear, I boarded the smoker.

I knew if the detective missed me, he would go at once to the hotel, and if he found my trunk there he would naturally wait around for an hour or so, thus giving me a pretty good start of him.

When about thirty miles from Grand Rapids I got off to get a paper. The newstand [sic] was next to the Western Union Telegraph office, and as I looked over the operator's shoulder, he received the following message: —

"Look out for man and black trunk. Left here this A. M. Arrest and hold him."

I may have looked queerly, but I inquired in a natural way, how far it was to—[Holmes omitted the location], my destination.

"Forty-eight miles," was the reply of the operator; and without raising his eyes, he called a boy to take the message to the station policeman.

But he was too late. The train started, I swung on, and immediately got hold of the baggage porter. I showed him my ticket, and asked him to put my trunk off at the next station, which was but eight miles distant. This he did, and it was a dismal place, indeed. When I got off the train it was raining. It had been raining hard, evidently, all night. The mud was hub deep on the lumber wagons, and the prospect of stopping there was not a pleasant one.

I learned, upon making inquiries, that I could get to a little town fifteen miles distant, which connected with another railroad, and to do this I would have to drive. I determined to go, however, as the detective, no doubt, would haunt every station between Grand Rapids and my destination until he got some trace of me, when he would learn that I had gotten away from him.

It was with difficulty that I secured a conveyance, which I did in the evening, as I did not want a driver, because I knew the trunk had become troublesome again on account of the odor of my dead companion.

Having carefully attached the trunk to the rear of a back-number buck-board, a dismal trip was begun. As I said, I had considerable difficulty in getting the rig, and as it was I had to leave a deposit large enough to buy several of that particular kind.

After seven hours of the worst riding it has been my misfortune to endure, I reached a small town from which a combination freight and passenger train was about to leave. It was one of those accommodating trains. I "saw" the conductor, who agreed to hold the train for half an hour.

This delay was for the purpose of giving me a chance to freshen my subject up a little. Ice was not procurable, and as there was no drug store in the town, I went down to the grocery store, got the proprietor up and bought several bottles of ammonia, which, when combined with one or two other simple things, made a solution that rendered my quiet friend quite acceptable so far as one's olfactories were concerned.

This operation of attempted preserving was done in the privacy of the baggage car, and all went well until we got about three miles from town. Through the negligence of some section hands a rail was left without the fish-plate being bolted on, and the whole train was ditched.

The engineer was killed, and the conductor was badly injured, as also were two or three passengers. I escaped through a window, and after helping some of the injured who needed surgical attendance, I went to the baggage car. It was a wreck. So was most of the baggage. My trunk and one or two others were intact, and while awaiting the arrival of the relief train and wrecking crew, my thoughts again got to wandering.

There was a score of us. Some were injured, one dead, and all of us anxious. The morning was just breaking; the rain had ceased to fall; and, as I looked away down the railroad, I could just distinguish a cloud of steam and smoke, through the fog, which showed the approach of a train.

Something seemed to tell me that I was about to be confronted with some disagreeable occurrence, and, in anticipation of this premonition becoming a fact, I quickly hauled my trunk to a little shed used by workmen, and impatiently awaited the wrecker. Therefore, I was not astonished when I saw that the first man to alight was my friend, the detective of Grand Rapids. He also saw me, but seemed to pay very little attention to me, as he knew I could not escape, for by this time it was broad daylight, and no trains coming or going.

Finally he accosted me, and we entered into "an agreement" to have my trunk taken to the junction of the road, which was done to my entire satisfaction, and, I have every reason to think, to his also. Just what that little agreement cost me I am not at liberty to say, for that officer still lives.

It was a dark and dreary day when I got into the wild wildernesses of Northern Michigan's lumber tracts. I was soon established in a hut, and it shortly became known that I was a lumber operator of considerable means, and was regarded with much consideration by the hardy hewers of trees and strippers of bark. The men were all honest, it seemed. So one day I went out in the evergreen forest and failed to return.

A week or so later what was purported to be my dead body was found pinioned to the earth by a fallen tree. Money and papers were found in the clothes on the body which established my identity beyond the question of a doubt.

Thus, by case No. 5, after a great deal of trouble and thrilling escapes from the law's officers, I added the neat little sum of $20,000 to my bank account by September 1st, as I had anticipated.

When I had finished with the trunk I presented it to a friend, but at the time did not tell to what use it had been put.

Some years afterwards I met him at his home, and told him all about it. Then he and his wife declared that often they had found it open—no one having touched it—when both declared it had been closed and locked the day previous.

One day in July, 1893, I met an old friend upon the street. I had not seen him for nearly two years, and I noticed at once that he had not prospered since I last saw him. I asked him to accompany me to lunch, and upon inquiry, he told me that his only means of support at that time consisted of what he could earn as a solicitor for the Fidelity Insurance Company of Philadelphia, and he asked me if I could not carry some insurance in his company, to which I replied that I was carrying all I felt able to pay for.

I gave him, however, the names of several parties whom he was to visit, some of whom he later insured. I invited him to come to the office and accompany me to lunch whenever he was in that part of the city, and later, at his solicitation, I abandoned the company in which I had been insured, and allowed him to place a policy for me with his company for two reasons: *first,* that he might be benefited by the premiums I paid; *second,* upon his showing me the advantages they offered. Considerably later, having exhausted all my resources so far as finding him customers was concerned, we were standing within the Chamber of Commerce Building, Chicago, when Pitezel, just returning from a successful Southern lumber trip, came in; and not having seen my friend for quite awhile, they talked for some time together, and finally he asked Pitezel if he could not carry some insurance. Pitezel answered that he did not care to do so then.

Up to that time Pitezel's insurance record was as follows: Upon all long trips, his instructions were to take out temporary insurance at the time he bought his transportation ticket or mileage, making the policies in favor of his family, and at my expense. He had occasionally carried yearly accident insurance, and upon one occasion some regular life insurance in the Washington Life Co. Soon after this meeting with Pitezel, my friend asked me to try and induce him to take some in his company. Pitezel was about to receive several hundred dollars, the greater part of which I knew would, in a very few days, be wasted, and considering the great help it would be to my friend during the coming winter, I decided to induce Pitezel to insure, telling my friend beforehand my reasons for doing so, and instructing him to place no more insurance than Pitezel would pay cash for at the time.

Later, a policy was issued for $10,000, for which a cash premium was paid. This policy differed very materially from one I should have chosen, if any fraud had been anticipated at the time. After this I do not think insurance was again mentioned between Pitezel and myself for six months.

Fig. 14. Mrs. Pitezel
Source: Herman W. Mudgett, *Holmes' Own Story*, 1895, p. 88.

My first intimate acquaintance with Mrs. Pitezel and her children began in the fall of 1893, although I had often seen them prior to that, especially the children, whom I liked and looked upon as remarkably bright when they had come to me from time to time upon errands. At this time Pitezel had gone to Indiana on some lumber business there among the farmers, and to aid him in establishing a credit, had taken with him some worthless checks to carelessly exhibit among his money, thus having it appear that he was a man of considerable means and worthy of credit in his business.

While under the influence of liquor he either lost or tried to use one of these checks or drafts, resulting in his being arrested.

This necessitated my making three special trips to Terre Haute, where his arrest occurred, and during this time a part of his family being sick, it was also necessary for me to visit them often as well. In November, 1893, I met Miss Williams by appointment at a hotel, where I made some preliminary arrangements that resulted later, after several more visits, in her accepting collateral security for all her real estate holdings in Texas, they being valueless to her for the reasons previously given.

> **Say the Checks Are Forgeries.**
>
> Inspector Shea has been called upon by the police authorities at Terre Haute, Ind., to investigate the case of Benjamin F Pitzel, alias Robert Jones, who is under arrest in that city charged with attempting to pass forged checks. Several merchants at Terre Haute complained that Pitzel had bought goods of them and offered checks in payment for the same. When taken into custody some $5,000 in commercial paper was found on his person. It is believed that all the checks are drawn by the Holbroah Lumber company and the Aimes Wheel company, and are accepted by the American Exchange National bank, all of this city. The bank people say the checks are forgeries, and that the acceptance stamps bears no resemblance to theirs whatever. Pitzel claims to have received the checks through a commercial transaction in this city. He also claims to have resided at Eighty-ninth and Carpenter streets.

Fig. 15. Benjamin Pitezel arrested in Terre Haute, Indiana, for check fraud
Source: "Say the Checks are Forgeries," *Daily Inter Ocean*, October 6, 1893, p. 5.

The last of these visits took place in Detroit in December, 1893 (nearly six months after the death of her sister), since which time I have not personally seen her. At the time of this visit a final settlement was reached. I told her, after having reached such a settlement, that I was very shortly to be married. This created so severe a scene that she not only threatened my life, but that of my prospective wife as well. These threats ceased only when I told her I should, upon my return to Chicago, give to the authorities the details of the tragedy that had occurred there in July.

The next day she seemed as pleasant as usual, and planned her own future course, which consisted in opening a massage establishment in a London hotel, Hatch to help her in conducting the enterprise.

About the middle of February I sent to her, from Fort Worth, $1,750, which, when deducted from my previous indebtedness due her, left me still considerably in her debt. This was secured by the Wilmette property, the title to which it was agreed she should hold until all was paid. I left Miss Williams in Detroit, apparently well pleased with her business arrangements, and at least passably satisfied that the many other matters between us had been settled.

Early in January, 1894, I sent Pitezel to Fort Worth, instructing him to sell the real estate there which previously had been conveyed to Benton T. Lyman, whom Pitezel was to personate, it not being safe for him to act in his own name on account of his recent trouble in Terre Haute, Ind. He did not succeed in readily finding a purchaser, and later in the same month, having been married in the meantime, I joined him there to aid him in his work. I had given Pitezel careful instructions as to his conduct while away, but I found upon reaching Fort Worth that he had not been governed by them. My first duty was to remove him from the boarding place he had chosen to one in a more respectable quarter, but the mischief had already been accomplished, and he was known by that time throughout the town as a liberal, free and easy drinking man, who, it was understood, had considerable property.

A party owning property adjoining that which we wished to sell had need of a portion of ours, but would not buy, depending upon renting it at a very small figure, as he had been doing heretofore. In order to force him to buy I directed Pitezel to withdraw his offer, and remain wholly away from him, quietly survey our lot, and proceed to excavate a portion of it, having it understood that he was about to erect a large building, covering all of the ground. Our neighbor was fully as crafty as ourselves, and not until we had caused elaborate drawings to be prepared by an architect, and some foundation laid encroaching upon the portion he needed, did he conclude to buy, and at a figure about twice what it was worth. With a portion of this money, the old encumbrance of $1,700, that had existed against the property, was paid. Then having had some tempting offers from prospective tenants, a larger loan was made and the building later nearly completed.

While the building was in progress there came to us a forlorn looking object, begging for work, and out of charity, we gave him some light labor to do. He grew stronger as soon as he procured food. Later he confided to me that he had recently been released from serving a ten-year term in a Southern prison.

I had at first called him "Mascot," which name clung to him thereafter, though I think his real name was Caldwell.

Early in March Pitezel came to me one morning to say that the day before while drunk he had been induced by some of the disreputable associates he had formed at his former boarding place to marry a woman of doubtful character, an adventuress some said, and that as soon as he became sober had come to me. He threatened to shoot both the woman and himself. I had him watched carefully for a few days, until I had reasoned him out of this idea. A little later I sent him home to his family in Chicago. He had in the meantime lived with this woman, and they were known as Mr. And Mrs. Lyman.

Upon reaching Chicago he did some work there, and in St. Louis where he afterwards went. He finally met me about May 1st, at Denver, where I had gone to prepare papers with which to secure a loan of $16,000 upon this Fort Worth building. I needing his signature to the papers, inasmuch as the property was (and still is) in his fictitious name, Lyman, upon meeting him in Denver, I wished to proceed at once to the Court House to have the necessary papers acknowledged, but he told me had, while away, devised a plan whereby he could not only gain $10,000, but at the same time forever do away with any fear of prosecution or trouble in consequence of his marriage in Fort Worth—a matter which had perpetually worried him.

I had times without number listened to his visionary schemes for obtaining vast wealth upon a day's notice, usually in connection with some new patent, until such matters had become a joke between us.

So I said to him, "Well, Col. Sellers, what is it now?" He replied that it was one of my own inventions, and if I would go to the hotel with him, he would tell me of it. He seemed so much in earnest that I, although in a great hurry, went with him.

His plan was this (I should say here that several years before, while making a Southern lumber trip with him, he had taken up some of the tedious hours of the journey in telling me of his wild gold-mining experiences, and, in reciprocation, I had told him something of my medical experience, including a part of the frustrated insurance scheme): He wished to hire an office in one of the highest buildings in Denver, having it understood that he was to use it as a wholesale book agent's office; that he should buy an awning to protect the room from the sun, and while placing it in position upon the outside of the window it should appear that he had fallen into the area way below, wishing me to have shipped to him from Chicago, or elsewhere, a body which he could use to aid in the fraud.

I do not think we talked of the matter to exceed fifteen minutes. He was accustomed to accept my judgment upon matters of importance without much hesitancy. I proceeded to give him several reasons why his plan was not a feasible one, principal among which was the fact that at the present time insurance companies are too well equipped and too much upon the alert not to detect this kind of fraud, nearly all of them having a corps of private detectives. Among other reasons I gave him was one he very well knew, that theretofore, when I had thought it wise to indulge in business transactions that were not strictly legitimate, I had always insisted upon two conditions being carried out: —

First, that such proceedings should be outside the regular beaten track followed by ordinary disreputable schemers, for in consequence thereof those engaged in them were closely watched. *Second,* that all such acts should stop short of anything that was punishable by either a large fine or imprisonment.

There was another reason I had for not entering into this fraud at that time, if no others had existed, I did not tell him of it, namely, that during the previous years he had been worth to me much more than $10,000 per year, and I could not afford to have him place himself in such a position as would necessarily be the case if this were carried out where I could not further use him. His idea in regard to this had been to go to South America and later have his family join him there.

Having dismissed the matter, I went on with my real estate work, and as soon as the papers were executed, returned to Fort Worth, Pitezel going back to St. Louis to attend to some work there.

Upon reaching Fort Worth, I found that some to whom money was owing had filed mechanics' and furnishers' liens against the property, and this so alarmed the party who was to have made the large loan that he withdrew from his agreement, and this resulted in a large number of the other creditors becoming alarmed, some two or three proposing to cause my arrest for having obtained the material for the building under false pretenses of payment.

I had never been arrested, and I had the same horror of it that I would of being shot. Especially terrible seemed the methods prevalent in the South, where I had seen, from time to time, convicts chained together, with hardly any clothing, and if I could believe the reports our "Mascot" had given us, with less food and more inhuman treatment than was accorded the slaves of that region forty years ago.

I therefore raised what money I could, paying all of it, save $200, to the poorer laborers who had worked for me, and immediately left the city, intending to secure the loan in St. Louis or Chicago.

From time to time, during my residence in Fort Worth, I had bought from different parties six good horses, paying for them, it is true, for the most part with notes guaranteed by Lynam [Lyman] as the owner of the real estate there. I make no claim that these notes have been paid, but I do claim that the transactions were lawful, that no mortgage or other encumbrance existed against any of the horses, but they were, however, subject to attachment by any parties whom I was owing, and to avoid this I instructed "Mascot" to take them to Denison, Texas, and ship them from there to St. Louis.

Upon reaching Denison he shipped five of the horses, but failed to accompany them himself, or send $300 worth of other material, including much of my clothing, one carriage, a watch I had loaned him, and $80 cash given him to pay the freight upon the stock; nor did I hear from him again until July, 1895, when, as an inmate of an Arkansas prison, he was willing in exchange for his liberty to tell of matters of which he could not have known even had they existed.

After reaching St. Louis, I immediately tried to negotiate the loan I had failed to secure in the South. Pitezel was feeling much annoyed at my failure there, for he had expected a rather more liberal payment therefrom than he had received during the few preceding months, owing to the fact that while he had been in Texas it had been necessary, in order to appear that he was the owner there, that he should carry the bank account in his name, and before he had known it, during his drunkenness, he had been robbed little by little of nearly $1,000. Therefore, when I told him that we should be short of money for some time longer, he again advocated the insurance scheme, saying that it could be carried out in the Southern Lumber Co.

He felt sure, and finally, against my better judgement, I told him we would take a trip to the region he had spoken of, partly upon lumber business and partly to look over the ground in connection with the insurance work. He was as pleased as a child, and all his morose feelings vanished at once. We first went down the Mississippi River to visit a lumber tract that had been offered to me the year before upon very easy terms, hoping to buy it, using some Chicago securities as payment, and by selling at once to raise the money we so much needed at Fort Worth. We found upon reaching our destination that this tract had been sold.

We then went East to the Tombigbee River in search of another similar tract, and here Pitezel wished to have it appear that while he was traveling upon horseback through the extensive swamps he had met his death accidentally, or had been killed for what money he was supposed to have carried. He was known in that locality under his own name, having transacted a number of legitimate lumber deals there the year before. After wandering with Pitezel for several days through those swamps, being eaten by fleas and terrified by snakes, he walking ahead, as he said, to drive them away, but, as I later found, to escape their anger by passing out of their reach, leaving them for me to contend with, I flatly refused to go farther with the scheme, but told him instead that I would interest some of the planters in a canning factory.

With the machinery which I was able to furnish from Chicago I felt sure that, before sixty days, we could realize $15,000 in cash and lumber therefrom. He would not hear to it, however, and opposed me more strongly than I had ever known him to do previously. He told me that at that time he was liable to arrest in Kansas, in Terre Haute, Ind., and Fort Worth, Texas, and that since his domestic trouble some years before in Chicago he had cared less than ever, and he had been determined ever since he left Texas, where he had drank more heavily than before (which also worried him), that he would leave the country, and now, if he could not do so, he would, upon my refusal to go on, go through with his scheme alone. His words were, "I can furnish a body, and, the way I feel now, I do not care how quickly I do it."

Seeing how downhearted he was I complained no more, but

talked with him of other things, and finally told him that I next day go to Mobile, and if I could procure a suitable body there, would return with it. If not, I should go direct from Mobile to St. Louis, where he must join me, and, after doing some work there, we would go to Chicago and organize a company among certain lumber firms we knew, and return South later and make what money we could by exchanging this stock and machinery for the canning factory into lumber and other products. I therefore left him, as he supposed, to go to Mobile. This I did not do, and have never been in that city in my life. I returned at once to St. Louis and, after a little delay, wrote to Pitezel that it had been impossible to obtain what I needed South and for him to join me at once. Nearly two weeks' delay occurred before he came. His wife had been receiving letters from him that he was sick during this time.

Later, after his death, I learned that upon receiving my letter that I could not do any more in the insurance matter he had made an effort to take his life at the hotel of Henry Rodgers, at Perkinsville, Ala., and for days, as a result of this ineffectual attempt, he was sick there, as he was later at the Gilmer House, at Columbus, Miss. As soon as I reached St. Louis I found that all efforts towards securing a loan there were useless, and being nearly out of money, owing to my having paid out so much before leaving Fort Worth, I had to look sharply about for some immediate source of revenue. I finally bought and took possession of a drug store in that city, paying for it with notes secured by a chattel mortgage and some other securities. Owing to the negligence of the firm of whom I bought, this mortgage was not recorded, and upon Pitezel reaching the city I sold to him all my right, title and interest (this being the wording of the bill of sale) in the store, which he immediately mortgaged for a considerable sum.

For this transaction I was arrested and confined in the St. Louis jail for several days until, although I perhaps could, by a legal fight, have shown that I had a right to sell the store under these circumstances, it became clear to me that it was safer to settle the matter, which was done.

My arrest occurred on a Saturday evening, and from then until Monday morning I was confined in the receiving portion of the jail, below the level of the street, and these few hours of my first imprisonment were far more trying to me than my subsequent experiences of like nature have been.

Here, all through that long, hot Sunday, all classes of prisoners, both male and female, were brought together, and allowed to indulge in the most filthy and obscene talk.

And at the open windows, opening directly upon the sidewalk, all day and far into the night, a crowd was standing, more than half of whom were tiny children, eagerly drinking in each word that was said. The next morning I had handcuffs placed upon my wrists, and was taken into Court and later into the jail proper, where better discipline was enforced. Here I was consigned to a very small iron cage (I know no better name for it), one of about three hundred, ranged tier above tier around a large area in which all, or nearly all, the prisoners are allowed to exercise together during certain hours of the day.

Here were to be seen many noted criminals, who were soon pointed out to me as "This is so and so, who is to be hung upon such a date." (About thirty murderers, one of whom was the prison barber, who if you paid him ten cents, would shave you with a very dull razor, while if you paid him more he would use a sharp one; and as I sat in his chair, I could not help thinking that which ever one he used was plenty sharp enough for him to commit one more murder with, if he chose, and I therefore directed him to use his sharpest razor at a price above his own figure, very much as I would have held out a tempting piece of meat to a vicious dog which I feared was about to bite me.)

Or, "That is the notorious forger or confidence man," as the case might be. Among others was one, a noted train robber [Marion Hedgepeth] then serving an eighteen years' sentence, and who a short time previously had become more notorious by a nearly successful attempt at escape from the prison. He is a young man, whom, to meet upon the street, one would suppose to be a bright mechanic or a farmer. He is very intelligent, and I took much interest in talking with him. He told me of the case that had resulted in his arrest; of his subsequent trial, and remarked that Blank & Blank in St. Louis were his attorneys; to which I replied that but for the fact of the senior members of the firm being absent on a vacation they would have been my attorneys as well, I having first sent for them, and finding this to be the case had employed Judge Harvey instead.

He afterwards asked me if, upon leaving the prison, I could not contribute $300, which, together with some other money he could obtain, would give him his liberty by bribing one of the keepers, making a claim that he had successfully done so before. My answer was, that at the present time I had less ready money than had been the case for years previously, owing to my having invested so much in the South. I told him if I could arrange to aid him later I would do so, but I made no engagement with him to furnish me with an attorney for the insurance work as has been claimed, for I was already acquainted with the firm.[8]

LETTER HEDGEPETH WROTE TO CHIEF OF POLICE:

St. Louis, Mo.,
Tuesday, October 9th, 1894.
MAJOR LAWRENCE HARRIGAN,
Chief of Police.

DEAR SIR:—

When H. M. Howard[9] was in here some two months ago, he came to me and told me he would like to talk to me, as he had read a great deal of me, etc.; also after we got well acquainted, he told me he had a scheme by which he could make $10,000, and he needed some lawyer who could be trusted, and said if I could, he would see that I got $500 for it. I then told him that J. D. Howe could be trusted, and he then went on and told me that B. F. Pitezel's life was insured for $10,000, and that Pitezel and him were going to work the insurance company for the $10,000, and just how they were going to do it; even going into minute details; that he was an expert at it, as he had worked it before, and that being a druggist, he could easily deceive the insurance company by having Pitezel fix himself up according to his directions and appear that he was mortally wounded by an explosion, and then put a corpse in place of Pitezel's body, etc., and then have it identified as that of Pitezel. I did not take much stock in what he told me, until after he went out on bond, which was in a few days, when J. D. Howe came to me and told me that that man Howard, that I had recommended him to, had come and told him that I had recommended Howe to him and had laid the whole plot open to him, and Howe told me that he never heard of a finer or smoother piece of work, and that it was sure to work, and that Howard was one of the smoothest and slickest men that he ever heard tell of, etc., and Howe told me that he would see that I got $500 if it worked, and that Howard was going on East to attend to it at once. (At this time I did not know what insurance company was to be worked, and am not sure yet as to which one it is, but Howe told me that it was the Fidelity Mutual of Philadelphia, whose office is, according to the city directory, at No. 520 Olive Street.) Howe came down and told me every two or three days, that everything was working smoothly and when notice appeared in the Globe Democrat and Chronicle of the death of B. F. Pitezel, Howe came down at once and told me that it was a matter of a few days until we would have the money, and that the only thing that might keep the company from paying it at once, was the fact that Howard and Pitezel were so hard up for money, that they could not pay the dues on the policy until a day or two before it was due, and then had to send it by telegram, and that the company might claim that they did not get the money until after the lapse of the policy; but they did not, and so Howe and a little girl (I think Pitezel's daughter) went back to Philadelphia and succeeded in identifying and having the body recognized as that of B. F. Pitezel. Howard told me that Pitezel's wife was privy to the whole thing. Howe tells me now that Howard would not let Mrs. Pitezel go back to identify the supposed body of her husband, and that he feels almost positive and certain that Howard deceived Pitezel and that Pitezel in following out Holme's instructions, was killed and that it was really the body of Pitezel.

The policy was made out to the wife and when the money was put in the bank, then Howard stepped out and left the wife to settle with Howe for his services. She was willing to pay him $1,000, but he wants $2,500 and so $2,500 of the money is held until they get over squabbling about it. Howard is now on his way to Germany, and Pitezel's wife is here in the city yet, and where Pitezel is or whether that is Pitezel's body I can't tell, but I don't believe it is Pitezel's body, but believe that he is alive and well and probably in Germany, where Howard is now on his way. It is hardly worth while to say that I never got the $500 that Howard held out to me for me to introduce him to Mr. Howe. Please excuse this poor writing as I have written this in a hurry and have to write on a book placed on my knee. This and a lot more I am willing to swear to. I wish you would see the Fidelity Mutual Life Insurance Company and see if they are the ones who have been made the victim of this swindle, and if so, tell them that I want to see them. I never asked what company it was until today, and it was after we had some words about the matter, and so Howe may not have told the proper company, but you can find out what company it is by asking or telephoning to the different companies. When I asked Mrs. Pitezel's address he waited a long time and finally said it was No. 6342 S. Michigan Ave. Please send an agent of the company to see me if you please.

Yours Resp., etc.,
MARION C. HEDGEPETH

Source: Frank P. Geyer. *The Holmes-Pitezel case; a history of the greatest crime of the century and of the search for the missing Pitezel children.* Philadelphia, PA: Publishers' Union, 1896.

Fig. 16. A smiling Marion Hedgepeth
Source: "You Can't Read Character by the Eye," *The Ogden Standard,* June 20, 1914, p. 19.

Fig. 17. Marion Hedgepeth booking photo, number 11,205
Source: Miller images.

Fig. 18. Jeptha D. Howe was the attorney Hedgepeth referred to in his letter ratting out Holmes to the Chief of Police. Howe represented Mrs. Pitezel after Benjamin Pitezel's death in order to claim insurance proceeds. For his part in the insurance swindle,

Howe was arrested in Philadelphia; however, authorities did not prosecute him due to lack of evidence. Only two witnesses claimed he knew about the swindle: H. H. Holmes and Marion Hedgepeth, both of whom where unreliable.
Source: "Jeptha D. Howe is Dead," *Kansas City Star,* March 12, 1919, p. 2.

The balance of my short stay in this prison was taken up by my reading "Les Miserables," a peculiarly interesting volume to me under the circumstances, and I judge it was to all prisoners who cared for reading, as was evidenced by the condition of the book itself, which I obtained from the prison library. I was also entertained by watching a huge negro being prepared to meet his death by hanging, by having alternately administered to him spiritual consolation from his confessors, large quantities of cigars to smoke, food to eat and liquor or beer to drink. A so-called death watch was kept also, but not so stringent but that he was allowed to go alone to the front of the compartments occupied by his favorite companions, and talk at some length with them.

Next morning, upon looking from my laticed [latticed] window across into the court yard, I saw him meet his death upon the gallows in the presence of a large and morbidly curious crowd of people. If I had been in need of any warning to deter me from almost immediately placing my self in a similar position, I know of no stronger one that I could have received than to witness this man's death struggles, to see the crowd making light of it, and almost before he was dead quarreling to possess small portions of the rope which sent his soul hence, and, I think, of his clothes. Gruesome relics they were, indeed.

Upon the day I was liberated from this place of confinement, I visited first my own attorney and later Blank & Blank, in the same street, at which time the following conversation took place.

Entering the office, and having explained who I was, I said: —

"I have called on you to perhaps make some arrangements that will aid in securing the liberty of your client," to which one of the firm to whom I spoke, replied, "I guess you have made a mistake in the office; I know nothing in regard to the matter." I said, "I am sure I have made no mistake in the office, and furthermore, have seen either you or your brother talking to him at the prison. However, my visit to you was to aid your client, and of no immediate value to me, and I have no desire to force the recognition of your client upon you, and will therefore bid you good day." Upon my withdrawing to the door, he followed me, and said, "Wait a moment; I will go down to the prison and see what my client means; you come here again, shortly."

I replied that I should be in Judge Harvey's office, and upon his return he could call there if he wished to talk further with me. I would then accompany him to his office. He did call for me, and upon reaching his private office was willing and ready to talk. Our conversation resulted in my placing in his hands for collection nearly $500 worth of good accounts, authorizing him to apply $300 of the proceeds to the robber's use. I also gave him my Chicago address, in case he wished to write me.

As I was leaving his office he said, "My client wished me to ask you, if he succeeds in gaining his liberty, if you will aid him in a certain piece of bank work he wishes to do." I replied that it was wholly out of my line, and I should be of no more service to him in such work than a dead man; moreover, my recent imprisonment had shown me the necessity of being even more careful to avoid laying myself liable to arrest in the future, but that I would furnish the chloroform and nitroglycerine he needed upon my arrival in Chicago, and have it placed in a safe place with a suit of clothes and other articles we had planned during our interview, and possibly might aid him later in disposing of certain bonds and stocks he expected to gain possession of; but that there would be ample time to plan for that after he had gained his liberty, for which I would watch the papers closely.

Upon this I left his office, and started for Chicago the same evening, where I had previously sent Pitezel to commence arrangements among the lumber men whom he knew for the formation of the stock company before mentioned. I reached Chicago August 1, 1894, and upon calling upon my attorney there and also my agent, both assured me that it was dangerous for me to stay in Chicago, as there were then Fort Worth parties there looking for me, and forming an alliance with some persons whom I was owing to cause my arrest, and thereby force me to procure the money due them.

My attorney instructed me to go elsewhere if I thought sufficient money could be made to satisfy these debts and organize my company, and upon my asking him where I should go, he told me that either New York or New Jersey were favorable States in which to organize companies to do business elsewhere. Having other business in New York I decided to go there, though under a different name, lest the granting of a charter to a company of which I was an officer should, by being published, be noticed by the Fort Worth parties.

I suggested to Pitezel that he should finish some patents, one of which I wished to use in this company, and it was later decided that he should go with me to New York to act as one of the incorporators and to work upon his patents in some small shop he was to hire for the purpose. Before leaving Chicago he reminded me that his insurance premium would be due before our return, and wished me to give him the money to pay it before he went away, remarking that he still thought I would be glad to fall back upon this plan of getting money after my company had failed me. I told him that, owing to the stringency of our money matters, I had allowed my own insurance to lapse and wished he would do the same. He was not willing to do this, advancing, besides the reason already given, that while it was safe for me to allow my insurance to lapse, as I had other things with which to protect those dependent upon me in case of my death, he had little or nothing. He also knew that I had collected a considerable sum of money since coming to Chicago, and could, if necessary, give him what was needed.

I finally settled the matter to his satisfaction in the following manner: Upon the day his insurance expired I was to give him sufficient money to take out a three months' accident policy for $5,000; it was supposed he at that time carried $1,000 of the same kind of insurance, and I agreed to be personally responsible to his family to the extent of $4,000 in case he died, this aggregating the sum of $10,000. He was satisfied with this, it being agreed that at the end of three months, when our money matters were in a more flourishing condition, his regular insurance should be renewed. During our trip to New York, in my talk with him, not having had much opportunity to plan and hold genial conversation together since he left Fort Worth months before, I noticed that he was not as pleasant as usual, was more inclined to sit by himself and smoke and think and frown and worry. I spoke to him of it, and asked him if he had encountered any new trouble at home, to which he answered that he had not.

We reached New York about August 5th, I think. I went to the Astor House and he secured a boarding place near Thirty-third street. I at once commenced to look about for some small space in a shop where he could carry on his work.

Up to this time, since I had sent Miss Williams the various sums aggregating $1,500 from Texas, during the preceding winter, I had received only two letters from her, both forwarded to me from New York through a friend in Denver, who had acted as my agent in the matter. About the time I left Fort Worth, I had written her asking that she send me $600. I found this amount awaiting me at New York in Bank of England notes, which I later converted into Unites States currency at Drexel & Co., in Philadelphia and in New York.

For the first few days of my stay in New York, I was busy

visiting several large machinery stores and in doing some other work pertaining to my company's business of years before. Upon the morning of the 9th of August, Pitezel reminded me that his insurance expired that day, and requested that I aid him in placing his temporary insurance.

I had been waiting for him to make this announcement. He had a very valuable, undeveloped patent, nearly finished, a machine for testing eggs, which I wished to use at once. I therefore said to him, suppose I pay you $500 cash for your share of the new patent (I by previous contract already owned one-half of it), then you can use the money as you choose, both for insurance and other matters. He answered that he ought not to take less than a $1,000. I finally gave him $600 for it, and upon his asking me which he should do, retain his old insurance or take out the new, I at once advised him to retain the old, for two reasons: *First,* it would help my old friend again. *Second,* if he took the third insurance, long before the expiration of that time his money would have been blown away, and I should feel obliged to give him more.

He then said, "I will go and telegraph to the company in Chicago, and see if they will keep my insurance in force until the money can reach them." I said, wire them the money instead. This was apparently a new idea to him, for after understanding it he not only wired them what was due, but also a small amount to St. Louis to his wife, I, as usual, cautioned him to be careful of the rest of the money, and make it last as long as he could. Besides this I had done all I could to cheer him up, and get him out of the morbid condition he had been in, and he voluntarily promised that for the following thirty days he would not drink liquor.

He told me afterwards that so hard did he try to keep his promise after I left him in New York that he went to the post-office there, and sent by registered letter to B. F. Perry[10] in Philadelphia, nearly all the money he had, so as to place himself beyond temptation for the first hard days of his struggle. At this time I had come to Philadelphia to meet my wife, to do some business with the Link Belt Engineering Company, with some stationers and with the Pennsylvania Railroad, all of whom were using a patent in which I was interested. Upon reaching Philadelphia I found that this and other work would detain me some time, and not knowing of Pitezel's precaution already taken, and fearing lest he should become drunk in New York, I wrote to him to come here. This he did, and, deciding to made our headquarters here, I hired some rooms for my wife and myself.

He immediately commenced to look about for a part of a shop in which to do his work. My wife was taken seriously ill about this time, and continued so during the remainder of our stay in Philadelphia. I was not able to be away from the house more than a few hours at a time, and therefore did not see as much of Pitezel as I otherwise should. About the middle of August he told me he had hired an entire house at 1316 Callowhill street, it being but little more expensive than a shop. That he had met another patent man who had promised to pay a part of the rent, remarking at the same time that when I got ready to help him in what he wished to do, he would buy out the other man's business or move elsewhere, and if I perfected my company and went South to unload it, he, if he could make any money in his patent exchange, would have his family come to Philadelphia for the winter, as under the name of Perry he did not fear trouble.

I did not have anything to do with the leasing of the house, nor was I in it to exceed four times prior to the day before his death.

Upon Saturday, September 1st, I called on him to execute some patent papers to send to Washington, and at this time he certainly was doing a good business. During the time I was there no less than twenty customers called, some of them being agents he was supplying with certain washing and cleaning compounds that he manufactured. He had also surrounded himself with a great number of models of patents he was trying to sell for other parties on commission. So busy was he, that after waiting patiently for a long time, I told him I would go to my house and would return next day to execute the work he wished to do. Just before leaving he asked me to lend him $30 or $35, saying he wished to use it to pay his rent that was then due and to place some advertisements in the next day's papers, explaining to me that all his money was in two large bills, which he did not wish to change until necessary, as, if once broken, he feared he would spend them faster.

I laughingly said to him, "Ben, you are sure they are not spent already?" he answered, "Oh, no! I have them placed away safely upstairs; I can go up and get them if you want me to[,]" and then started as if to do so. I gave him the money, saying that I did not require him to verify his statement.

That evening he came to my place of residence at about 8:30. I noticed at once that he had been drinking, and spoke to him of it, though not in anger, as it had always been my custom to wait until he became sober before chiding him. He told me that he had received word that one of his children was sick, and it might become necessary for him to go home. I asked him which child it was, and also told him he had better telegraph and instruct his wife to wire him if she thought it was necessary for him to go. He then spoke of leaving his business, and asked me what he should do about it if the man he was expecting to take an interest with him did not come on at once. I told him I thought it best for him to select the most trustworthy of his agents to leave in the office for a few days, reminding him that I had to go to St. Louis upon some legal business early in the week, and therefore could not aid him. I then bade him good night, telling him I had to go to the market near by before it should be closed. He said he would go with me. He waited at the market while I made my purchases, and returned with me almost without speaking. I then again said "[G]ood night."

He said, "Can't you come out again? I want to see you."

I told him as my wife was not well, I could not very well be absent longer, attributing his unusual request to his having been drinking; I also reminded him that I was to see him early the next day.

He said in reply, "Then come out a moment now, and I will go home."

I did so, and he said, "You will have to let me have some money in case I have to go to St. Louis."

I said, "[T]hat will hardly be necessary; use what you have, and if the child dies or other unforeseen expense arises, I shall be in St. Louis during the week, and can then see to it."

He replied, "Well, I will have to tell you; I have not got any money save what you gave me to-day, and I have used part of that for liquor instead of paying my rent with it."

I said, "Ben, this makes over $1,600 you have wasted in debauchery and drink within the last seven months while your family have needed it. I am done. I told you in Fort Worth if it occurred again I should settle our business affairs, and thereafter you would have to care for yourself. I don't want to talk with you to-night, but to-morrow I will go to your house, and I want to settle up not only the patent work, as we had intended, but all our other affairs, and in the future if I can spare any money it will be given to your family instead of to you, but I will go to see them upon my arrival in St. Louis, and will, if the child is dangerously sick, send you money to go home with."

He said they had no money then to live on.

I said, "If I find this to be so, I will give them some. It will not be the first time I have done so, and far in excess of what would have come to them had you been working elsewhere. For your own part, you will have to keep sober here in Philadelphia in order to make a living, which I know you can do if you try." He was crying at the time. He then asked me if I would not help him to carry out the insurance work, having it appear he had been robbed there in the Callowhill street house. I replied, that inasmuch as he was persisting in drinking, it would not be a month after it was carried out before he told some one of it. He said, "You are in earnest; you will not help me any more; I can do nothing alone."

I replied, "I am in earnest, and will talk it all over with you tomorrow, and plan as best we can for the family," and again bade him good night, and as he reluctantly started away I asked him to promise me not to drink again that evening, and to go at once to his home and to bed.

He promised to do this after first going again to the telegraph office to see if there were any messages for him. He then left me, and that is the last time I ever saw him alive.

I wish to say, however, that while I thought it wise and for his advantage for him to suppose he had got to care for himself in the future, I had no intention of abandoning him, if for no other reason than that he was too valuable a man, even with his failings taken into consideration, for me to dispense with. I should have gone through a form of settlement with him next day, and upon my return from St. Louis, if I found him sober, have gone on as before.

The next morning I went to the Callowhill street house, reaching there about 11 o'clock, entering with a key he had given me some weeks before to use if I came there in his absence. I found no one in the front portion of the house, and passed back into the kitchen; finding that also deserted, I went to the stairway and called him by name; receiving no answer, I went up the stairs so that I could look into the room where he slept.

He was not there, and I was much worried, thinking that, instead of coming home as he had promised, he had gone about the city and perhaps had been arrested. Upon returning to the kitchen, however, I noticed that there were evidences of a fire having recently been built in the stove, and, therefore, did not think more of the matter, concluding that he had gone to the postoffice or telegraph office.

I then left the house, but before doing so I placed a chair in a narrow passageway at the end of a counter, to denote to him, if he returned before I did, that I had been there. I went to the Mercantile Library and read the foreign papers for about an hour, went to a place on Eleventh street where I had a box for my private mail, and then, buying a Philadelphia Sunday paper, I returned to the Callowhill street house, entering as before.

The chair was as I had left it. I sat down for a few minutes to read, then went into the kitchen and rekindled the fire, so that he could prepare us a light lunch as soon as he returned, while I was making up the necessary papers.

The fire soon making the lower rooms uncomfortably warm, I went up stairs and lay down upon his bed and resumed the reading of the paper.

Fig. 19. Holmes Burning Benjamin Pitezel's Clothing
Source: Herman W. Mudgett, *Holmes' Own Story*, 1895, p. 124.

Fig. 20. Mercantile Library where Holmes read foreign papers
Source: The Miriam and Ira D. Wallach Division of Art, Prints and Photographs: Photography Collection, *The New York Public Library*. "Mercantile Library, Philadelphia, Pa." New York Public Library Digital Collections.

While there I noticed an unusual odor and finally got up. Upon going into the adjoining room I found perhaps two dozen small bottles containing a certain cleaning fluid upon the mantel, some of which were uncorked. This fluid contained some chloroform, ammonia and benzine among other ingredients, all being of a volatile nature.

I don't know how long I stayed there, nor what time it was when I finally thought it best to go home, and I then went down stairs to his desk to write him a note. There among the paper I found a note written in a cipher we sometimes used, which read, "Get letter in bottle in cupboard," or words to that effect. (This note being one that no one could read without my aid, I carried it in the small watch pocket of my pantaloons, until in Toronto, having a new suit of clothing made, from which my tailor had omitted such a pocket, I placed the note in a tin box of papers that later was taken by the authorities. The note is now, or should be, in their hands.)

I went to the kitchen cupboard, which was the only one I had noticed in the house, and there I found a whiskey flask, within which I could see some paper.

To get at it I quickly broke the bottle, and upon opening the letter I read, "I am going to kill myself, if I can do it. You will find me up stairs. I am worth more dead than alive." I did not wait to finish the letter at that time, but went hurriedly up stairs. The only place on the second floor I had not had occasion to visit that morning was a small room under the stairway, and looking into it I found it empty.

I then ran up this stairway to the third story, a portion of the house I had never before been in.

It consisted of two low, small rooms, each having one small window. The door to one of these rooms was open. I instinctively turned to the room that was closed. Thrusting open the door and stepping within, I saw Pitezel lying upon the floor. I rushed to him, but before I had remained longer than to remove a large towel that was wrapped around his head, and not having time to find if he were alive, I was forced, owing to the overpowering odor of chloroform, together with the shock of coming upon him so suddenly and in such a condition, to leave the room, falling upon my knees and crawling a portion of the way until I finally reached the window in the adjoining room, which I opened, and in a few minutes had recovered myself sufficiently to return to the room where Pitezel lay, but again was forced to leave before I could make a satisfactory examination.

This time I had opened the window in this room as well, and presently was able to ascertain that he was dead. I then went to the hallway and sat down upon the stairs. I do not know how long I sat there, nor what I thought in the meantime. I had not yet wholly recovered from the effects of the chloroform, and was dazed. This was not due to having come suddenly upon a dead body, for my medical experience of years before had rendered me accustomed to disagreeable sights and scenes—but the man had been to me far more than an ordinary employee; one whom, although most of our tastes were dissimilar, I had always liked and had had fewer disagreements with than would likely have been the case had he been my own brother. And to come upon him thus had unmanned me.

I know the thought never came to me while sitting there that it might be dangerous for my own safety, the street door being then unlocked. After a time I returned to the room and made a careful examination.

He lay upon his back, his lower limbs fully extended, one arm folded upon his chest, the other thrown out at his side.

His head was slightly raised by means of a coarse colored blanket, closely folded. He was fully dressed, except his coat and vest which hung on a chair beside him. The pockets of his trousers were turned inside out, and in the waistband was a letter within an envelope addressed "C. A. P."[11]

If asked to express an absolutely true opinion as to how long he had been dead, I should say not more than six hours.

Upon the chair was a large gallon bottle laying upon its side, so arranged that it would nearly empty itself, it being held in position upon one side by a hammer and upon the other by a small block of wood; from the bottle, and connected thereto by a perforated cork in which an ordinary quill toothpick had been inserted, there trailed a long piece of small rubber tubing, terminating at its free end in the towel I had removed upon first entering the room. This tube was constricted midway by a piece of cord tied about it, so that the flow of liquid would be slow.

Owing to the time that had elapsed after his death all the chloroform that could escape from the bottle, in the position in which it lay, had passed through the tube, filling his mouth and, as I later learned from the Coroner's physician, his stomach as well; this one fact alone being sufficient to prove to any scientific person, or physician at least, that any one having a medical training would not, if obliged to use chloroform for such a purpose, carry it to such an extent if he wished it to appear later that the man died as the result of inhaling the vaporous fumes of chloroform and benzine, that had exploded in a bottle held in the victim's hands.

The excess of the liquid had then run out upon the floor and on the blanket underneath his head. The only other articles in the room besides those already enumerated were some small pocket belongings, a knife, memoranda book, match box, containing some of our patent stamps, and perhaps twenty small coins; all these were placed on the chair beside the bottle. Upon the windowsill was a small handful of tacks with which he had fastened some newspapers upon the sash in lieu of a curtain.

By this time, owing to the excoriating effect of the chloroform his face had become somewhat discolored, and I went to the rooms below and procured a wet towel, and after covering the face with it I started down the stairs fully intending to call in some of the neighbors. Then came the thought that, instead of filling the house with a crowd of curious people, it would be better to go direct to the Coroner.

I know this thought was in my mind as I passed down the

stairway, for I distinctly remember wondering in what part of the city the Coroner's office was located, whether at the City Hall or elsewhere, and if it would be open on Sunday.

Reaching the kitchen I picked up the letter which, in my haste, I had let fall before going up stairs in search of him. The substance of the letter, beside that already given, was that he had tried to take his life in Mississippi during the previous June, and now with his drinking habit growing so much stronger day by day, he could not hope to make a living without my aid. He wished me to so arrange his body in one of two ways that it would appear that his death had been either accidental or that he had been attacked by burglars and killed, giving the details of how I was to carry out either course: —

First, that his family should not at present know of his death;[12] second, that the children should never know he had committed suicide (this he also repeated in the letter left for his wife); that the insurance money should be used to place the Fort Worth building in an earning condition, and that I should exchange some Chicago property we owned for some house in a city with good school advantages; that none of the money should be so placed that relatives could borrow it away from his wife. He spoke of our close connection for years, and that he could depend upon my aiding him now and in the future, ending his directions with the words:—

"Do enough with me so there won't be any slip-up on the insurance; I shan't feel it."

The letter was poorly written, and it took me some minutes to decipher it, and upon finishing it, I sat down for a time and re-read parts of it. This gave me time to consider my own position, and as soon as it came into my mind, but before I had decided to carry out his instructions, I went into the front office and locked the street door.

The thought that troubled me most at that time was, that under no conditions, whether the insurance part was carried out or not, was I the one discover his dead body. I was here in Philadelphia under an assumed name. A few years earlier I had stopped at some hotels and met people under the name of Holmes. Some years before that I had done business here under still another name, and at another time, earlier yet, I had visited relatives here under my true name.

And now at this time, to be called as a witness before a Coroner's jury, would almost certainly cause me to be identified by some one; and if under the name of Holmes, it was more than likely to be seen in the papers by some Fort Worth people, and would probably result in my arrest upon the charges there, and my arrest at this time I was satisfied would mean death to my wife.

Again, I had an engagement in St. Louis for the following Thursday morning, to fail to keep which would result in the loss of a considerable sum of money, and also prove a source of great annoyance to my attorney, who was personally responsible for my appearance there.

Besides this, Pitezel was dead; nothing I could do here would aid him, while in St. Louis I could be of the utmost benefit to his family, by forestalling the announcement of his death reaching them through the newspapers, by seeing them personally, and also caring for the child that was sick, if need be. This portion of the matter was settled in my mind at once, then came the question whether I should do anything to aid in the deception of the insurance matter or simply remove the letter he had written to his wife, lest it contain matters that should not be made public and go away.

One of his plans I did not entertain for a moment, the one involving striking him upon the head severely enough to crush his skull. Had my own life depended upon it, I could not have forced myself to strike his dead body even had I been sure there was no suicide clause in his insurance policy. I should have preferred to have told his family at once of his death, contrary to his wishes, in preference to doing anything to mislead the authorities, involving, as it necessarily must, some mutilation of the body.

I had never seen the policy, but from my friend the insurance agent's statement that it was similar to mine, I judged it contained such a clause. Nor did I know whether or not the suicide clause was inoperative in Pennsylvania as it is in many other States. (All these things I most certainly should have found out previously if I had been intending to immediately carry out the fraud.) After considerable deliberation, I went to the room in the second story that he had partially prepared, uncorked the small bottles I had previously found there, and also found the pipe he had filled with tobacco, the top of which was slightly burned as though he had just lighted it before his accident occurred.

Fig. 21. Callowhill Street House in Philadelphia Where Benjamin Pitezel's Body Was Found
Source: Herman W. Mudgett, *Holmes' Own Story*, 1895, p. 135.

Fig. 22. 1316 Callowhill Street House (see white arrow), Philadelphia, 1894
Source: City of Philadelphia, Department of Records, August 24, 1894.

September 4. Superintendent of Police Linden instructed the police not to permit the carrying of red flags in parades.

— The remains of B. F. Perry, who kept a small store at 1316 Callowhill street, found in a partially decomposed condition. The face and left arm had been burned, probably by an explosion while he was filling a bottle with benzine.

September 7. Ex-Attorney General F. Carroll Brewster celebrated the fiftieth anniversary of his

Fig. 23. Announcement of B. F. Perry found dead
Source: "Remains of B.F. Perry," *Philadelphia Public Ledger,*
September 4, 1894.

He did this part of the work previous to his death, knowing that I did not smoke or knew little of filling pipes intelligently enough to deceive any one. Having placed the room in the condition necessary (breaking the large bottle, placing pipe upon the floor, etc.), I moved his body as carefully as possible to this second-story room. I found that the chloroform had given the side of the face and neck and part of the chest quite the appearance of having been burned, and this made my task the easier, although it seemed terrible enough in any event.

At last I forced myself to burn the clothing upon one side of the body, smothering the flames when they reached the flesh, and in this way produced partially successful results; then hastily gathering together several small articles that I wished to take away with me, I placed the room somewhat in order, and after going again to the room where he lay to see him, as I then supposed for the last time, I at once left the house, disguising myself to some extent by wearing one of his hats, for I had been fully alive to the necessity of care after I had first had time to think of the matter. Among the things taken from the house was a bottle of chloroform, which he had previously bought in Philadelphia, and prepared to send to Chicago to be placed with the clothing and other things for Hedgpeth's [Hedgepeth's] use.

In going out of the house I was careful to leave the door both unlocked and open, in order to call attention to the condition of affairs within as soon as possible. Upon reaching the more pure air of the street I was seized with a feeling of nausea and dizziness, resulting probably as an after-effect of the chloroform-laden air within.

I knew my general appearance must have been that of an intoxicated person. To become relieved of this feeling somewhat if possible, I decided to walk a portion of the distance to my residence, and while doing so decided that it was best, my wife being well enough, to leave Philadelphia at once, thinking that Pitezel had no doubt spoken of me to some of his newly-made friends, and perhaps told them where I lived. I, therefore, went to the Broad Street Station and ascertained that a train would leave in half an hour (so I know now that I left the Callowhill street house at about 3:45 o'clock [P.M.], as the train referred to was the regular 4:30 Western train); I found that another train left for the West at 10:25 P. M.; and although my wife was not able to do so, I took her as carefully as I could to this train and left at that hour.

I have often since that day tried to analyze the feelings which I had at the time of Pitezel's death. I felt it to be a terrible matter, and certainly could not have deplored it more had he been a relative, but I did not then, nor have I since felt the great horror concerning it that I experienced at the time of Nannie Williams' death in Chicago, which was wholly unprovoked and for which I felt that I was the indirect cause; while in this case, his death occurred as the result of his own premeditation, in consequence of his having allowed himself to slowly drift into pernicious habits for which he was more than any one else to blame.

Upon reaching Indianapolis, I was occupied until Wednesday noon, September 5th, in arranging comfortable quarters for my wife, at which time I started for St. Louis, reaching that city about 7 P. M., having brought upon the train a St. Louis *Globe-Democrat,* giving in a Philadelphia dispatch an account of the finding of Pitezel's (Perry's) body in the Callowhill street house upon the previous day.

After a short delay I went at once to Mrs. Pitezel's place of residence, about an hour's ride from the centre of the city, hoping to be in time to tell them of the matter myself. Upon reaching the house, however, I found all in a state of commotion.

The neighbors were there, a physician had been summoned, and it was some time before I could obtain a suitable opportunity to talk with Mrs. Pitezel. I found her in a very nervous and overwrought condition, and I thought it best to palliate her fears for a time, and, therefore, said to her, "Perhaps Ben is not dead. There may be a mistake in the person, as I saw him alive last week."

To which she answered, "Oh, no! I am sure it is he, for I have been writing to him under that name and at that address."

Just at this moment Dessie, the oldest daughter, called me to one side and said, "Do you think papa is really dead?"

HOLMES' "CASTLE" CHICAGO.

Fig. 24. Holmes' Castle in Chicago, Illinois
Source: Herman W. Mudgett, *Holmes' Own Story*, 1895, p. 140.

Fig. 25. Holmes' Castle was located at 601-603 West 63rd Street (cross-street Wallace), Chicago, 1896. In 1938, it was sold to make way for the Englewood Post Office.
Source: Frank P. Geyer. *The Holmes-Pitezel Case*. 1896, p. 91.

According to a report in the *Daily Inter Ocean,* Holmes' Castle was owned by Lucy T. Belknap, Holmes second wife's mother from Wilmette, Illinois. In December 1889, Lucy and her husband, John S. Belknap obtained a $12,000 loan secured by trust deed signed by Lucy and John. The interest on the loan was not paid when it became due and as a result, the trustee began foreclosure proceedings in 1892. It was sold to William H. Rose, then to Chandler. After execution of the trust deed, H. H. Holmes obtained possession and control again and an incendiary fire occurred, which destroyed the roof and part of the third floor. The damage was never repaired. Someone collected rents for a time from occupants of stores within the portion of the building that was not damaged. Source: "Was Known as Pratt," *Daily Inter Ocean*, August 2, 1895.

Fig. 26. Holmes' Castle in 1937
Source: Frank Cipriani. "The Murder Castle," *Chicago Tribune*, March 21, 1937 p. 7.

I replied that I feared so, but that her mother should not be told until we were certain of it.

She said, " I don't think he is. Last spring, when I was sick and he was leaving me, he told me that if I ever heard that he was dead not to believe it, as some work he was going to do might require him to have people think so for a time."

I asked her if he had told her mother of this, and she said, "No; her father had told her not to tell any one."

As soon as a favorable opportunity occurred, I said to Mrs. Pitezel, "Did Ben ever say anything to you about not worrying if you heard of his death?"

[S]he replied, "Yes," and, after stopping a moment, added, "If he has gone and done that without letting us know, leaving us to worry ourselves to death, I could almost wish he was dead. Is it the insurance matter?"

"I guess it is," I replied, in such a tone that she would think that I knew it to be so.

She then asked if he would get the money all right, and I told her that it would be paid to her, if anyone.

She asked, "Where is Ben now?"

I replied that it was his plan to go South at once.

She said, "Well, I do not want him writing to me; all his letters for me must go to you; and the children need not know but that he is really dead, for they would certainly tell of it; they are young, and will soon get over the worry."

I asked if the insurance policy was there in the house, and she said, "I do not know; I will see; he ought to have given it to you if he was going through with it so soon; it may be in Chicago among some things stored in a warehouse there."

I did not allow her to look for it at that time, as she was too ill yet from her shock to do so, but instructed her to look for it next morning, and if well enough, to bring all the papers she had to my attorney's office.

Some question then arose as to whether she could find this office, and she remembered that at the time of my arrest her husband had called there and had brought home one of their cards, which she said was still among some of his papers, and with this she could find her way.[13]

At about 9 o'clock, the family being more quiet at the time, I returned to the hotel for the night, and I feel sure that Mrs. Pitezel at the time of this visit, which was the first confidential talk I had ever had with her, had no previous knowledge of an intention to perpetrate a fraud upon this company other than a vague idea that under certain conditions and at a more remote time it might have been carried out, which was the exact condition of affairs as they had existed upon the day of Pitezel's death.

She is not a woman of extraordinary gifts, and any simulation on her part at this time would not have deceived me.

The next morning I went to Judge Harvey's office and found that owing to his absence my case had been postponed. I left word there for Mrs. Pitezel, if she called during the day, to wait for me, and I went to the offices of another attorney and spoke of the insurance claim and told him if it was promptly paid I could use some of that money. He said insurance companies are slow and it will probably be some time before it is settled.

He asked how large an amount it was, and upon my stating it was $10,000, he said, "You will need an attorney in fixing the papers; can't I do it for you?"

I re-replied that I was about to consult Judge Harvey.

He said, "Let me have it; I have just settled a fire insurance loss and had first-rate success, besides you are really my client, as we sent you to Judge Harvey because my partner was away at the time."

After returning to Judge Harvey's office and not finding him there, I saw him again and told him that the claim was a false one, that the man was, in reality, not dead.

He made a number of inquiries as to the details of the fraud and finally said, "Well, if you have any one to attend to it here it had better be me, for neither Judge Harvey or my partner would dare to take hold of it. I do not belong to this firm, although I have an office here with them. You will notice my letter-heads appear with my own name alone; still I can avail myself of their judgment in important cases, and on account of this supposed death occurring under a fictitious name, you will find you need help."

I then explained that Mrs. Pitezel was to come into the city that morning, if she was able, with the papers, and he remarked, "Well, she must not know that I have any knowledge that the claim is not a legitimate one."

It was then arranged that he should write some letters to the company's office in Chicago, to ascertain if Pitezel had, in reality, paid the premium as he had stated, there being no receipts showing this had been done, and also to write to the authorities in Philadelphia.

I asked him in regard to his fee, and he stated that it would depend upon how much work had to be done, but that being a young attorney he would make it a reasonable sum. Later, in going out of the building, I met Mrs. Pitezel and explained to her that this lawyer would take care of the case for her, and that she should not have him know that she was aware of his knowing the true state of the case. In other words, she, while in his presence, was to appear and speak as though it were a genuine loss.

So, at this stage of the case, I knew Pitezel was dead; Mrs. Pitezel and the attorney each supposed him to be alive, but, by a separate agreement each had voluntarily made with me, both were to deceive each other in this respect, making a most unique case of conspiracy, if conspiracy it was.

I was not present during all of the attorney's first interview with Mrs. Pitezel, but she authorized him to write the necessary letters, and I told her that he had made satisfactory arrangements with me in regard to his fee, which I would be responsible to him for.

I then gave Mrs. Pitezel some money for her immediate wants

and left the city, intending to return again in ten days, at which time my case was to be called in Court. Before going away I told the attorney he could address me at Indianapolis at any time. About five days thereafter I received a letter from him, stating that he had received an answer to his letter of inquiry sent to the Philadelphia authorities, in which they stated that the man referred to was only known to them under the name of Perry, and would be buried as that person unless some one identified him at once as Pitezel. He also stated that Mrs. Pitezel instructed him to ask me to return to St. Louis and aid her if I could do so.

This I did at once, and upon meeting him he told me it would be necessary for some one to go to Philadelphia at once, and wished me to furnish the money for him and one of the family to make the trip. I told him that until the first of the following month I could not well do this, but suggested a person with whom Pitezel had formerly dealt that I thought would advance the necessary sum, if it was agreed that it should be returned to him with interest as soon as the insurance was collected. The attorney later negotiated such a loan, receiving $300.

At this time I saw Mrs. Pitezel, and she not being strong enough to take the trip, it was decided that the daughter, Alice, should go. This choice of the children being principally due to arrangements previously made by Pitezel, that if Miss Williams came to this country, and returned to her old occupation as a teacher, that Alice should live with her for a year to go to school. I had received a letter from Miss Williams that she had decided to do this, and at the time of Pitezel's death had asked her to come to settle in Cincinnati, thinking thus she would break away from her old life, making it safer for me to be also where she could help in regard to some Texas papers, which I had found must at any hazard, be duplicated. Therefore, a few days later, when Alice left St. Louis, it was with the full understanding that she was to stay East with Miss Williams, or go with her to Cincinnati, if all located there.

At the time I was about to leave, having made these arrangements, I received a letter that had been forwarded to me from Chicago, asking for my assistance in identifying Pitezel, it being known to the Chicago office that he had been in my employ. To intelligently answer this letter, I went to the attorney's office, at which time I first closely examined the insurance policy. I then wrote to the company as accurate a description as I could give of him.

At this time the attorney said, "Why don't you go to Philadelphia, also?"

I replied that it would be an unnecessary expense, and I wished to go to Cincinnati at that time to arrange for a house for the family.

He said, "I had better wait until the money was paid," and I replied that the family would have to have a house whether the money was paid or not.

Finally it was decided I should go to Philadelphia via Cincinnati, which I did, writing to the company from the latter place that I had business calling me toward Philadelphia, and I would call upon them in a few days, and if possible aid them in identifying the body.

Later in the same day I met Alice *en route*. The next day, early in the afternoon, I called upon the Insurance Company in Philadelphia.

I was introduced, after a little delay, to Colonel Bosbyshell, one of the officers. He talked with me for some time regarding the case, and finally, having asked me a good many questions as to Pitezel's general appearance, said, "Well, I think that it is either a case of mistaken identity or a fraud. The man found here, and who has been buried under the name of B. F. Perry, was a man who weighed forty pounds more than Mr. Pitezel, both according to your judgment and according to his application for insurance; and moreover, this man had red hair while Pitezel's was black. An attorney and some of Mr. Pitezel's relations are expected here at any time, and I wish you could stay and aid us in clearing up the matter.["]

He then left the office, and in a few minutes returned with some money, which he tendered me, saying they would be glad to have me stay at their expense. I replied that I would not take the money, but having other work to attend to, I would call from day to day, and if I was put to much expense or loss of time, I would ask them to pay me, otherwise no charge would be made, explaining further that Pitezel was indebted to me, and if the claim was a genuine one I would be willing to devote some time to it in order that I could collect my money, which I had no doubt his wife would pay.

That afternoon I saw our attorney, he and Alice having arrived in the interim. I told him of my interview, and he at once said, "We shan't collect a dollar. They have either substituted a body for the one you used, or your choice was so poor it had not deceived them." He was in favor of abandoning the case and returning to St. Louis.

Fig. 27. Alice Pitezel
Source: Herman W. Mudgett, *Holmes' Own Story*, 1895, p. 151.

Fig. 28. Alice Pitezel
Source: Frank P. Geyer. *The Holmes-Pitezel Case*. 1896, p. 38.

Finally it was decided that he should see the company the next day, but he insisted, as he said, for his own safety, that if we met at the company's office he should not have it appear he had ever seen me before. The next day, about half an hour after I called at the insurance office, the president of the company, who I had met the day before, and our attorney entered the room where I was seated, and the following conversation took place:—

Mr. [Holmes omitted the last name], the president, then introduced me to our attorney, saying:—

"This is Mr. Holmes, of Chicago, who carries insurance in our company, and who formerly was well acquainted with Mr. Pitezel."

Upon our shaking hands, he said, "I am glad to know you, sir."

After some general conversation, I said, "The officers of the company inform me that you have certain letters and other papers in Mr. Pitezel's handwriting, and I think, if agreeable to you, I can identify them if belonging to him."

Our attorney then turned to the president, saying, "Who is this man? Before I show any papers or have anything more to do with one who is apparently an outsider, I wish to know more about him."

The president then said in a conciliatory manner, "Oh! I think you can depend upon Mr. Holmes acting independently and for the interest of all in the case. He is a man formerly in business in Chicago, and for whom Mr. Pitezel worked for a long time, and if any one is able to give an accurate description of him, Mr. Holmes should be able to do so."

"My inquiry was a precautionary one," said our attorney, "I am willing under those circumstances that Mr. Holmes should examine the papers and aid us if he can."

During that afternoon our attorney entered into an agreement in writing with the company, stipulating, that in order to establish his claim, certain marks of identification should be found upon the body, which it had been arranged to have disinterred the next day. Among those marks should appear a large wart, or mole, upon the back of the neck, jet black hair, a cowlick upon the forhead [sic], a peculiarly decayed condition of the teeth, a bruised thumb nail and a scar upon one of the lower extremities.

That evening, quite late, our attorney came to me freshly

terrified, and again ready to abandon the case. He had met a man named Smith, who, in conversation with him, had stated that while in Pitezel's place of business he had seen a man come in and hold some conversation with him, who he had understood was a friend then living in the city. Smith had stated that the friend had not come forward at the time of his death and he thought it strange, and also remarked that if he ever saw the man again he would know him.

Mr. Smith was to be at the Coroner's office next day, and was also to be present at the time the body was viewed. I told him that from what I remembered of the man Smith, I did not think he was a very close observer or overburdened with general intelligence, and I would take the chances of his recognizing me, rather than give up the case at that stage of it. Next morning we all met at the Coroner's office. My judgment had been correct in regard to Smith. He noticed me only as he would have done any stranger, and upon being introduced to him, and being in his company and holding a general conversation with him, I met with the same result.

It was decided at the meeting at the Coroner's office that later in the day those interested should go to the cemetery where the body would be exhumed for identification. This was done, there being in the party the president and two others, representing the insurance company, a physician and a Deputy Coroner representing the city; our attorney, Alice Pitezel and myself, besides Mr. Smith before referred to.

Upon reaching the cemetery we were told that the body had already been placed in a small house and was ready to be seen.

I felt, that there being two other physicians present, it was not necessary for me to take part in the identification, unless called upon to do so; and had, upon first arriving together with Mr. Perry, taken the daughter to a distant quarter of the enclosure. The physician made the examination of the body, which lay in a well-lighted room; and, after taking abundant time for this purpose, came out of the building and announced that all marks of identification were wanting. After some further conversation, the president said to our attorney that they were satisfied before they came there that such would be the case, and a general movement was made preparatory to leaving the place.

The attorney asked me what I thought should be done, and upon my answering him, he told the president that he would like to have me examine the body as well. I asked the doctor if he would object, and he said, "No," but that I would not find it a pleasant task.

I entered the building, and hardly had passed the door before I was positive that the doctor had been mistaken in the color of the hair. Upon a close examination, all the marks were easily found: the wart upon the neck, equal in diameter to that of a lead pencil, and projecting fully a quarter of an inch from the surface; the cowlick, the bruised nail, the teeth decayed exactly as had been described; and lastly, the scar an inch and a half in length upon the foot.

I could do no less than call the doctor in, and one by one he grudgingly admitted their presence; and that there should be no further question as to the identity of the man, I asked him to remove the wart for microscopical examination, some of the hair, the nail and the scar. He said he had no implement with him that he cared to use for this purpose. I had only a very small lancet, but I removed the necessary portions, and later turned them over to the Coroner's representative.

I then endeavored to have a decision reached at once in order to save the necessity of the daughter seeing the body, feeling it to be cruel to have her do so, and if possible to prevent it. The president would not agree to this, but it was finally arranged that she should see only the teeth. All other portions of the body were therefore excluded from view, and I led the child into the building.

It was a terribly hard thing that I had to do, for she was but a delicate child of perhaps fourteen or fifteen years, yet she was courageous and very willing to do what she could.

Upon reaching the body she said, "Yes, those are papa's teeth, I am sure of it."

I at once led her away, but I found the impression left upon her tender mind would remain as long as she lived, and have always felt it to have been a wholly unnecessary requirement upon the part of the company.

Without regard to what the reasons were, the doctor's report was destined to cost me dearly, as will later be seen in this history. This ended the examination at the grave-yard, and we all returned to the city.

Even at that time the officers of the company would not express themselves as willing to allow the claim, but later in the day they reluctantly admitted that they were satisfied with the identification. Upon reaching the Coroner's office again, the Coroner very kindly offered to take my testimony the next morning, which was Sunday, in order that I could leave the city without further loss of time.

After making this arrangement, I went to the insurance company's office where I was reweighed, remeasured and in other ways readjusted my own insurance, and later went to an undertaker's office, and made every arrangement to have the body properly buried in a good locality, well satisfied to be able to perform this final act for my friend.

The next day at 4:30 P. M., having previously gone to the Coroner's office, I left Philadelphia, taking Alice Pitezel with me. I had not heard from Miss Williams as I felt sure I should do, informing me of her expected arrival in New York, and thus not hearing, I addressed her there, asking both she and Hatch to come to Cincinnati as soon as they conveniently could, stating my reasons for asking them to do so.

Alice did not like to return to St. Louis on account of having told every one she knew before leaving that she was going away for the winter, although she would have been very glad to have seen her mother; and upon reaching Indianapolis I told her she could choose between returning to St. Louis or remaining there for the few intervening days while I went to St. Louis and returned with some of the rest of the family upon our way to Cincinnati, it having previously been arranged with Mrs. Pitezel that this move should be made at once to save commencing another month in St. Louis, where she was paying rent.

Alice having decided to remain in Indianapolis, I took her to Stubbin's Hotel and left her there in charge of those whom I had become acquainted with during my previous stay in that city.

The next day I received a telegram from the attorney, stating that the company had paid him the insurance, after deducting several hundred dollars for expenses, which, I think, was wholly unjust towards Mrs. Pitezel, the whole amount, if any, being due her.

I then returned to St. Louis, where, owing to my absence, my own case had again been postponed, and I therefore decided to return to Cincinnati.

Taking the two children, Nellie and Howard, I started for that city via Indianapolis, telegraphing to the hotel to have some one accompany Alice to the train in the morning to join us. This was done, and at about 8 A. M. we reached the Cincinnati station where Hatch met us. It was the first I had seen of him since early in December of the previous year.

Miss Williams had remained in New York, being unwilling to go to Cincinnati where she had previously played, and therefore was known to some people.

Being in haste to commence my work among the real estate men, I gave the children into Hatch's charge, and he took them to a small hotel near the station. But not liking the surroundings, I returned to the Hotel Bristol.

I spent a very busy day, but was not successful in finding property to exchange for Chicago property, and at last I thought it safer to rent a house for a time, and then, by advertising my property, find something more suitable for the children's wants. I therefore hired a house, paying one month's rent and six months' water tax. I also made arrangements for its being comfortably furnished.

Miss Williams not having come, I looked around for some trustworthy person to care for the children until their mother could reach them. Mrs. Pitezel having a desire to visit her parents before going elsewhere, did so.

Not finding such a person as I wished, and not liking to leave the children without proper attention, I decided to take them with me to Indianapolis, where I expected to be engaged in some real estate work for the following two weeks. This I did, Hatch accompanying us, and then going on to Chicago from whence he returned in a few days.

We reached Indianapolis about October 1st; the children stayed one day at English's Hotel, and then I engaged permanent board for them at the Circle House, my wife and myself being at another hotel near by, so that I could visit the children each day and know they were properly cared for. This form of life was new to the children, and they thoroughly enjoyed it, going about the city either by themselves, Hatch's or my own company.

I shortly afterwards returned to St. Louis, and, upon entering the attorney's office, he said, "Well, I am glad you have come; my partner had been wishing that you would return."

I said, "Why?"

He replied, "Because he wants to get this matter settled up and get our fee out of it. You know how close work it was to get the company to believe the claim was straight, and something may occur to make them change their minds.["]

But, I said, "Why has he to be considered, even in that event?"

He replied, "Because, in a case as big as this, he will have to be considered; besides, if it had not been for his letter of introduction to Superintendent Linden in Philadelphia, the money would not have been paid."

I then told him that I had not yet seen Mrs. Pitezel, but we would arrange the settlement when I did so, and I would have her come in and sign the necessary papers later.

"Well," said he, "what do you think we should receive?"

I said, "I have no idea; you must set your price, not I."

He then said, "Well, usually in these insurance cases the attorneys get fifty per cent. [sic] of the claim. I have asked three disinterested lawyers about it, and they say I ought to have that much, they not knowing it as a fraudulent claim, which makes it all the worse."

My answer was, "Well, if it comes to taking $5,000, which, from your own statement to me, is more money than you ever before earned in your life, you will have the opportunity to keep the balance as well."

After some further conversation, he offered to choose an attorney if I would choose one, and leave the fee to their decision, and with this understanding I went away to return the next morning.

When I returned he met me with the announcement that his partner would not agree to his proposition. I then said, "I wish to see him if he is the principal." At that time I had never been introduced to him. He left his office in a few minutes and returned and conducted me into his partner's private office. He was seated at his desk, apparently much too busy to leave his work for so small a matter as the settlement of a $5,000 fee.

Finally he turned upon me and, in an an [sic] overbearing, bull-dozing manner, said, "What is all this trouble about? Don't you expect to pay your attorney after you have hired him?" I was angry at his insolent manner, and at once told him that I would have no words with him. If they wished to receive $500 for their services (reminding him that had it not been for my presence in Philadelphia they would not have collected the claim, as he had shown so very little tact in treating with the company—so much so that they had been twice upon the point of ordering him from their offices) then that amount could be deducted, but no more.

He then said, "I will allow no man to come into my office and dictate to me in regard to a fee after the work has been done for him, and as for $500 it is an insult to offer it."

I then reminded him that I was not making it as an offer to him, one of the most prominent lawyers of St. Louis, but to his partner, a recent law graduate, to whom a $500 fee would be a large one, inasmuch as his expenses upon the trip had been elaborately provided for.

He said, "Well, we will take $3,000 for this work and nothing less."

I replied, "It cannot be paid."

He said, "Then there is no further use for us to discuss the matter."

Turning to his partner, he then said, "Go to the bank and get a New York draft for what you have left; I am going to return the money."

I said, "Very well, sir, nothing could be more to my advantage than this, and upon Mrs. Pitezel receiving the money direct from the company I shall tender to you your fee of $500."

He replied, "You will never have a chance to do this; when the money is sent back I shall at the same time write a letter to my old friend, Captain Linden of the Philadelphia Police Department, stating that since my return we have found out that the claim is crooked and cannot handle such money, and that we think it our duty to aid him by placing him in immediate possession of all the facts pertaining to the matter; moreover, you are wanted in Fort Worth, Texas, and I shall at once cause your arrest before you can leave the city."

I replied, "You could only cause me trouble in regard to the insurance matter at the cost of your partner's disgrace."

He said, "It is not so; it would be the word of our firm, which is well known throughout the country, against your single statement, and you a man that has already been under arrest once and will be again inside of an hour."

This so angered me that I said, "You can send back the money, you can arrest me, but you cannot intimidate or browbeat me. I will spend ten years in the penitentiary before giving in to you now."

Upon this I left the office.

Mrs. Pitezel was seated in the outer room, having come in in [sic] the meantime. I asked her to come at once to Judge Harvey's office, and upon her hesitating to do so, when he asked her to remain a moment, I told her to make no settlement that involved a greater reduction than $500 from the amount the company had paid.

Upon my doing this I left the office, and waited a long time for Mrs. Pitezel; and when she met me she was in tears and said that they would not let her leave the office until she allowed them to deduct $2,500 from the insurance money, and that she had also signed a long typewritten agreement of some kind. She then had the remainder of the money, about $6,000, with her, the lawyers having previously paid some bills upon her giving them a written order to do so.

Some days previous to this I had made arrangements that the amount of money to be used at Fort Worth should be paid at a bank at St. Louis in exchange for a note her husband had executed while there.[14]

Mrs. Pitezel went to the bank and lifted this note, and of the balance gave me $225 for my expenses, as she supposed.

As a matter of fact, the $5,000 thus paid upon the note came to me, I having months before had to satisfy the claim by the use of other property. That afternoon, some time later, I left St. Louis, intending to return to Cincinnati and complete the arrangements there for the home of the Pitezel family. Before leaving St. Louis, however, I arranged that Mrs. Pitezel and the two other children should go to Galva, Ill., upon their intended visit to Mrs. Pitezel's mother, and also made private arrangements to be informed of any movements that should be made by the attorneys detrimental to my interests.

Upon my returning to Indianapolis I found that both the children were apparently enjoying themselves. Hatch had received a letter from Miss Williams (to whom he claimed he was married) asking that we both meet her in Detroit. This meeting was delayed, as I had some more real estate work to do in Indianapolis which had been neglected, owing to the insurance work. While attending to this work I received word that the attorneys were intending to make trouble for me, and almost at the same time word came from Chicago that some Fort Worth detectives were again there, and had heard of my being in Cincinnati, Indianapolis and St. Louis.

After consulting with Hatch, who was very much worried lest if I were arrested it would implicate him as being with me, and perhaps Miss Williams as well, we concluded that we should go away at once. Finally I decided to abandon the Cincinnati house, and have the Pitezel family locate elsewhere, as the attorneys knew of my former trips to that city. I therefore wrote Mrs. Pitezel at Galva, advising her to change her plans and go to Detroit.

Up to this time, all that I had done for Mrs. Pitezel she had been aware of, but I did not now think it prudent that she should know of the probability of trouble arising from the insurance company. I preferred having her locate in some large city at that time, and explain to her afterwards about her husband's death as he had requested me to do, and also of the necessity of remaining quiet until I could ascertain if any real danger existed.

Quite early upon the morning of October 10th, I went to the children's hotel, and found them eating their breakfast. I told them we were going away that day, and went with them to their rooms and instructed them to divide their belongings into three separate packages, they having previously been contained in a very old trunk, which was not in a condition to be taken further. There was left in this trunk some old clothing, among which was a suit of heavy clothes which had belonged to Pitezel.

I then asked the children whether they would go with me to

Chicago, and then to Detroit, or go with Hatch. Howard Pitezel chose to go with Hatch, while the girls desired to go to Chicago, hoping, while there, to have time to visit some of their former acquaintances.

Having some purchases to make before leaving, I therefore, after telling the girls at what time to meet me at the station, left the hotel, having instructed Howard not to leave until Hatch should come, in order that he could direct him to come to the station before my train left.

I met Hatch and Howard later upon the street. This was the last time I ever saw the boy Howard, at which time he was both well and contented. The first few days after his leaving home he had been homesick.

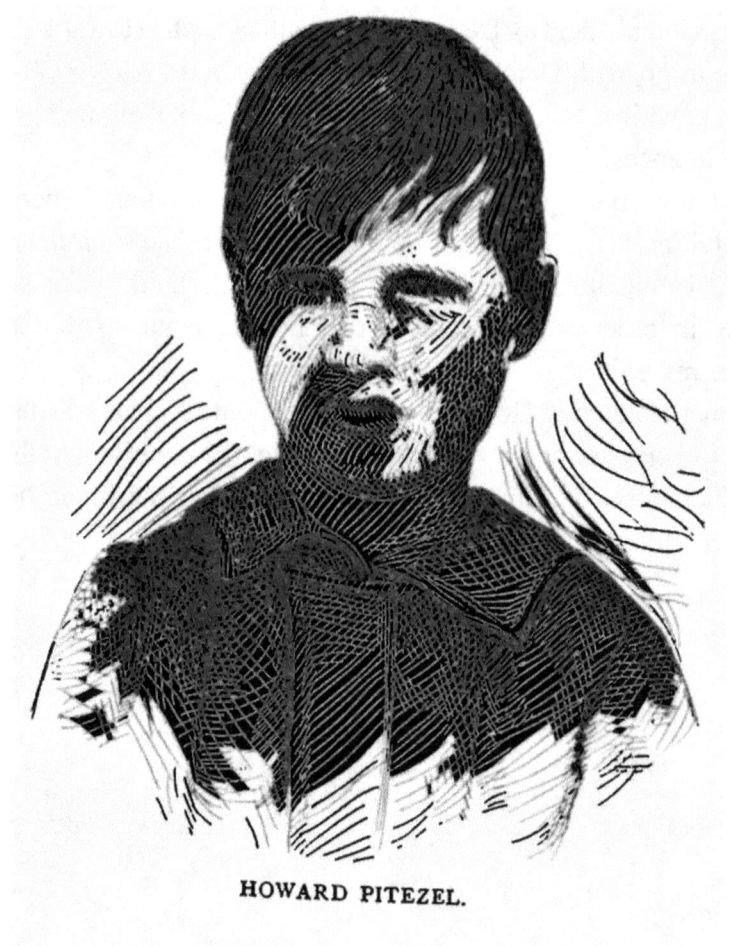

HOWARD PITEZEL.

Fig. 29. Howard Pitezel
Source: Herman W. Mudgett, *Holmes' Own Story*, 1895, p. 171.

Fig. 30. Howard Pitezel
Source: Frank P. Geyer. The Holmes-Pitezel Case. 1896, p. 218.

While I was in the barber shop at the station upon this same morning, I asked Hatch to go to the hotel and have the nearly empty trunk taken to the station and have it checked to any destination he might choose, there being nothing of value in it, and it not being desirable to have it left at the hotel.

Upon reaching Chicago, I took the two girls to a hotel, as I had business in a distant part of the city. I stayed during the one night I remained there at a new hotel upon the west side of North Clark street, less than a block north of the Lincoln avenue car junction.[15]

Not deeming it prudent, owing to the late news I had heard at Indianapolis, to go to my attorney's office, I had both him and my agent meet me elsewhere, and arranging my work as quickly as possible, I left Chicago upon Friday, October 12th, going directly to Detroit, taking the girls with me.

During the latter part of this trip my wife was upon the same train, she having left Indiana that morning in response to a request from me to do so.

Anticipating this, I had made arrangements with Hatch before leaving Indianapolis to be at the Detroit Station to take charge of the children.

Upon our reaching Detroit I at once took my wife to a hotel about one mile from the station, and as I was leaving the train I saw Hatch helping the girls from the car in which they had traveled. About a half hour later Hatch met me at the Western Union telegraph office in response to a note I had given to Alice for him.

It was very late at night, and I returned with him to the hotel, where he had taken the girls, to see that they were all right, and while going there he told me that he had been delayed twenty-four hours at some junction between Indianapolis and Detroit, so that he had only reached Detroit that afternoon, and Miss Williams not wishing by any accident to meet my wife had gone to Buffalo to visit some theatrical friends, taking Howard with her. I did not think strange of this, for I knew Howard had known and liked Miss Williams the year before, when she was in my office in Chicago.

The next day I engaged permanent board for both myself and wife, and also for the children, in two separate portions of the city, as I expected to remain there for some time, and enlisting Hatch's services, we proceeded to look for a house that, if possible, could be bought in exchange for Chicago property, and by so doing save money.

If this could not be accomplished, then a house that should be rented for a few months, until such a trade could be made. A small house was found so favorably located, with school advantages for the children, that I thought it best to pay the small deposit required, five dollars, to hold it for a few days.

On Sunday morning Mrs. Pitezel came to Detroit, and I did not think it wise to tell her positively that she was to settle there until I should have heard again from both St. Louis and Chicago.

During the interval, I had her board at a hotel; nor did I think it wise to tell her the other children were in the city, until I knew that no further move was to be made, lest she not understanding the danger of arrest—if such danger I should find still existing—she would be unwilling to go elsewhere, unless she supposed the children and her husband, or both, had already gone.

I had brought with me a package of papers from Chicago, which I did not care to carry in my own trunks, and it was arranged to conceal them in the house lately rented in Detroit. I took them there in company with Hatch, and proceeded to place them above the ceiling of the upper story, when he suggested that in case of fire they would be lost, and volunteered to prepare a place next day in the basement for their safe-keeping. And this he did by first buying a new shovel, and then making a small excavation in the earth, not using this shovel, as it afterward appeared, but another found in the basement.

Upon the morning of October 17th I received startling intelligence from both St. Louis and Chicago, and, upon holding a consultation, it was with reluctance that we decided to leave Detroit and go either to Canada or Europe; for I felt that any move, without regard to expenses, was better than to have Mrs. Pitezel arrested and myself as well.

This day was a very busy one. Before Mrs. Pitezel left St. Louis

I had bought a large trunk, which I loaned to her to carry part of her personal effects to her new house.

When it was decided to make a move into other lands, I arranged with Hatch that, while I was busy about other matters, he should take the trunk to his room and repack it, and exclude a multitude of worthless articles, after having told Mrs. Pitezel that this was to be done.

It also became necessary to go to a city called Ypsilanti upon that same day to get a package of valuable papers I had ordered forwarded to me there, and, being so busy about other matters, I requested Hatch to make the trip for me.

He hesitated considerably about doing it, saying he must see to repacking this trunk.

I told him that I could better take the time to do this than to go to Ypsilanti.

He replied that I could not well take it to his room, as I was not known to the people of whom he rented.

I told him I would arrange it otherwise, and he then started for Ypsilanti.

At about one o'clock I found an expressman, and accompanying him to a feed store near by bought a flour barrel with the address of a party in Hartford, Conn., upon one end of it.

We then drove to Mrs. Pitezel's hotel and had the trunk taken to the depot. There, upon the platform, I took such worthless articles as Mrs. Pitezel had placed in a separate part of the trunk and put them in the barrel, and leaving the trunk at the depot had the expressman take the barrel to either the United States or American Express Company's office, and ship it to Hartford, Conn.

At about 2 P. M. I went to a livery stable on [Holmes omitted the street name] street, and hiring a horse and buggy drove to the house that had been rented and took the two girls with me for a drive. I entered the house and procured the papers I had previously left there. I also left a note instructing Hatch to the effect that if he came there from Ypsilanti with the other papers, not to bury them.

I then drove to Hatch's room and left a small note, and this accounts for the note being later found in the house where I directed the authorities to search.

Earlier in the same day Hatch and I visited several large stores, and at one obtained a $500 and two $200 bills, which, together with other small bills, making in all $1,000, which sum he took to Miss Williams to pay upon what was due her on the Fort Worth transaction.

Before leaving Detroit, Hatch brought to the depot the new shovel wrapped in a paper, and wished to put it in the trunk, but upon my remarking that it seemed more useless than things I had just taken out to make more room, he said he had paid for it and did not care to throw it away.

The next morning my wife and I left Detroit for Toronto at 10 o'clock. Mrs. Pitezel and the two children started two hours later.

The next morning Hatch took the two girls, Alice and Nellie, to the train and they made the journey to the same city alone twenty-four hours later, and over the same road I had come, while Hatch came to Toronto by the way of Buffalo, where he stopped to see Miss Williams.

I reached Toronto early Thursday evening, October 18th, and went at once to the Walker House. After taking dinner, I went to the station and met Mrs. Pitezel, taking her to a hotel near by, and returned to the Walker House for the night.

Next morning we breakfasted at about 8:30.

Fig. 31. Nellie Pitezel
Source: Herman W. Mudgett, *Holmes' Own Story*, 1895, p. 179.

Fig. 32. Nellie Pitezel
Source: Frank P. Geyer. *The Holmes-Pitezel Case*. 1896, p. 199.

Fig. 33. Minnie R. Williams
Source: Herman W. Mudgett, *Holmes' Own Story*, 1895, p. 258.

I visited Mrs. Pitezel at her hotel about a half hour, and then with my wife visited several fur stores, purchasing a fur cape and returned with her to the Walker House for the mid-day meal. Immediately thereafter we went for a long country drive, and did not return until about 6 P. M. I ate dinner and then, as upon the preceding evening, went to the station.

This time I met the two girls, Alice and Nellie, with whom Hatch had started from Detroit that morning, as stated.

Upon their arrival I placed them in an omnibus running to the Albion Hotel, in care of the runner for that house, and returning to the Walker House had hardly time to prepare for the theatre, which I attended that evening with my wife.

The next morning, after eating a late breakfast,[16] my first occupation upon this day was to go to the Hotel Albion and visit the children. I found them in their room, greatly interested in watching the immense open market across the street. I remained with them until almost, if not quite, 10 A. M. I then went to the post-office, making a few calls at some haberdashers on the way.

I reached the post-office not later than 10:30, when I met Hatch, in accordance with an arrangement made before leaving Detroit. He had visited Miss Williams at Buffalo, upon the trip to Toronto; and, in answer to my inquiry, stated that the boy Howard was well, and that he had wanted to come to Toronto with him, but he had thought it best for him to wait and accompany Miss Williams if she came.

Fig. 34. Albion Hotel in Toronto, Ontario Canada, where Holmes kept Alice and Nellie Pitezel
Source: Toronto Public Library, Virtual Reference Library, Albion Hotel, 1873, public domain.

He then left me, as he stated, to find for himself a private room, agreeing to meet me at the same place at 2 P. M.

Now, in this short time between 10:30 A. M. and 2 P. M., it appears from the testimony recently taken in Toronto at an inquest, that a visit was made to a real estate agent then in a distant part of the city; a call was made upon the owner of the house at Vincent street of sufficient length to arrange for renting the property, and to enter into a detailed description of the family supposed to be the future tenants, and become well acquainted with the owner; then to take possession of the house, to call upon a neighbor and make their acquaintance as well, and, presumably, to eat a lunch at some restaurant, and buy a small amount of furniture for the house just hired. Add to this the almost certain probability that the lessee had visited other houses as well, it being hardly possible that he could have found a house at once so well adapted to the purpose as this seems to have been, and there is little time left for other work before 2 P. M. of the same day.

My movements during these same hours were as follows: Leaving Hatch at the post-office, I went to Mrs. Pitezel's hotel, fully one mile away, stopping upon my way at the telegraph office for fully fifteen minutes, while a search was instituted in a different part of the building for undelivered telegrams.

After making a short call at the hotel, I returned to the Walker House, went again to the fur store where our purchase of the day previous had been made (one of two stores located very near each other about two blocks west of the post-office and north of K street).

Here fully one-half hour was taken up in the work done there, which included the purchase of two storm garments. We then went to King street, made several calls at furnishing stores and one large dry goods store, and then, after spending some time in selecting a good pocket compass, returned to the Walker House for lunch; to do which, and to write two letters, certainly occupied fully an hour, probably more.

I then went again to the Albion Hotel, stopping to buy the children some fruit and toys upon the way. At the appointed hour, I went to meet Hatch at the post-office. He was late in keeping his appointment, and I made several purchases in that neighborhood, and I think at this time selected the material and was measured for a suit of clothes at a custom tailor shop, upon the west side of Young street, near junction of the street leading to the post-office.

Upon meeting Hatch, I told him I was to be absent from the city on Sunday, and asked if he could see to the children while I was away, and if they wished to go for a street car ride, he would accompany them. This he agreed to do, and after making some further plans with him for the following week, I went to the Hotel Albion again and told the children of the arrangement made for their ride, then went to the furnishing store on King street kept by a man named Dickson, I think.

When I found the grade of goods I had been in search of, and after purchasing some, I returned to the Walker House with hardly time left to be shaved and go to Mrs. Pitezel's hotel, to let her know I was to be out of the city the next day, and to catch the 4 or 4:30 train for Niagara Falls.

At this time my wife's trunk and the large trunk from Detroit, were both at the Toronto Depot, and I asked that they be checked to Niagara.

I remarked to the baggage agent that I had no need to take the large one, save to avoid storage.

He asked how long I desired to leave it there, and I replied that was uncertain, but perhaps a week.

He asked for a half dollar and said that there are no further charges if it was taken away in a week's time.

The trunk never left the Toronto Depot during my stay there. Sunday, October 21st, was passed by us at the Falls, returning to Toronto by the way of Hamilton in the early evening, at which time I went to the Palmer House.

During Monday I was busy about the city, returning to my hotel often during the day. Part of the time I was with Hatch searching for a suitable location in which he and Miss Williams could open a respectable massage establishment, if they all settled there, which was the real object of the Toronto trip, as I have reason to believe.

During the day he asked me if I would not spend Tuesday night with him in and about the city. I gave him to understand that I might do so. Tuesday morning we met, as had become our custom, at the post-office between 10 and 11 o'clock.

I received additional and disquieting messages from the West, and by noon-time we had made up our minds that the conditions favorable to the business we had hoped to find did not exist in Toronto, and had decided to go to England instead.

Hatch particularly favored this plan, as they had had a prosperous business there during the foregoing year, and he at once wrote Miss Williams to that effect, and for her to meet the two girls at Niagara at as early a day as possible, which she was to appoint by letter.

She was to take the three children to London, while Mrs. Pitezel took the others there a little later on, or as soon as we could become settled again.

When Hatch again urged me to stay with him during the night, I finally told him that since my terrible experience of the year before, which the indirect results of my loose living had been Nannie Williams' death, and more particularly since my marriage, I had endeavored to live a clean life, and thought best not to deviate in this instance.

I returned to the Palmer House not later than 4:30 P. M. Later, in thinking the matter over, I thought, inasmuch as he had helped me so much during the preceding weeks, it seemed like ill-treatment towards him, and decided that if he brought the matter up next day I would spend a part of the evening with him.

Acting upon this decision, I told my wife next morning, Wednesday, that I might not return until late, but later in the day I reconsidered my former plan and returned to the Palmer House at about 2:30 P. M., and my wife being absent and the room locked at the time, I threw some flowers I had just bought into the room through the open transom, my wife finding them upon her return a short time later.

During the day I had been buying a quantity of small articles to send to my relatives in New Hampshire, and had gotten them together temporarily at the furnishing store previously mentioned.

At noon-time I had eaten lunch with the children and in the afternoon Hatch had taken them for a drive.

In the evening I accompanied my wife to the theatre, enjoying myself far more than the case would be had I been going about the city together with Hatch and a guilty conscience.

On Thursday, October 24th, the day when it is reasonable to suppose the two girls were killed, I was busy about the city during the forenoon. The girls came to the post-office at about 10:30, and either went with Hatch for a drive or a street-car ride, they having been in Hatch's care more than with me while in Toronto, for the reason that their hotel was so distant it encroached upon my time to ride to visit both them and Mrs. Pitezel and do what work I wished.

That morning we heard that Miss Williams would meet the girls at Niagara upon the arrival of the afternoon train. They ate lunch with me between 1 and 2 o'clock, Hatch being elsewhere at the time.

The girls returned to their hotel afterwards for a few minutes to change part of their attire for some that was warmer, which I had bought for them in anticipation of their sea voyage. Later they joined me again and I bought them a number of presents. I also bought Miss Williams a small brooch, which I gave to Alice, together with a note, which she was to deliver personally to Miss Williams.

My object in sending it in this way was that Hatch knew of our former relations, and I had avoided sending by him as he then claimed she was his wife.

About half an hour before train time, which I think was 4:30 P. M., we were upon Young street. I sent the girls to a restaurant or bakery near by to get some lunch prepared to take with them upon the train, instructing them to then come to a large store which I pointed out to them, where I would await their arrival.

I then entered this store and bought some small articles for the children, having in my hands at the time some underwear I had previously purchased to send to Howard, the boy, when I heard a familiar voice, and turning, saw Mrs. Pitezel and the other two children.

I quote from her recent statement, made in Toronto, as to what took place between us then, and state that it could only have been on this day, for while there I asked her if she could get ready to leave Toronto that evening:—

"I am convinced that my two children where right here in Toronto while I was here," said Mrs. Pitezel. "One day while I was shopping in a large store here, I suddenly saw Holmes. He said you wait here a little while until I return. I believe my children were right there in that store at the time, and Holmes took them out some other way so I should not see them."

As a matter of fact, they were at the bakery before spoken of, and I can only wish now that they had been with me, and met their mother, though at the time I should have considered it an unfortunate circumstance for the same reasons that obtained in Detroit.

I at once left the store and took the children to the depot, where Hatch met me with some bundles of goods he had bought.

I took the children to the ladies' waiting room and giving Alice $400, directed her to go into the private waiting room and fasten it securely within her dress, and later give it to Miss Williams.

I also gave each of the girls a small amount of spending money. I I [sic] wrote a telegram, directing it to myself at the hotel opposite the Palmer House, for Alice to send me early next morning from Niagara, if anything happened to prevent Miss Williams meeting them as had been agreed upon.

I also gave them explicit directions as to where to stay, and told them that I would surely go to them at once if any trouble arose. I then asked if they were afraid to go alone.

Alice answered, "Oh, no; I wish you or Mr. Hatch were going along, though."

The train came so quickly that I had little time to bid them good-bye, and therefore got upon the train and accompanied them perhaps a mile to a station where the train slowed up; Hatch going sill farther, at his suggestion, to see that the conductor took their tickets and agreed to transfer them at Hamilton to the right train.

I sat in the seat with Nellie during this time, Alice being in the seat in front. They spoke of their prospective voyage, gave me messages for their mother and the baby, and asked how long it would be before we all came to London. I told them to help Miss Williams all they could, and especially cautioned Nellie about quarreling with Howard, which she was apt to do when they were together, finally telling them upon my arrival there the three who had not quarreled would receive a present of considerable value.

My opportunity to leave the train having now arrived, I hastily bade them good-bye, and started to leave the car.

Little Nellie followed me to the door, and said, "Don't forget about baby," and reaching up kissed me good-bye, and ran back to the seat again.

With all truthfulness, I most earnestly state that under the circumstances, and at this time, about 4:30 P. M., Thursday, October 25th, I last saw these children.

I immediately returned to the Palmer House, telling my wife we should leave the city next morning, and said to her that if she had any more purchases to make, she should attend to it at once, as certain of the stores closed early.

For the next hour I was busy collecting my various purchases about the city, and taking them to the depot to place in the large trunk, and at not later than 6:30 Hatch was again at the depot, and stated that the conductor had taken the children in charge before he left the train. He then left me, agreeing to meet me early next morning at the hotel to learn if the children arrived all right. I then returned at once to the Palmer House and ate dinner.

Without delay I went to Mrs. Pitezel's hotel and assisted her in packing her trunk and having it taken to the train before 8 o'clock, the larger trunk going upon the same train; but Mrs. Pitezel and Dessie remarked to me later that they saw that trunk upon their arrival at Prescott early next morning, and a day later the Custom's officer at Ogdensburg, during his inspection, came across the shovel Hatch had insisted in placing in it at Detroit, remarking that he did not know but that it was dutiable on account of being new.

If this trunk had been at the Vincent street house there would have been no necessity of one's going to the neighbors to borrow a spade with which to conceal the evidence of the terrible crime committed there.

I returned to the Palmer House before Mrs. Pitezel had started —not later than 8:15 P. M.—and during the evening aided my wife in her preparations for the next day's journey; and only left the hotel before taking the train next morning at 8 o'clock, for about two minutes, to step across the street and ascertain if the girls had met Miss Williams, as was reasonable to suppose as no telegram was there.

Hatch was waiting for me at the hotel, and said he should wait one or two days in Toronto to get his mail and to buy some dutiable goods to take across the border.

I did no smuggling while upon this trip, nor was I even absent from my hotel any evening or night, save when accompanied by my wife to some place of amusement; nor did I ever leave my hotel before 8:30 A. M., save upon this last morning.

Thus it will be seen that this is not an unimportant statement, for according to a witness named Rodgers, if his testimony at the inquest at Toronto is correctly reported, he saw the two children at 1 P. M., Thursday, and that early next morning a spade that had been previously borrowed had been returned to him.

In an informal talk upon this subject, Mr. Rodgers has several times stated that this occurred quite early before working hours.

The hackneyed expression that, "a spade is a spade" may be true, but I feel that it but poorly expresses the full value and significance of this particular article.

Again, Mr. Rogers states that "Some time—in one published account some days later—the keys were left with me; I fully believe that the children met their death and were buried during the night, Thursday, October 25th; the spade returned before 8 o'clock —for Hatch was at that time at the hotel—that during the day their clothes were slowly burned"—and this, while I was journeying towards Prescott, Canada, a railroad trip of about eight hours, and where I registered at the Imperial Hotel not later than 4:30 P. M. that day.

It may be asked how at this late date I can fully remember what occurred upon one certain Saturday, nearly a year previous to the writing of these pages, to distinguish it from the preceding day or any other day that is less important?

Upon first hearing of the children's death, I was no more in a position to be positive in regard to this particular day than any other, until after thinking of the matter for hours and days together, as I believe only a man can force himself to think when he feels that perhaps his life depends upon such exertion, I arranged the facts in my mind in something like the following order:—

Being first sure, from some written memoranda, that I arrived in Toronto upon Thursday, October 18th, upon the next day, which was Friday, I was sure that no purchases had been made, save the fur garment referred to, because this took up the entire morning, and our ride occurred the same day, which fact was firmly impressed upon my mind by remembering that the livery conveyance came to the Walker House. This could not have occurred on any other day, as next afternoon we were going to Niagara, and at all later dates we were at the Palmer House.

I also remember that the second purchases at the fur store, that of the storm coats, were made upon the day following our previous purchase; this being further strengthened and impressed upon my mind by remembering that upon my return from Niagara the day following these purchases, a delay had occurred of several hours at Hamilton. The weather being such as to require it, I went to the baggage car, and after considerable conversation with the baggage man, was allowed to open our trunk for this garment.

This date brought to my mind that the compass had been used

while at Niagara, showing that that, too, was bought upon the day previous. This in its turn made me think that the purchase of the compass had occurred while passing from one furnishing store to another, looking for the special grade of underwear I wished, and which was bought later in the day, showing me clearly that at least a dozen other calls had been made at different other establishments for a like purpose, and which must of necessity have occurred prior to the purchase which ended my search.

My suit of clothes was promised to be delivered to me upon the following Tuesday, if possible, and upon Wednesday at the latest, and I was required to call once in the meantime to have them fitted.

If instead of Saturday I had been measured Monday, and told to call the next day to be fitted, they could not have been promised to me upon Tuesday, and so on in regard to the other visits made after this day, until I became so thoroughly convinced that I have not yet verified them by tracing the several stores, not knowing their names; but I fully believe that the order books and delivery slips of at least three responsible establishments will show that I must have been transacting business in their stores at the very hours when it had been sworn I was in remote parts of the city paying friendly visits to the owner and neighbor of the Vincent street house.

From there the remainder of my journey was by private conveyance, hired for that purpose, and through a blinding snow storm.

My pen cannot adequately portray the meeting with my aged parents, nor, were it possible, would I allow it to do so for publication. Suffice it to say that I came to them as one from the dead, they for years having considered me as such, until I had written them a few days before.

That after embracing them, as I looked into their dear faces once more, my eyes grew dim with the tears kindly sent to shut out for the moment the signs of added years I knew my uncalled for silence of the past seven years had done much to unnecessarily increase.

For the next two days I tried to feel that I was a boy again, and when I could go away by myself for a few minutes, I would wander from room to room, taking up or passing my hands lovingly over each familiar object, opening each cupboard and drawer with the same freedom I would have used twenty years before.

Here I found some letters written to my mother when I was a boy, and later as a young man; then as a physician, giving her careful directions regarding her health; then the letter written the day before my supposed death, all bearing evidence of the many times she had sorrowfully read them.

There also I found toys that years before had seemed so precious to me, and old garments carefully laid away, principally those which I had worn, and which I felt sure mother had purposely caused to be placed separately, thinking me dead, for if such had been the case it would have been the first death in our family.

And, moreover, I had always been looked upon by the others as "mother's boy."

When I went to the room where, times without number, I had been given such faithful teachings, and prayed with so earnestly, and had I been the earnest Christian my mother had then entreated me to become, I could have prayed for guidance beside the same dear old chair in which she had so often sat with me. I could not stay here, I felt it was too sacred a place to be entered now, and with tears in my eyes, that come again as I write, I reluctantly closed the door and went away.

Later, I visited what had been my own room, finding it much as I had left it twenty years before. Many of my old school books were here, but my most precious though worthless possessions I had carefully placed elsewhere; and now I took them, dust laden, from their places of concealment.

First, a complicated contrivance that when finished was to have solved the problem of perpetual motion, then a piece of a windmill so arranged as to make a noise when in operation sufficient to scare the crows from the corn field; going further I came to some small boxes containing almost everything from a tooth, the first I remember of having extracted, to a small bunch of very tenderly-worded notes and a picture of my little twelve-year-old sweetheart.

These experiences were repeated next day when I drove to the old farm my grandfather had owned during his life-time. Here mother had lived as a child, a girl, and a young woman, and accompanying me she no doubt saw many things as dear to her. I, too, had lived here for a time, and could not leave the place until I had found my "marks" denoting my height at various times—the first of which was less than three feet.

I also explored the yards and barns. Here many changes had taken place; even my initials that had been deeply cut in one of the large elm trees that grow so slowly had become obliterated. This touched me deeply, seeming so much in keeping with what had in reality occurred to the name itself; and feeling that I must find one unchanging remembrance, I went to a huge boulder upon a hill near by, having to cross the brook with much difficulty that in earlier years had offered no impediment to the progress of my unclad feet.

Reaching the rock I raised my voice, uttering the same words I had used as a child, and listened for the echoing answer. It did not come; it, too, was dead, owing, no doubt, to the woods upon the surrounding hills having disappeared meantime.

Returning I found my brother had come in answer to my request that he should visit me. He was accompanied by several sturdy boys whom I had never seen, and in whose faces I could see my brother and myself of years ago; but when, in conversation, they spoke to and of their father as "Arthur," his given name, I could but wonder if he thought of what would have been our portion had we ever addressed our parents in like manner.

The day before I came away father told me of what disposition he had made, when he thought me dead, of the portion of his property that would have belonged to me if I had lived, and told me that he would rearrange it. This I begged him not to do, and a good occasion having thus been brought about, I had him bring from his trunk of private papers the several promissory notes that he had guaranteed for me years previous, and later had paid, and after adding the interest, I insisted upon his taking the money so represented.

The next day, after a leave-taking nearly as pathetic and hard to bear as my meeting had been, I left them.

I have seen neither of them since, nor do I ever expect to do so. Each prison mail delivery I receive with trembling hands, expecting it to be an announcement of their death, caused by this great sorrow and shame so cruelly forced upon them.

The morning following my return to Burlington I visited the post-office and received my mail. It had been handed to me and I had stepped to a small desk to open some of it when, glancing toward the delivery window, I saw what seemed to me to be the entire office force staring with all wonder at me.

I knew instantly that I was in danger, and this was made more sure to me by the manner in which they at once sought to dispel this feeling by dispersing from the window. I at once resumed my reading, for I felt that it would be hazardous to have them know I was aware of their acts.

As soon as I could do so safely I went to Mrs. Pitezel's house and told her I had been hastily called to Boston and New York; that she should remain in Burlington until I should return or send for her prior to her going to the children.

At this time (when I knew that momentarily there was a possibility of officers coming to the house for me) she reminded me that the supply of coal was nearly exhausted and not wishing to go upon the street to order more, I accompanied her to the basement and, after removing some of the decayed boards from the floor of the coal bin, I shoveled together a considerable quantity of coal that had accumulated there[.]

It was this circumstance that later, when she was suffering so acutely in Toronto, she distorted into the statement that she believed I was then preparing to take her life.

The dispatches I had received in my Burlington mail left no doubt in my mind that detectives were following my movements, although I could not determine then how they had undermined my apparently safe plans.

Later I found that, by making absolutely erroneous statements to the Post-Office Department at Washington, they had been given the right to examine all of a certain line of mail matter, thus accomplishing their purpose.

Having made these arrangements with Mrs. Pitezel, I left Burlington Tuesday morning, November 13th, and reached Boston the same evening at the Adams House.

The next day I secured some rooms in a quiet street for my wife and myself, and proceeded at once to arrange for Mrs. Pitezel's departure for Europe. But that evening while writing some letters at the Parker House, a careless shadower, in his earnestness to learn their address, allowed me to know that I was being watched. As in Burlington, I tried not to have it known that I had observed it, but from that moment I knew I was in their hands.

After leaving the hotel and entering several crowded stores to ascertain the number and vigilance of my followers, I adopted the only feasible plan I considered was left open to me. I wrote Mrs. Pitezel a letter, asking her to meet me upon a certain day at Lowell, Mass., intending to see her and instruct her as to taking the trip alone.

After throwing off my followers, I sent this letter to Burlington by express, including tickets and full directions for their journey. I then returned to my rooms, intending to tell my wife of my threatened trouble and the causes that had led up to it. I could not do it.

We had been married less than a year, and during that time I had endeavored to shield her from all annoying influences, and to cause her such great unhappiness now, until I absolutely knew it was upon me, was impossible.

The next day I was continually shadowed, and finally returned to my room, and while my wife was absent made a small opening in the now famous trunk.[17]

I then went to a relative, living in a suburb, intending to ask him to aid me in making my escape, by means of the trunk, if absolutely necessary. Here again my courage failed me, when I had visited him, lest it should involve him in some difficulty, and I returned to my room resolved to meet whatever was in store for me.

Saturday P. M., November 17th, I left the house intending to send two letters, if possible.

I had proceeded hardly a block when I was surrounded by four greatly excited men, two of whom said, "We want you, you are under arrest, and it will be useless for you to try to escape, as there are four of us."

I said, "I shall make no effort to escape."

We were near the police headquarters, where I was at once taken into Inspector Watts' private office. I knew that no time would be lost in sending to my room to search my belongings, and I therefore asked that my wife be called to me, preferring to tell her myself of what was in store for her. The request was granted, and in a few minutes she was ushered into the room.

Of this scene I also cannot write. No one was present save Inspector Watts, and I can never forget or fail to appreciate his efforts to make it as easy for her—for us both, for that matter—as was possible.

Before she had left me I told her what had brought about my arrest and also my right name.

Only true-hearted, loving wives, who have been made to suffer in the same way, can know what the blow meant to her. They also alone can understand her feelings expressed to me in a letter months afterwards, from which, sacred though it is to me, I quote these words, "Our idols once shattered, though cherishing the broken fragments as best we may, can never be the same."

After she had returned to our rooms I had a long conversation with Inspector Watts, a representative of the Insurance Company and a Pinkerton detective. I found I had been arrested upon the charge of stealing horses in Texas; that I was to be held upon this charge until requisition and other papers could be obtained from Pennsylvania in order to have me tried in that State upon the charge of conspiring to defraud the Insurance Company in Philadelphia.

I at once waived the necessity of requisition papers, and told them I was ready to go with them.

I was then closely questioned regarding the whereabouts of the Pitezel family, and knowing that Mrs. Pitezel would in a few days be in Lowell with no one to plan and care for her, and fearing lest she should see an account of my arrest and become alarmed thereby, I thought it best to tell them where she was, asking them to meet her upon her arrival.

They thought it best to go to Burlington, and it was there arranged that they should escort her to Boston, but it was agreed not to place her under arrest.

I told them that Pitezel and the other children were in the South, not wishing to deviate from Mrs. Pitezel's understanding of his condition until I could see her.

In my interview with Mr. [O. LaForrest] Perry, the company's representative, it was agreed that in consideration of my aiding them in clearing up the case, that I could depend upon the company's influence and aid in selecting a suitable location for a home for my wife in Philadelphia. That my name, then only known to a few persons, should be withheld, allowing me to appear before the public as H. H. Holmes, thus shielding my relatives from disgrace. That I should, upon reaching Philadelphia, see and talk with Mrs. Pitezel, and plan for her future, and that my wife should visit me upon my arrival there.

No one of these promises was kept save to obtain a boarding place for my wife, and that principally that they could use their best endeavors to so prejudice her against me that she would not care to visit me.

Upon the following Monday evening I started for Philadelphia in company with Detective Crawford, being chained to him, in fact.

Upon this trip my wife came into the car in which I was traveling to visit me for a few minutes, and while there saw Mrs. Pitezel and her two children for the first time in her life—they being then in the same car. Nor had she even known of the existence of such a family until my arrest in Boston. She had known of Pitezel in Fort Worth as a man working for me by the name of Lyman.

Upon reaching Philadelphia I was placed in a darkened cell in the City Hall, and here, figuratively speaking, the thumb-screws were applied.

I was not allowed to see or hear from my wife, save that she was seriously ill.

Mrs. Pitezel and the two children I knew were in the same place of confinement, but only by hearing their voices or cries of the child, as I was not allowed to speak to them.

After a time I was taken to the photograph department and weighed and measured, a process which had been too often described for publication to be of interest, save to say that so scientifically is it done that a person once placed under the ban in this way has little chance of ever escaping recognition.

Later my photograph was also taken with what must have been a magical camera, judging from the thousand and one different reproductions from time to time appearing in print.

Returning to my cell, Superintendent Linden visited me and advised me to see no attorney, and wishing to return his good-will, if possible, I for a time gave heed to this. He also urged me strongly to tell him Pitezel's exact location.

Upon Friday, October 23d, I was committed to prison upon the conspiracy charge, but before I went I made a detailed statement of our attorney's connection with the case, for I had found that he had been the cause of my trouble, and was then standing back, as he had said he should do, relying upon his reputation as a member of an influential firm of lawyers, to escape trouble himself.

What followed during the next weary months of my life I feel that I can best express by copying from my prison diary, kept during this time, which now lies before me.

I give such portions as relate more particularly to my case, stating first, however, that during all my life I had always been active and had taken much out-of-door exercise, and that on this account, together with worrying about my wife's safety, and financial affairs, it seemed for a time after my imprisonment commenced that I should die from the effect thereof.

O. LA FOREST PERRY.

Fig. 35. Ophir La Forrest Perry, Fidelity Mutual Life Insurance Association
Source: "Mrs. Pitezel Faces Holmes," *New York Herald,* October 31, 1895, p. 3.

WILLIAM B. WATTS.

Fig. 36. Boston Chief Inspector, William B. Watts, from Pinkerton National Detective Agency, allowed Holmes' wife to see him after his arrest. Source: William B. Watts and Benjamin P. Eldridge. *Our Rival, The Rascal*. Boston, Massachusetts: Pemberton Publishing Company, 1897, p. i.

Moyamensing Prison Diary Appendix

Saturday Evening, November 24, 1894.—A week ago to-day I was placed under arrest in Boston, and after preliminary hearing was brought here to Philadelphia, where I was confined at City Hall police headquarters.

Yesterday P. M. I was placed in a crowded conveyance filled with a filthy lot of humanity, and after what seemed to me an endless drive reached the county prison, located at Tenth and Reed streets, which is known as Moyamensing.

I was assigned to a thoroughly clean, whitewashed room, about 9 x 14 feet in size, lighted by one very narrow grated window. The entrance to the room is closed by a small latticed iron door, beyond which is still another solid door of wood, which, when closed, excludes nearly all sound, and thus renders the room practically a place of solitary confinement.

A register furnishes furnace heat, and one sixteen candle power electric burner gives light during a part of the evening, it being turned off promptly at 9 P. M.

The superintendent of the prison came to my door for a few moments this morning, and spoke to me of some of the prison rules and regulations.

My attorney, Mr. Shoemaker, also called on me, also assured me that my wife should see me on Monday, and that she was no longer seriously ill, to hear which makes my heavy load seem lighter.

I have now had three meals served to me since coming here, and can judge something of what my food will be if I have to stay here any length of time. For breakfast a plentiful supply of plain coffee and a quantity of course white bread; at the noon hour a small pail well filled with soup, thickened with barley and a few beans, and containing a large piece of beef; at 5 P. M.

I was agreeably surprised at receiving a liberal quantity of cocoa, made, I judge, from cocoa shells—a most healthful drink for one in such close confinement. This was accompanied by another piece of bread, which completed the day's rations.

One thing is certain, even if not a great variety, the quantity is sufficient, and is cleanly cooked and served.

Fig. 37. Moyamensing Prison, which was located at 1400 South Tenth Street
Source: J. C. Wild. *"Panorama and Views of Philadelphia and its Vicinity,"* 1938.

Fig. 38. Philadelphia City Hall, 1884
Source: William B. Smith. *First Annual Message of William B. Smith, Mayor of Phildelphia with the Accompanying Documents, for the Year 1884*. Philadelphia, PA: Dunlap & Clarke, Printers, 1885, p. i.

William A. Shoemaker

Fig. 39. Holmes' Attorney, William A. Shoemaker
Source: "Shoemaker's Fate," *Philadelphia Inquirer*, March 15, 1896, p. 1.

Sunday, November 25, 1894.—A long, still day, doubly hard to bear, inasmuch as since my marriage it has, owing to our long talks, reading and driving, grown to be a day of delight to me.

At 3 P. M. the outer door to my room was opened about four inches in order to admit the sound of the religious services held at that hour and lasting until 4 o'clock, which consists principally of singing, some of which is quite good.

November 26, 1894.—My wife [Georgiana Yoke] came to see me at 9:30 this morning. I had not been allowed to see her since my arrival in Philadelphia, and it required all the courage I could command to go to her under such humiliating circumstances.

Our meeting took place in the presence of one of the prison officials.

She has suffered, and though she tried heroically to keep me from seeing it, it was of no avail; and in a few minutes to again bid her good-bye and know she was going out into the world with so heavy a load to bear, caused me more suffering than any death struggles can ever do.

Each day until I know she is safe from harm and annoyance will be a living death to me.

I am promised that for the present she shall visit me two times a week, each week, not to exceed fifteen minutes in duration. If she can bear the humiliation of coming here it will be a Godsend to me, but I shall not urge her to do so against her will.

Tuesday, November 27, 1894.—My attorney called to see me to-day. He only is allowed to visit my room and converse with me alone.

Our time was principally occupied in planning to furnish bail for Mrs. Pitezel, who must be set at liberty at all hazards.

I am threatened with arrest upon the charge of murder, if I give bail myself, which is only another form of saying that I must stay here until it is their pleasure to call my case for trial; for if charged with murder, bail would not be accepted.

Had letters sent to Miss Williams.

The other two children are here in Philadelphia, and I am assured are well cared for.

Was agreeably surprised to-day to find that unsentenced prisoners are allowed to receive eatables, at their own expense, from outside the prison, and I shall make arrangements to have this brought about. I also can have all newspapers and periodicals I wish. Money here in the prison, aside from these uses, is absolutely without value.

MRS. PITEZEL AND DAUGHTER IN THE CELL.

Fig. 40. Mrs. Pitezel, her daughter, Jeannette 'Dessie' (16), and Mrs. Pitezel's son (1) are shown here in jail
Source: "Crime is His Passion," *New York Herald,* November 25, 1894, p. 1.

November 30, 1894.—My wife came, looking brighter and stronger. This time a seat was given her outside my door, though a keeper was present during the entire interview.

I can see only too plainly what an effort it is for her to come into this terrible place, for she sees more of the prison in passing in and out than I do myself, and to one of her sensitive nature it is a most trying experience.

Was instructed to-day that, after I have completed several important business letters I am writing, I must restrict all of my correspondence to one letter a week. All mail is inspected in the prison office.

I think my weight is twenty pounds less than at time of my arrest; but I am getting more used to my unnatural surroundings and to my bed of straw, and am sleeping better.

The great humiliation of feeling that I am a prisoner is killing me far more than any other discomforts I have to endure.

I notice quite a difference, however, between my wooden stool and a comfortable office or rocking chair, but still feel that I have much to be thankful for, as thus far I have been allowed to wear my own clothing and to keep my watch and other small belongings. The escape from wearing the convict garb I greatly appreciate.

December 3, 1894.—I have commenced to write a careful and truthful account of all matters pertaining to my case, including the fact that Pitezel is dead and that the children are with Miss Williams, and as soon as I have completed it I shall ask my attorney to place it in the hands of the authorities that they may verify what I have written.

I feel that I could very easily have carried out the statements I made relative to his being alive and the substitution of a body if there was anything to be gained by it, but Mrs. Pitezel, at all events, should know of it before the children return, lest the question arise as to where he was, and give occasion for the prosecution to feel that other motives than this had caused me to conceal the true state of affairs.

December 25, 1894—Christmas. I shall receive no presents, and caused only a few flowers to be sent to [Holmes omitted the name], as I feel that any reminder of a year ago to-day would make it harder for her to bear. Nor will I trust myself to write at length to-night.

I did not have a dinner sent in to-day.

To-morrow will also be another sad anniversary, and a day hard to bear.

January 1, 1895.—The New Year. I have been busy nearly all day in prison formulating a methodical plan for my daily life while in prison, to which I shall hereafter rigidly adhere, for the terrible solitude of these dark winter days will otherwise soon break me down.

I shall rise at 6:30, and after taking my usual sponge bath shall clean my room and arrange it for the day. My meal hours shall be 7:30 A. M., 12, and 5 and 9 P. M. I shall eat no more meat of any kind while I am so closely confined. Until 10 A. M. all the time not otherwise disposed of shall be devoted to exercise and reading the morning papers. From 10 to 12 and 2 to 4, six days in the week, I shall confine myself to my old medical works and other college studies, including stenography, French and German, the balance of my day shall be taken up with reading the periodicals and library books with which [Holmes omitted the name] keeps me well supplied. I shall retire at 9 P. M. and shall as soon as possible force myself into the habit of sleeping throughout the entire night.

Received a most kind and tender letter from my wife, filled with encouraging words. But each day seems to make it harder to bear.

January 9th.—We have abandoned for the time being all hopes of procuring Mrs. Pitezel her liberty. The insurance company, misconstruing our motives, are determined to keep her under their control.

Efforts are being made to keep me from making satisfactory settlements of my business matters, as well as trying to induce my wife to abandon me.

Came across these two lines in my reading to-day:—

> "I only know the sky has lost its blue,
> The days are weary and the night is drear."

They so thoroughly described my own condition that I cannot refrain from copying them tonight.

January 25th.—Had a long, quiet talk with my wife at City Hall to-day, where I had been taken to be interviewed by the authorities.

I feel better and stronger to-night than for many days.

Caused advertisement to be sent to Miss Williams, and also sent out a large number of business letters, there being no restriction against doing so while there.

In February Mr. Shoemaker started West and South to settle up my business matters for me; I expect him to be absent fully two weeks. Owing to the interference of the insurance company, property that I would have refused $50,000 for three months ago, some of which I would not have sold at all, will have to be sacrificed, so that not more than one-half that sum will be realized for it.

March 1st.—Commenced to-day to arrange for my trial. Mr. S. P. Rotan is to act with Mr. Shoemaker as associate counsel. Thus far I have devoted but little time to this work, but shall now give my 10 to 12 study hour to it each day.

March 11th.—Read Trilby [a book by George du Maurier], and was much pleased with parts of it.

My wife also brought me some very nice flowers, speaking so strongly to me of our former life that I have had to put them from my sight.

March 23d.—The days are fast lengthening; the sun shone into my room for a few minutes to-day for the first time since I came here.

May 16th.—My birthday. Am 34 years old. I wonder if, as in former years, mother will write me.

Was at the City Hall and pleaded with the Assistant District Attorney again that my present case be abandoned and that I be at once tried upon the charge of killing Pitezel, as I feel that I cannot too soon have this matter settled, inasmuch as they so boldly accuse me of it. This they flatly refused to do, saying I only wished to avoid serving a sentence upon the minor charge.

Then the only satisfaction I could obtain when I urged that the conspiracy charge be tried at once in order that Mrs. Pitezel may be set at liberty was, "Don't you worry yourself about Mrs. Pitezel; we will care for her and will also give you all you want to do before we are through with you.["]

Have retained Mr. R. O. Moon as special counsel.

May 21st.—My case was called in Court to-day, and I entered a formal plea of "not guilty." The trial was postponed until a later date.

[May 27th.] On Monday, May 27th, my case was called for trial. I went to the City Hall, where the Court was held, in the same kind of conveyance that had brought me here over six months before, and was conducted by two officers into the Court room, and placed in a small enclosure in the centre of the room.

After a little delay, the Court was called to order, Judge Hare presiding. Little time was lost in securing a jury, as those first called, almost without exception, appeared to be intelligent and honest.

After administering the oaths, the District Attorney arose and addressed the Court. Theretofore I had not looked upon my case as serious, for after I had placed before the authorities my written statement, some months earlier, stating that Pitezel was actually dead, some of the prosecution and the insurance company had openly stated that they believed it to be true, and knowing myself that his death had actually occurred, it left little, save the charge of conspiracy, to be disposed of; but when the prosecution drew into the case matters altogether foreign to the conspiracy charges, I felt that it could not help but influence the jury.

The authorities had also brought Mrs. Pitezel into Court, and had seated her in a prominent portion of the room, and later, while giving his testimony, one of the witnesses led the Court to understand that with a knife I had proceeded, in a cold-blooded manner, to mutilate the body of Pitezel at the time of examination for the purpose of identification.

I saw that the prosecution were determined to magnify and dilate each point that could be turned in their favor.

During the afternoon session I learned that a subpoena had been issued requiring my wife to appear in Court, contrary to a distinct arrangement that I had previously made with the insurance company that she should not be used as a witness or annoyed in regard to the case, and I felt that I would rather serve a longer term of imprisonment than thus humiliate her.

At the close of the Court for the day I learned that the prosecution were prepared to place upon the witness stand the doctors before referred to, who had seen the body at Callowhill street, both of whom would swear the body found there could not have been Pitezel, a matter I could not disprove, and that evening, after considering all the proceedings of the day, I resolved to ask my counsel to allow me to change my plea, relying upon them to show the Court when I should, at a later date, be brought before the Judge to be sentenced, that while there had existed an agreement to perpetrate a fraud under certain circumstances, there was no active conspiracy at the time when Pitezel's death had occurred, and that the death being genuine, the insurance company had not been defrauded.

This, together with the fact that I should save at least a week's valuable time to the Court by ending my trial as I did, I hoped would cause the Judge to reduce my sentence to one-half the fullest extent, thus allowing me to go to Texas in October, 1895, which would be in season to attended to my business matters there before they would seriously suffer from the delay.

Before leaving the Court the Judge stated that I should be allowed the six months I had already been in prison, which I could not but appreciate, as it was wholly discretionary with him.

Later during the day I was called before the District Attorney, in his private office, and there made a statement as to the probable whereabouts of the children, telling them as truthfully as I knew all the facts I could think of that would aid them in the search, and later gave them the cipher I had formerly used in communicating with Miss Williams. I then returned to my prison room at Moyamensing.

[June 18th.] Upon the 18th of June I was taken to the Court House as a witness in the case against Howe; but a long continuance being taken, I was not called upon to testify.

Shortly thereafter one of my attorneys, after careful preparation, went to London, and did considerable hard work for me in endeavoring to locate the missing children by searching for the old addresses given me by Hatch; and the assertion made by the Assistant District Attorney that I had deceived my counsel and sent him upon a search I knew to be useless, is simply one of many statements he has made both to me and for publication that are [sic] painful evidence of the want of discernment and good judgment one had a right to expect from the occupant of so important a position.

[Late June.] Later in June Detective Guyer [Geyer] called on me, and, in a long conversation with him, I made a most honest endeavor to place him in possession of all the facts I could think of that would be instrumental in facilitating the proposed search, which I looked upon and welcomed as one of corroboration of the same statements I had previously made, feeling that upon his following my movements from place to place, and finding that I had not misled him in any way, he would return more free to believe other statements that were not so easily verified; and I do not think I need to state to any intelligent reader that had I known of the death and burial of the little ones in the Toronto cellar, and wished to conceal the same, I should have avoided all mention of other houses where furniture had been brought and, in one instance, an excavation made, and I feel that if Mr. Guyer [Geyer] were called upon for a truthful statement, he could not fail to say that but for my aid, freely given him at this time, together with detailed statements and drawings previously made relating to those places where I had forgotten the exact location, his search would have been a failure, inasmuch as he would have had no incentive to prosecute a similar investigation in Toronto.

[July 16th.] On the morning of the 16th of July, my newspaper was delivered to me at about 8:30 A. M., and I had hardly opened it before I saw in large headlines the announcement of the finding of the children in Toronto. For the moment it seemed so impossible, that I was inclined to think it one of the frequent newspaper excitements that had attended the earlier part of the case, but, in attempting to quickly gain some accurate comprehension of what was stated in the article, I became convinced that at least certain bodies had been found there, and upon comparing the date when the house was hired I knew it to be the same as when the children had been in Toronto; and thus being forced to realize the awfulness of what had probably happened, I gave up trying to read the article, and saw instead the two little faces as they had looked when I hurriedly left them—felt the innocent child's kiss so timidly given and heard again their earnest words of farewell, and I realized that I had received another burden to carry to my grave with me, equal, if not worse, than the horrors of Nannie Williams' death.

I think at this time I should have lost my senses utterly had I not been hurriedly called to prepare to be taken to the District Attorney's office.

I went there securely handcuffed and accompanied by two officers for further safety, and not until these extra precautions were taken did I realize the new and terrible change that had occurred affecting the entire aspect of my case.

Upon reaching the City Hall the Assistant District Attorney met me. I was in no condition to bear his accusations, nor disposed to answer many of his questions. I felt it right that he should know that I had already seen the morning papers, and upon his demanding that I tell him where the body of the boy could be found, I answered, that in the light of the Toronto development, I had reason to think he would be found buried in or about the house that had been hired in Detroit.

He then accused me of killing him in Detroit and destroying his body by burning it in a furnace that was in the cellar.

This I denied, and moreover felt sure and told him that the body could not have been destroyed there in that way by any one else, as I had been in the house upon two occasions and knew that if human remains had been cremated there even at a considerably earlier date the odor would have been noticeable.

I did not see the District Attorney at this interview and was very soon taken to the prison again.

For the next forty-eight hours I reasoned and thought, studying minutely each step of our journey from the time Hatch had joined us; but what seemed utterly incomprehensible to me then, and even now, was how any sane man would take such awful chances, even if he had no other scruples to restrain him, yet I well knew it could have been no one else that committed the crime, for in that event the non-arrival of the children would have been known to us.

I knew also that the small sum of $400, that was given to the girls just previous to their death, could have been no incentive for the commission of the act, and was forced to look further for the motive.

I could only think that it had been done at Miss Williams' suggestion and in furtherance of her threat of the previous year, which, owing to friendliness at a later date, I had believed wholly abandoned, probably also intending to give color to a theory (if later for her safety such had to be advanced) that I, and not she, had killed her sister, pointing to these disappearances that had occurred at a time when I was known to have had the children in my charge as corroborative of the same, though I felt sure that her hellish wish for vengeance for the imagined desertion of the previous year was much the more potent of the two motives.

Finally I commenced at the time I had first asked them to come here, and following carefully each step and conversation we had held, I became certain that when Hatch had first met me in Cincinnati he could have had no matured plans.

Then going over our route I could see no change until after reaching Indiana. He had gone away for a few days to Chicago, as he then said, but, as I now believe, to Detroit, to consult with Miss Williams, as it occurred directly after he had first known I was liable to be arrested.

He then commenced taking more interest in the children, taking them about with him and buying them presents.

It was at this time, also, that he took a private room, saying that inasmuch as I was liable to be watched, it was unsafe for any of us to be at a hotel.

It was then that he had his beard removed from his chin[18] in the barber shop at the Indianapolis depot, each act being a trifle in itself, yet taken together showed to me that then was when the change had commenced.

Following still further, I had at first wished to go to Chicago alone, thinking it safer to do so than to be accompanied by the children. I had asked him to take them all to Detroit with him, to which he replied that if this was done it would keep him from looking about for a house there for Mrs. Pitezel, which we were anxious to obtain as quickly as possible; that he could take the boy with him easily, for he could accompany him about the city in his search.

This, together with the girls' desire to go to Chicago, led me to carry out the arrangement in this way.

Then came our arrival in Detroit, two days later, when Hatch stated that the boy had gone with Miss Williams to Buffalo, and that he had been delayed twenty-four hours *en route* to Detroit at some junction where a wreck had occurred, thus accounting for his having made no search for a house.

Then of another circumstance, which ordinarily I should not have considered more than a coincidence. While in Cincinnati, Alice and the boy had disputed as to which should wear an old watch that had belonged to their father. Alice advancing her claim of superior years, Howard, that he was the boy of the family, accompanied by the remembrance that his father had promised it to him when he grew older.

I settled the matter by taking the watch in charge and buying each of them a small nickel open-faced watch and chain. This left little Nellie with a broken heart, and as soon as I noticed her trouble, I told her that before our journey was ended I would also buy one for her, or something else equally pleasing to her, if she preferred.

The day after our arrival in Detroit she came to me much elated, saying Mr. Hatch had bought her a watch. Upon looking at it, it proved to be of the same make and design as the one Alice had, and I now believe it was the same watch I had given Howard some days before.

Then in Detroit occurred the buying of the spade and his insisting upon taking it to Toronto, giving the weak excuse that he had paid for it and did not wish to throw it away, when he could have sold it at a second-hand store much easier than to have taken it so far to the depot to place it in the trunk.

Then, the letter from Miss Williams, asking that I pay the $1,000 due upon the Fort Worth property then, instead of later, as she wished to use a part of it; it seeming hardly probable, if this had been the real reason of requiring the money at that time, that so much trouble would have been taken in trying to convert the money I gave into a $1,000 bill.

The only other circumstance I could then think of was his almost querulous objection to my buying a jacket in Detroit for one of the girls, and later heavier clothing in Toronto, he saying that Miss Williams could better understand their needs, and his efforts to borrow $500 from me in Burlington, and also that Alice had told me in Toronto that Mr. Hatch had given her a letter or a postal card to write for him, as he had no writing materials at his room.

I asked her what it was about, and she answered, as near as I can remember, that it was to a Mr. Cooke about a house that he did not need longer and about a sale of furniture or that it had been sold.

If I thought sufficiently of the matter at the time, I supposed it referred to the Detroit house, as this was the only one I had reason to think he had engaged, and I think it will be later found that at Logansport or Peru, or some other junction town in Indiana, a house was hired upon October 10th or 11th, while I was in Chicago, and the body of the boy shipped from the hotel in Indianapolis in accordance with the report that a large trunk was that day shipped to an unknown destination, and the remains buried similarly to the Toronto case, and that this was the true cause of his delay in reaching Detroit.

Some days later I told the authorities that such was my belief, giving them my reasons for thinking so, and for my pains I was severely taken to task for having previously stated that I thought he would be found in or about the Detroit house.

From this I have been characterized by them as a supreme falsifier.

With the one exception of the statements made at the time of my arrest, and adhered to until I knew Mrs. Pitezel could be no longer saved from worriment by so doing, I know of no material misstatements made, save that the children were in England, which I most honestly believed to be true.

The next day I saw an account in the papers of my wife's coming here in answer to a telegram from the District Attorney's office. This said to me far more than was printed in the paper. I knew she must have been intimidated to have come at this time and in answer to a summons from them.

My fears were confirmed a few days later when I learned from a trusted source that such was the case, and that the threat had been made that if she made any effort to see or communicate with me she would be arrested and held as a witness. (It will here be remembered that our prison interviews were invariably held in the presence of a keeper.) And upon the other hand if she remained away from me and aided them, all her expenses would be paid by the prosecution or the insurance company.

I knew that the latter would have no weight with her, but I feared that the threats they made would cause her to worry until she became ill, and I therefore felt justified in resorting to almost any means to see her and try and quiet her fears.

With this in view I wrote the District Attorney that if I could have an interview with him, my wife being present, I would endeavor to make it plain to him where they could expect to find the remains of the boy.

This interview was promptly accorded me and, upon being taken into his private office, I met my wife, and it needed but one glance to know what she had been and was then suffering, which caused a feeling of almost uncontrollable anger to take possession of me, both towards the authorities for unjustly causing her hard lot to be made worse, and towards myself that for the sake of business gains I had ever allowed myself to enter into the petty transactions that had been the cause of all her troubles.

My first inquiry, as could naturally be expected, was as to her physical condition and if she was in comfortable quarters and free from actual restraint. I also told her that until the world at large ceased to look upon me as a murderer I should not in the presence of others greet her as was my usual custom.

If at this time my wife shrank from me as though in fear, as was given out from the District Attorney's office for publication, I, in my blindness, did not see it, and in the days and nights that followed until I again heard of her welfare almost my only source of comfort was the remembrance of the few kind words she had said, and, what was even more to me, that she had worn both her engagement and her wedding rings, and as many of the gifts I had presented to her during our happier days as she could without exciting undue notice, choosing those that would convey to me from their associations the kind thoughts she knew she would have no opportunity to say in words.

This was particularly plain to me, inasmuch as it was wholly contrary to her usual custom to appear thus attired at that early hour of the day, and in so public a place, and until she tells me that such is not the case I shall hold to the belief that she is yet loyal to me.

There were present at this meeting, beside the District Attorney, Mr. Shoemaker and Supt. Linden, and for a part of the time Mr. Fouse and the Assistant District Attorney.

I endeavored to state to them, in as few words as possible, the circumstances of Hatch's delay of twenty-four hours, and the letters sent from either Detroit or Toronto about a house.

They at once branded my statements concerning Hatch as untrue, and said that he was a mythical person, asking me to name any one who had ever seen him.

In reply I said, "I do not consider that you have any more grounds for doubting the fact that he was at these places than to doubt that Mrs. Pitezel or these children were there, because they did not happen to meet. However, you need not rely upon my statements."

Last November or December Mr. Perry, a representative of the insurance company, came to the prison, in company with another witness, to question me about some other matters pertaining to the case, and while there said to me, "Who was the man you met at the Burlington depot you seemed so surprised to see, and immediately went to the telegraph office and took up a message you had previously written?"

I told him it was a man named Hatch, a friend of Miss Williams, who was not connected with my case in any important way. I also stated in further answer to the District Attorney's question that I felt sure that the barber in the Indianapolis depot would remember his coming there with me, it being so unusual an occurrence for me to be accompanied by any one; that the proprietor or clerk of the small hotel where he had taken the children upon their arrival in Detroit would remember him, and probably the woman where they boarded during most of their stay in that city, as he accompanied them to the train the day following my departure for Toronto. That Mrs. Pitezel will remember his calling at her house at Burlington, and upon her going to the door he made some trivial excuse and went away, having expected to meet me there. And that my wife will remember my leaving her upon the steamboat landing at B. for a moment to step across to the depot to speak to him, and upon two subsequent occasions while in that city of recognizing him upon the street, she remarking upon my knowing any one there, and parties who have lately testified that they knew of my visiting Miss Williams in New York in 1888, and later in Denver, will know that it was Hatch and not myself, as I never was in Denver until January, 1894, and never saw Miss Williams prior to January, 1893.

"Call him Hatch, Jones, or Smith, if you will, but you have known for months that there was such a person at certain places during the trip with whom I communicated, and with whom I was seen, and whose existence you cannot now ignore."

I then tried to explain to them that for want of time alone, even if I were the bloodthirsty villain they were inclined to make me appear, I could not be guilty of the Toronto murders, and begged them to allow me to go there before by any chance evidence that could now be obtained should become unavailable to me.

To this the District Attorney replied, "I shall not do it; I shall try you here."

What more could be said? If a man as broad-minded as I knew

the District Attorney to be, both from common report and from my own observation, would not consider so important a statement, what could I expect from others having a less thorough knowledge of the case?

I was much disappointed, both at not being allowed to go there, and at the harsh and unjust way he looked upon the matter, and the feeling was increased a few minutes later when I asked to be allowed to provide for my wife's support while here, by having him tell me that he did not consider it any part of my business at the present time to either know of or care for her welfare; and some weeks later by his refusing to allow my relatives and business agent to visit me at the prison, and by a number of trivial matters like withholding my newspaper and intercepting and keeping letters that, after reading, he could see did not pertain to, and could not influence my case in any way, saying that if I, were given hardships enough and kept long enough away from others, I would confess these crimes.

Feeling it was useless to prolong the interview, and noticing that my wife was suffering intensely, I brought it to a close as quickly as possible. I bade her good-bye and was again handcuffed and taken to prison.

During the previous days the part of the Toronto matters that had seemed the most unaccountable to me was how Hatch could have returned to the depot so soon after I had left both him and the children upon the train, and what excuse he could have given to them to forego their journey.

This information my interview had supplied.

In questioning me, Superintendent Linden had said, "Who was that light young man standing upon the corner of the street near the house where the children were killed, that you spoke with at some length and then went away to hire an expressman?"

I hesitated in my answer to him, and finally told him that I had not met any one there, but if he knew that such a meeting had taken place it was of the most vital importance to my case.

There had instantly come into my mind when he had asked this question a remembrance of two years previous, but owing to their scoffs at the possibility of Hatch's existence, I felt it wise to refrain from speaking of it to him until I could hear from those by whom I could prove the statement I would have liked to have made at the time

One day in the spring of '93, soon after Miss Williams' trunks, containing her theatrical costumes, had been brought to our rooms in the block in Chicago, returning from the city one afternoon, I met upon the stairway leading to my office a jauntily dressed young man, whom, as I passed, I asked to cease smoking his cigarette within the building, and a few minutes later was being saucily laughed at in my office by Miss Williams.

So clever had the deception been, both in clothing and change in facial expression by aid of her color box, that upon her wishing to do so, I allowed her to accompany me upon a trip to Aurora, Ill., and later to St. Joseph, Mich., costumed in this manner.

That both of these trips, made under these circumstances, actually occurred, I am able to prove by competent and disinterested persons, and I feel sure that Miss Williams was in Toronto, probably meeting the children at Hamilton, and returning with them, and keeping one with her while the other was killed; and next day, while I must necessarily have been hundreds of miles away, inasmuch as I registered at Prescott at 4 P. M., she, if any one, met Hatch near this house, disguised in this manner.

On August 15th, Mr. Cops, a Fort Worth attorney, obtained permission of the District Attorney to interview me, and, after questioning me for a time, said he would like to tell me his theory of how I had killed my Chicago victims, which was that while they were in my office I had in some way induced them to step inside the vault and then caused their death by suffocation.

He said, "Why, Holmes, it is the plainest case I ever heard of, even the footprints of one of them are to be seen upon the door, where in their desperation they had tried to make their escape."

I asked him when he believed the last of these deaths had occurred there.

He replied, "Probably in July, 1893. In fact, if you could show me that Minnie Williams was alive after that date, I would be much inclined to believe that she was alive now and that she killed her sister, as you say, for, if alive, only that could have been a sufficient motive to induce her to conceal her whereabouts for so long from her Texas friends."

I said, "Will you grant me that I am not guilty of taking life there since I left Chicago about January 1, 1894, for Texas."

He replied, "Yes, I think that would be safe from the evidence I have gathered in Chicago."

I said, "In August, 1893, a fire occurred in the building, causing the destruction of many valuable letters and papers, and upon the building being repaired I bought this vault, in October or November, 1893, from a safe and vault company whose offices were one block west of La Salle street, between Madison and Adams, in Chicago. The purchase was made in the name of the Campbell-Yates Company, and in December, 1893, it was put in place and plastered by a workman names Kriss.

"A very few days thereafter I left Chicago and have never been in the rooms since. There was never any other vault in the building, save one upon the first floor that for years had been under the entire control of tenants occupying the drug and jewelry store in which it is located. I cannot give you the name or exact address of this company, but it is plainly printed upon the door of the vault, and upon your return to Chicago, if you care to do so, you can satisfy yourself of the truthfulness of my statement regarding it."

He said, "Until I can do this I cannot believe it to be true, but if I do find that such is the case I shall be inclined to return to Fort Worth and abandon my case, and upon the strength of what you have told me, I will say to you that I have lately learned that there has been found at Fort Worth among mail that was sent to you after you left that city, a London letter from Miss Williams, but being so sure in my own mind that she died nearly a year previous to that time, I have supposed it be a clever forgery sent there by you to mislead those who found it."

I told him that Miss Williams had sent me three letters there which were forwarded by Mr. John L. Judd, my Denver agent, 1609 Lawrence street, that city, to whom he could write to or visit to corroborate my statement. That two of these letters I had received and had supposed the other had been sent to the Dead Letter Office and destroyed; that if he would take the letter to Mr. [Holmes omitted the name] and others in Fort Worth, who knew her writing, they would at once tell him it was not a forgery.

A few days later I heard of the explosion and fire at the block in Chicago, and felt, as has lately been the case whenever I hear of any loss of life, strange disappearances or other misdemeanors not easily accounted for, throughout the Unites States—anywhere in the world in fact—almost thankful that the strong doors of my prison room make it impossible for such acts to now be ascribed to me.

Other Disappearances

A Miss Van Tassand to the best of my knowledge I never saw. Certain it is that I hired no fruit store in Chicago, nor did I have a person of that name in my employ at any time.

A Mrs. Lee, said to have disappeared some time in 1893, I do not know of ever having seen.

Cora Quinlin is said by the newspapers to be alive. No insurance of any kind was ever caused to be placed upon the life of this child by me nor did I know that such had been placed by others.

A Miss Cigrand was sent to me by the National Typewriter Exchange in Chicago in May, 1892. She worked faithfully in my interests until November, 1892, when, much against my wishes, she left my employ to be married, as I understood at the time.

Some days after going away she returned for her mail, and at this time gave me one of her wedding cards, and also two or three others for tenants in the building who were not then in their rooms; and in response to inquiries lately made I have learned that at least five persons in and about Lafayette, Ind., received such cards, the post mark and her handwriting upon the envelope in which they were enclosed showing that she must have sent them herself after leaving my employ.

While working for me she had also acted as the secretary of the Campbell-Yates Co., a corporation in which I was interested; and in 1893 certain papers relating to the business of this company that had been overlooked required her signature, and after considerable delay she came to the office in November, which was about one year after she left my employ.

She accompanied me to lunch at Thompson's restaurant, where I had eaten regularly for years, and where during the previous year she had often eaten with me.

Here the man known as Henry, who for a long time has been head usher in this estabment [sic] and knew us both well, remarked to her, as he gave us our seats, "It is a long time since you were here."

She replied, "About one year."

A few days later she met me elsewhere in Chicago, at which time Arthur S. Kirk, a member of the well-known soap manufacturers, Kirk & Co., and two employees were present, and upon my recalling to Mr. Kirk's memory certain business transactions I had with him at about this time, he, as well as his employees, will remember the circumstances, and be able to fix the exact date and give an accurate description of Miss Cigrand.

Before leaving Chicago, she expressed a desire to re-enter my employ, stating that unless more kindly treated she should not longer live with her husband, but should either return to office work or re-enter the convent, where she had been educated, or some other similar institution.

She also told me that she had written her people, but should not visit them until she could give them financial aid, as she had been in the habit of doing before her marriage, and I think she will let me know her location and present name before I am made to suffer for her disappearance.

Miss Mary and Miss Kate Dunkee are both acknowledged by the Philadelphia authorities to be alive.

Charles Cole is also known to be alive.

The Redman family, the child or its abductress, I never saw, and know nothing of the case save from the accounts published at the time.

Robert Latimer, a former janitor, a Mr. Brummager, one in my employ as a stenographer, also a Miss Mary Horacamp, from Hamilton, Canada, are alive, as shown by letters recently received from friends or relatives of each.

Miss Anna Betz, formerly of Englewood, Ill., whose death I have been so persistently charged with during the past year, the claims being made that it had been caused by a criminal operation performed by me at the instigation of [Holmes omitted the name], of Chicago, for which I received a release of the sum of $2,500 that I owed him, I was but little acquainted with, and if her death was occasioned in such a manner I certainly am not the cause of it, and checks given upon my order by F. W. Devoe & Co., of New York, will show when and how my indebtedness to Mr. [Holmes omitted the name] was canceled.

The same charge concerning a domestic named Lizzie is untrue, although I have no means of verifying it save that it has been proven that she was alive and in Chicago some months after I left that city, early in 1894.

Photographic Identifications

In 1883 there were conducted within my knowledge a series of experiments illustrative of the unreliability of photographic identifications, and other similar experiments have often been made.

These consisted in calling upon ten students who had witnessed two skillful sign writers executing some work upon a street window to later identify them from photographs.

An open album was first handed to the student who was told to choose which one of two pictures before him was the party in question, they all made a prompt decision as to one or the other being the person they had seen, the fact being that neither of the pictures were of these men.

To another group of ten that had also seen the painters under like circumstances was given a frame containing forty photographs, they being instructed that the picture of one of the men they had seen was among the number.

Only one chose the right picture, and none looked for or found more than one, although without their knowledge pictures of both were plainly before them in the group.

The result of the entire number of experiments was that over 95 per cent. [sic] failed in their efforts at identification.

In my own case by means of pictures, a man in Milwaukee is or was ready to make oath that I was in that city, accompanied by the two children, at a time when the Philadelphia authorities know we were elsewhere.

A woman in Chicago is equally positive that I was several days at her boarding house with Miss Williams and the two children, at a time the authorities know I was in Cincinnati, Ohio.

In the same manner two Detroit parties are ready to swear that Miss Williams was in that city, accompanied by a man answering my description of Hatch, at a time when I know he was with me in Indianapolis.

In all these instances, and in the Toronto identifications, I believe that the parties have been honest in the statements made, but it must be remembered that they have been led to understand that no other decision was possible.

A good example of the methods employed was furnished some

months ago when at police headquarters here.

I was taken before some twenty or thirty people by a detective who, when near enough for them to hear, said, "Mr. Holmes, these people are witnesses in the case for which you are to be tried here, and I wish to see if they can identify you."

Motives

Had my early life and associations been such as to predispose me towards such criminal proceedings, still the want of motive remains.

I can show that no motive did exist.

Those who knew me personally can see that it could not have been avarice, for whenever I possessed even a small surplus of ready money, those whom I was owing or friends in need of same could always receive the most or all I possessed.

Any ungovernable temper is excluded, for I do not possess it.

Appetence cannot be ascribed as a motive, age and other circumstances to a great extent excluding same.

The principal motive thus far ascribed, namely, that I had first involved my alleged victims in, or made them parties to, dishonest transactions can be excluded, from the fact that all such transactions are matters of recent date, and almost without exception they are found to have done nothing criminal.

Either one of the foregoing I should prefer having my supposed shortcomings attributed to than the only remaining motive I can think of, namely, insanity, to which, either hereditary or acquired, I can plead not guilty, and be substantiated in so doing by a sufficient number of medical experts, whose testimony cannot be lightly overlooked.

Of the three more important cases, first that of the Williams sisters. Nannie Williams was wholly without means.

The following account will show that had I given Hatch the $500 he wished to borrow of me in Burlington, there would have been little due Nannie Williams; nothing in fact, if I had included various small sums paid her from time to time, of which no account was kept.

It should also be borne in mind that she still holds the title to the $10,000 Wilmette property, which, on this account, is valueless to me.

RECEIVED OF M. R. WILLIAMS.

April, 1893, Cash, ... $2,500
April, 1893, Real Estate, . . 7,000
August, 1894, Cash, ... 600
                              _____ $10,100

PAID M. R. WILLIAMS.

May, 1893, Cash, ... $2,500
July, 1893, Cash, ... 1,000
December, 1893, Cash, . . . 750
January, 1894, Fort Worth
   Incumbrance, ... 1,725
February, 1894, Cash, . . 1,750
October, 1894, Cash, . . . 1,000
October, 1894, Cash, ... 412
                              _____ $9,137

                              $963

Shown by cashed drafts and checks endorsed by M. Williams, and other forms of evidence.

In the case of Benj. F. Pitezel, the motive is said to have been the money to be derived from his insurance, and more than this form his Texas real-estate holdings.

In regard to the former, I can only reiterate that he was worth more to me each year he lived than the amount he was insured for, and each year he was becoming more valuable to me; therefore, why should I take his life?

His real estate was not of one dollar's value to him, and could only be of value to me after he had signed certain papers, the want of which I felt within thirty days after his death.

This is also true of his patents and other belongings.

The claim that I designed to kill the six other members of the Pitezel family to avoid being held accountable for the small sum of $5,200, seems too unlikely a motive to call for a denial, and, excluding this, it will be hard to find another, when the care and attention I have given them for years is considered.

Moyamensing Diary Conclusion

In conclusion, I wish to say that I am but a very ordinary man, even below the average in physical strength and mental ability, and to have planned and executed the stupendous amount of wrongdoing that has been attributed to me would have been wholly beyond my power, and even had I been able to have performed it, a still greater task would have been the successful elaboration of a story at the time of my arrest that, if untrue, would have provided for the many exigencies that at that time I could not have known would have occurred later in the case; and I feel justified in asking from the general public a suspension of judgment as to my guilt or innocence, not while the various charges can be proven against me, but while I can disprove them, a task which I feel able to satisfactorily and expeditiously accomplish.

And here I cannot say finis—it is not the end—for besides doing this there is also the work of bringing to justice those for whose wrong-doings I am to-day suffering, and this not to prolong or save my own life, for since the day I heard of the Toronto horror I have not cared to live; but that to those who have looked up to and honored me in the past it shall not in the future be said that I suffered the ignominious death of a murderer.

Fig. 41. Georgiana Yoke, Holmes third wife who visited him in prison
Source: "Tears Dim Holmes Eyes," *Philadelphia Inquirer*, November 1, 1895, p. 1.

Fig. 42. Holmes' Attorney, Samuel P. Rotan. In 1909, Rotan was elected to the Office of District Attorney for Philadelphia and served in that position until his death in 1926. He also served as a Pennsylvania District Six Republican Delegate.
Source: Sam Hudson. *Pennsylvania and Its Public Men.* Philadelphia: unknown publisher, 1909, p. 75.

PART TWO
CONFESSED 27 MURDERS

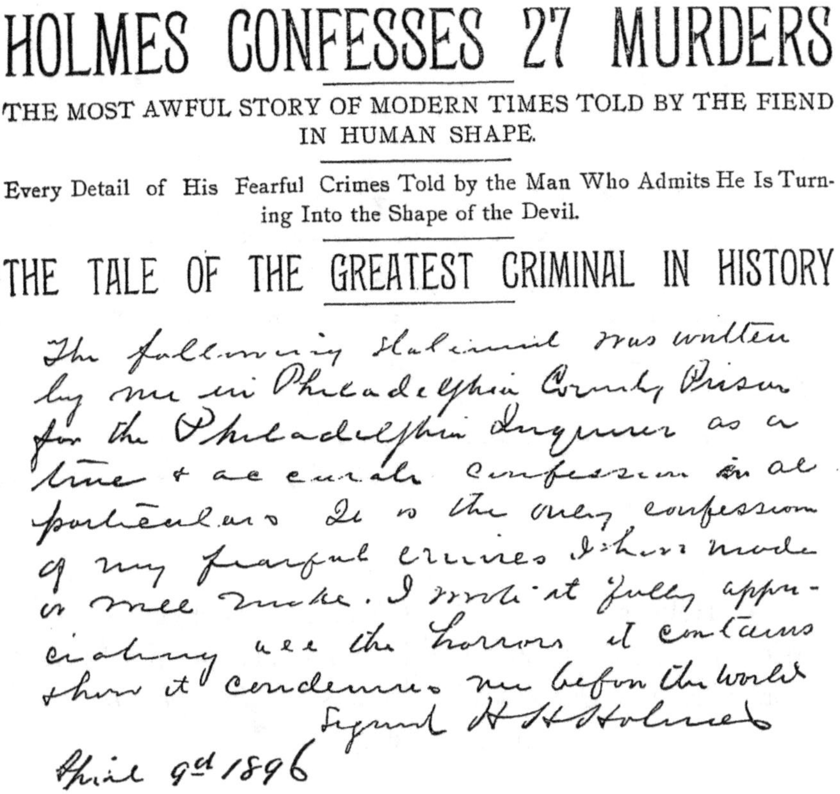

HOLMES CONFESSES 27 MURDERS

THE MOST AWFUL STORY OF MODERN TIMES TOLD BY THE FIEND IN HUMAN SHAPE.

Every Detail of His Fearful Crimes Told by the Man Who Admits He Is Turning Into the Shape of the Devil.

THE TALE OF THE GREATEST CRIMINAL IN HISTORY

The following statement was written by me in Philadelphia County Prison for the Philadelphia Inquirer as a true & accurate confession in all particulars. It is the only confession of my fearful crimes I have made or will make. I write it fully appreciating all the horrors it contains though it condemns me before the world.
Signed H H Holmes
April 9th 1896

Fig. 43. *Philadelphia Inquirer* news confession headline
Source: "Holmes Confesses 27 Murders," *Philadelphia Inquirer,* April 12, 1896, p. 1.

Transcription of his handwritten statement:

The following statement was written by me in Philadelphia County Prison for the *Philadelphia Inquirer* as a true & accurate confession in all particulars. It is the only confession of my fearful crimes I have made or will make. I write it fully appreciating all the horrors it contains though it condemns me before the world.

Signed H. H. Holmes
April 9th 1896

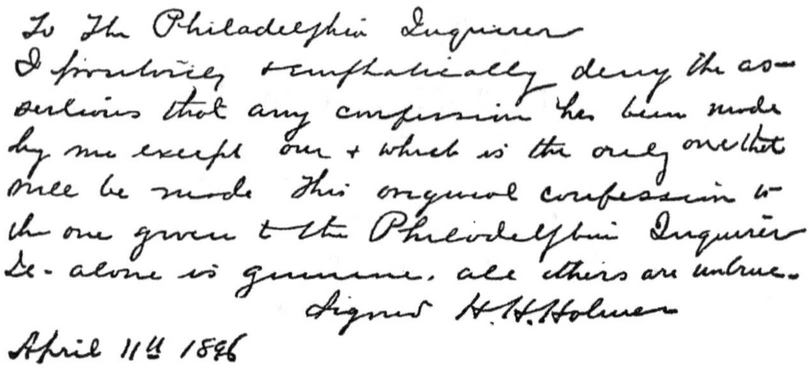
To the Philadelphia Inquirer
I formally & emphatically deny the assertions that any confession has been made by me except one & which is the only one that will be made This original confession is the one given to the Philadelphia Inquirer It alone is genuine, all others are untrue.
Signed H. H. Holmes
April 11th 1896

Fig. 44. Holmes' note to *Philadelphia Inquirer* denying all other versions of his confession that were also printed on April 12, 1896 Source: "Holmes Confesses 27 Murders," *Philadelphia Inquirer,* April 12, 1896, p. 9.

Transcription of his handwritten denial:

To the Philadelphia Inquirer

I formally & emphatically deny the assertions that any confession has been made by me except one & which is the only one that will be made[.] This original confession is the one given to the Philadelphia Inquirer[.] It alone is genuine, all others are untrue.

Signed H. H. Holmes

April 11th 1896

Fig. 45. Herman Mudgett, *alias* H. H. Holmes
Source: "Holmes Confesses 27 Murders," *Philadelphia Inquirer,* April 12, 1896, p. 1.

Fig. 46. Holmes Writing His Confession
Source: "Holmes Confesses 27 Murders," *Philadelphia Inquirer*, April 12, 1896, p. 1.

The Tale of the Greatest Criminal in History

(Copyright, 1896, by W. R. Hearst and James Elverson, Jr.)

During the past few months the desire has been repeatedly expressed that I make a detailed confession of all the graver crimes that have with such marvelous skill been traced out and brought home to me.

I have been tried for murder, convicted, sentenced, and the first step of my execution upon May seventh, namely, the reading of my death warrant, has been carried out, and it now seems a fitting time, if ever, to make known the details of the twenty-seven murders, of which it would be useless to longer say I am not guilty, in the face of the overwhelming amount of proof that has been brought together, not only in one but in each and every case; and because in this confession I speak only of cases that have been thus investigated and of no others, I trust it will not give rise to a supposition that I am still guilty of other murders, which I am withholding.

To those inclined to think thus, I will say that the detectives have gone over my entire life, hardly a day or an act has escaped their closest scrutiny, and to judge that I am guilty of more than these cases which they have traced out is to cast discredit upon their work.

So marvelous has been the success of these men into whose hands the proving of my guilt was given, that as I look back upon their year's work it seems almost impossible that men gifted with only human intelligence could have been so skillful, and I feel that I can here call attention to what the prosecution at the close of my trial was denied the pleasure of stating, concerning their ability, through no words of mine can fittingly express what the world at large owes to these impartial and untiring representatives, and more especially to Assistant District Attorney Barlow and

Detective Frank Geyer and to O. La Forrest Perry, of the Fidelity Mutual Life Association of Philadelphia; for it is principally owing to their unerring judgment, skill and perseverence [sic] that in a few days I am to be forever placed beyond the power of committing other, and, perhaps, if possible, more horrid wrongs.

Surely justice, if attended by such servants as these could no longer, in the sense of making mistakes, be appropriately portrayed as being blind.

I am moved to make this confession for a variety of reasons, but among them are not those of bravado or a dasire [sic] to parade my wrongdoings before the public gaze, and he who reads the following lines will, I beg, make a distinction between such motives and a determination upon my part to enter plainly and minutely into the details of each case without favor towards myself.

And having done so I have chosen to make it public by publishing it in THE PHILADELPHIA INQUIRER.

A word as to the motives or causes that have led to the commission of these many crimes and I will proceed to the most difficult and distasteful task of my life, the setting forth in all its horrid nakedness the recital of the premeditated killing of twenty-seven human beings and the unsuccessful attempts to take the lives of six others, thus branding myself as the most detestable criminal of modern times—a task so hard and distasteful that beside it the certainty that in a few days I am to be hanged by the neck until I am dead seems but a pastime.

Acquired homicidal mania, all other causes, save the occasional opportunity for pecuniary gain having by others been excluded for me, is the only constant cause, and in advancing it at this time I do not do so with the expectation of a mitigation of public condemnation, or that it will in any way react in my favor. Had this been my intention I should have considered it at the time of my trial, and had it used as my defense.

All criminologists who have examined me here seem to be

unanimous in the opinions they have formed, although one inexplicable condition presents itself, viz.: that while committing the crimes these symptoms were not present, but commenced to develop after my arrest.

Ten years ago I was thoroughly examined by four men of marked ability and by them pronounced as being both mentally and physically a normal and healthy man. To-day I have every attribute of a degenerate—a moral idiot. Is it possible that the crimes, instead of being the result of these abnormal conditions, are in themselves the occasion of the degeneracy?[19]

Even at the time of my arrest in 1894 no defects were noticeable under the searching Bertillon system of measurements to which I was subjected, but later, and more noticeably within the past few months, these defects have increased with startling rapidity, as is made known to me by each succeeding examination until I have become thankful that I am no longer allowed a glass with which to note my rapidly deteriorating condition, though nature, ever kind, provides in this, as in the ordinary forms of insanity where the sufferer believes himself always sane, so that unless called to my attention, I do not notice my infirmity nor suffer therefrom.

The principal defects that have thus far developed and which are all established signs of degeneracy, are a decided prominence upon one side of my head and a corresponding diminution upon the other side; a marked deficiency of one side of my nose and of one ear, together with an abnormal increase of each upon the opposite side; a difference of one and one-half inches in the length of my arms and an equal shortening of one leg from knee to heel; also a most malevolent distortion of one side of my face and one eye—so marked and terrible that in writing of it for publication, Hall Caine [a famous British novelist][20], although I wore a beard at the time to conceal it as best I could, described that side of my face as marked by a deep line of crime and being that of a devil—so apparent that an expert criminologist in the employ of the United

States Government who had never previously seen me said within thirty seconds after entering my cell: "I know you are guilty."

Would it not, then, be the height of folly for me to die without speaking, if only for the purpose of justifying these scientific deductions and accrediting what is due to those to whom society owes so much for bringing me to justice?

Murder 1: Dr. Robert Leacock

The first taking of human life that is attributed to me is in the case of Dr. Robert Leacock, of New Baltimore, Mich., a friend and former schoolmate.

I knew that his life was insured for a large sum and after enticing him to Chicago I killed him by giving him an overwhelming dose of laudanum.

My subsequently taking his dead body from place to place in and about Grand Rapids, Mich., as has been so often printed heretofore, and the risk and excitement attendant upon the collection of the forty-thousand dollars of insurance, were very insignificant matters compared with the torturing thought that I had taken human life.

This, it will be understood, was before, by constant wrongdoing, I had become wholly deaf to the promptings of conscience, for prior to this death, which occurred in 1886, I beg to be believed in stating that I had never sinned so heavily either by thought or deed.

Later, like the man-eating tiger of the tropical jungle, whose appetite for blood has once been aroused, I roamed about the world seeking whom I could destroy.

Think of the awful list that follows.

Twenty-seven lives, men and women, young girls and innocent children, blotted out by one monster's hand, and you, my reader of a tender and delicate nature, will do well to read no further, for I will in no way spare myself, and he who reads to the end, if he be charitable, will, in the words of the District Attorney at my trial, when the evidence of all these many crimes had been collected and placed before him by his trusty assistants, exclaim: "God help such a man!"

If uncharitable or only just will he not rather say: "May he be utterly damned," and that it is almost sufficient to cause one to doubt the wisdom of Providence that such a man should have so long been allowed to live.

If so I earnestly pray that this condemnation and censure may not extend to those whose only crime has been that they knew and trusted, aye in some instances, loved me, and who to-day are more deserving of the world's compassion than censure.

Fig. 47. Dr. Robert Leacock
Source: "Holmes Great Crimes," *Philadelphia Inquirer,* April 26,

1896, p. 26.

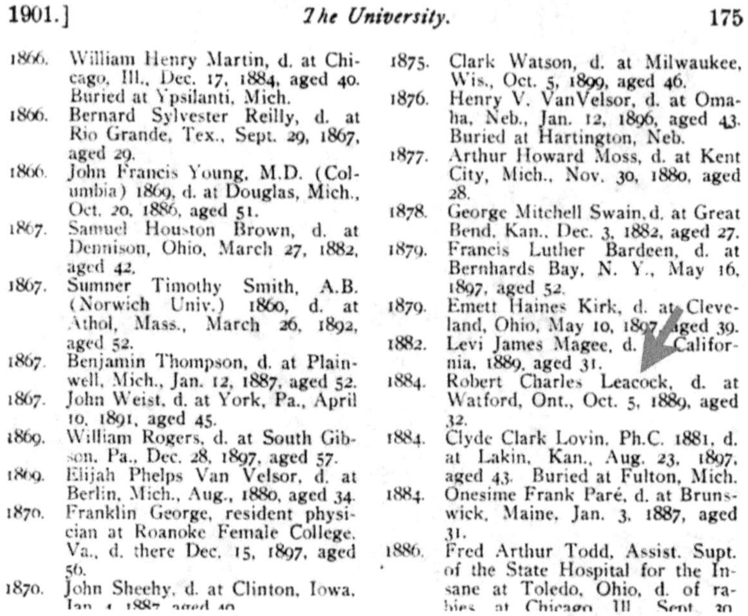

| 1901.] | *The University.* | 175 |

1866. William Henry Martin, d. at Chicago, Ill., Dec. 17, 1884, aged 40. Buried at Ypsilanti, Mich.
1866. Bernard Sylvester Reilly, d. at Rio Grande, Tex., Sept. 29, 1867, aged 29.
1866. John Francis Young, M.D. (Columbia) 1869, d. at Douglas, Mich., Oct. 20, 1886, aged 51.
1867. Samuel Houston Brown, d. at Dennison, Ohio, March 27, 1882, aged 42.
1867. Sumner Timothy Smith, A.B. (Norwich Univ.) 1860, d. at Athol, Mass., March 26, 1892, aged 52.
1867. Benjamin Thompson, d. at Plainwell, Mich., Jan. 12, 1887, aged 52.
1867. John Weist, d. at York, Pa., April 10, 1891, aged 45.
1869. William Rogers, d. at South Gibson, Pa., Dec. 28, 1897, aged 57.
1869. Elijah Phelps Van Velsor, d. at Berlin, Mich., Aug., 1880, aged 34.
1870. Franklin George, resident physician at Roanoke Female College, Va., d. there Dec. 15, 1897, aged 56.
1870. John Sheehy, d. at Clinton, Iowa, Jan. 4, 1887, aged 40.

1875. Clark Watson, d. at Milwaukee, Wis., Oct. 5, 1899, aged 46.
1876. Henry V. VanVelsor, d. at Omaha, Neb., Jan. 12, 1896, aged 43. Buried at Hartington, Neb.
1877. Arthur Howard Moss, d. at Kent City, Mich., Nov. 30, 1880, aged 28.
1878. George Mitchell Swain, d. at Great Bend, Kan., Dec. 3, 1882, aged 27.
1879. Francis Luther Bardeen, d. at Bernhards Bay, N. Y., May 16, 1897, aged 52.
1879. Emett Haines Kirk, d. at Cleveland, Ohio, May 10, 1897, aged 39.
1882. Levi James Magee, d. in California, 1889, aged 31.
1884. Robert Charles Leacock, d. at Watford, Ont., Oct. 5, 1889, aged 32.
1884. Clyde Clark Lovin, Ph.C. 1881, d. at Lakin, Kan., Aug. 23, 1897, aged 43. Buried at Fulton, Mich.
1884. Onesime Frank Paré, d. at Brunswick, Maine, Jan. 3, 1887, aged 31.
1886. Fred Arthur Todd, Assist. Supt. of the State Hospital for the Insane at Toledo, Ohio, d. of rabies at Chicago, Ill., Sept. 30,

Fig. 48. Dr. Robert Leacock, class of 1884, died October 5, 1889 in Watford, Ontario Canada
Source: "Necrology," *The Michigan Alumnus*, Vol. VII, No. 57, (1900-1901): p. 175.

Murder 2: Dr. Russell

My second victim was Dr. Russell, a tenant in the Chicago building recently renamed "The Castle."

During a controversy concerning the non-payment of rent due me, I struck him to the floor with a heavy chair, when he, with one cry for help, ending in a groan of anguish, ceased to breathe.

This quarrel and death occurred in a small outer office, and as soon as I realized that my blow had been a fatal one and I had recovered somewhat from the horror of having still another victim's blood upon my hands, I was forced to look about for some safe means of concealing the crime.

I locked the doors of the office, and my first intention was to dispose of the body to a Chicago medical college, from one of whose officers I had previously obtained dissecting material, as they believed, but in reality to be used in insurance work.

I found it difficult, if not impossible, to thus dispose of it, and was directed to call upon a party to whom I sold the bodies and whose name I withhold, but I have confessed his name to parties in whom I have confidence.

To him I sold this man's body, as well as others at later dates.

In short, in this writing, in each instance when the manner of the disposal of their remains is not otherwise specified, it will be understood that they were turned over to him, he paying me from $25 to $45 for each body, and right easily could he, during the recent investigations, go from room to room in the building when each was more or less grewsomely [sic] familiar to him.

It is not necessary for me to add that the efforts of his friends to shield him when it became evident that he had talked too freely for his own safety should not have saved him from being compelled to turn over the remains of these persons for decent burial or to point out the various museums where they were sold.

Murders 3 and 4: Mrs. Julia L. Connor and Daughter, Pearl

The third death was to a certain extent due to a criminal operation. A man and woman were cognizant of and partially responsible for both the operation and the death.

The victim was Mrs. Julia L. Connor.[21]

A reference to almost any newspaper of August, 1895, will give the minute details of the horrors of this case, as they were worked out by the detectives, therefore making it unnecessary to repeat it here, save to add that the death of the child Pearl, her little daughter, who is the fourth victim, was caused by poison, and that the man and woman above referred to were equally responsible with myself for its administration, although it was at my instigation that it was done, as I believed the child was old enough to remember of her mother's sickness and death.

They wished, at first, to place the child in the care of their aged parents, who lived south of the city, but were overruled by my opposition.

Owing to the suddenness of the third death, a certain note of considerable value, well secured by property south of the Castle, was uncollectible, and at the time of my death it will be sent to such of her relatives as it may appear have the greater right to receive it.

Fig. 49. Mrs. Julia Connor
Source: "Holmes Confesses 27 Murders," *Philadelphia Inquirer*, April 12, 1896, p. 9.

Fig. 50. Pearl Connor
Source: "Holmes Confesses 27 Murders," *Philadelphia Inquirer,*
April 12, 1896, p. 9.

Murder 5: Rogers

The fifth murder, that of Rodgers, of West Morgantown, Va., occurred in 1888, at which time I was boarding there for a few weeks.

Learning that the man had some money I induced him to go upon a fishing trip with me, and, being successful in allaying his suspicions, I finally ended his life by a sudden blow upon the head with an oar.

The body was found about a month thereafter, but I was not suspected until after my trial here, and even then by a fortunate circumstance succeeded in having the report publicly denied, but did not succeed in changing the opinion of fifty or more persons living in the town who had recognized my picture in the daily papers.

Murder 6: Charles Cole

The sixth case is that of Charles Cole, a Southern speculator.

After considerable correspondence this man came to Chicago, and I enticed him into the Castle, where, while I was engaging him in conversation, a confederate struck him a most vicious blow upon the head with a piece of gas pipe.

So heavy was the blow it not only caused his death without a groan and hardly a movement, but it crushed his skull to such an extent that his body was almost useless to the party who bought the body.

This is the first instance in which I knew this confederate had committed murder, though in several other instances he was fully as guilty as myself, and, if possible, more heartless and bloodthirsty, and I have no doubt is still engaged in the same nefarious work, and if so is probably aided by a Chicago business man.

Murder 7: Lizzie

A domestic, named Lizzie, was the seventh victim.

She, for a time, worked in the Castle restaurant and I soon learned that Quinlan [his janitor] was paying her too close attention and fearing lest it should progress so far that it would necessitate his leaving my employ I thought it wise to end the life of the girl.

This I did by calling her to my office and suffocating her in the vault of which so much has since been printed, she being the first victim that died therein.

Before her death I compelled her to write letters to her relations and to Quinlan, stating that she had left Chicago for a Western State and should not return. A few months ago the prosecution, believing from certain letters purporting to have been written by her that she was alive, at once showed me their willingness to give me a fair trial by having this publicly known, she being a witness that I could have used to great advantage in the Pitezel case, here.

Murders 8, 9, and 10: Mrs. Sarah Cook, her child and Niece

The eighth, ninth and tenth cases are Mrs. Sarah Cook, her unborn child, and Miss Mary Haracamp, of Hamilton, Canada.

In 1888 Mr. Frank Cook became a tenant in the Castle. He was engaged to be married to a young lady living at some distance from Chicago who later came there and was married to him in my presence, by the Rev. Dr. Taylor, of Englewood, Ill [Illinois].

They kept house in the Castle, and for a time I boarded with them.

Shortly Miss Mary Haracamp, of Hamilton, a niece of Mrs. Sarah Cook, came to Chicago and entered my employ as a stenographer. But Mrs. Cook and her niece had access to all the rooms by means of a master key and one evening while I was busily engaged preparing my last victim for shipment, the door suddenly opened and they stood before me.

It was a time for quick action, rather than for words of explanation upon my part, and before they had recovered from the horror of the sight, they were within the fatal vault, so lately tenanted by the dead body, and then, after writing a letter my dictation to Mr. Cook that they had tired of their life with him and had gone away not expecting to return, their lives were sacrificed instead of giving them their liberty in exchange for their promise to at once and forever leave Chicago, which had been promised them in return for writing the letter.

These were particularly sad deaths, both on account of the victims being exceptionally upright and virtuous women and because Mrs. Sarah Cook, had she lived, would have soon become a mother.

Murder 11: Miss Emeline Cigrand

Soon after this Miss Emmeline [sic] Cigrand, of Dwight, Ill., was sent to me by a Chicago typewriter firm to fill the vacancy of stenographer.

She had formerly been employed at Dwight where she had become acquainted with a man who visited her from time to time while she was in my employ.

She was finally engaged to him and the day set for their wedding.

This attachment was particularly obnoxious to me, both because Miss Cigrand had become almost indispensable in my office work, and because she had become my mistress as well as stenographer.

I endeavored upon several occasions to take the life of the young man and failing in this I finally resolved that I would kill her instead, and upon the day of their wedding, even after cards had been sent out announcing that it had occurred, she came to my office to bid me good bye.

While there I asked her to step inside the vault for some papers for me.

There I detained her, telling her that if she would write her husband that at the last moment she had found that it would be impossible to live happily with him and consequently had left Chicago in such a way that search for her would be useless, I would take her to a distant city and live openly with her as my wife.

She was very willing to do this and prepared to leave the vault upon completing the letter only to learn that the door would never be again opened until she had ceased to suffer the tortures of a slow and lingering death.

NOTE: After Emeline disappeared, her father, Peter Cigrand, wrote a letter to Holmes to ask if he knew where she was. Holmes responded with the following two letters, which were later published in the *Indianapolis News*:[22]

> THE CAMPBELL-YATES CO.,
> 701-703 Sixty-third street, Chicago, Ill.,
> March 18, 1893.
>
> Mr. Peter Cigrand, Oxford, Ind.:
> Dear Sir—In answer to your letter of the 16th inst. [of the current month] would say that Miss Emma left our employ on December 1.
> I received her wedding cards about December 10. She called at the office about ten days later for her mail, after her return from Michigan, where she was married, and again about January 1, at which time she was disappointed at not finding any mail here for her, and my impression is that she spoke of having written to you previous to that time.
> Before going away in December she told me personally that the intention was that she and her husband should go to England on business with which he was connected, but when she called here the last time she spoke as though the trip had been given up.
> Please let me know within a few days if you did not hear from her, and give me her uncle's address here in the city and I will see him personally and ask if she has been there, as I know she was in the habit of calling upon him quite often. Yours truly, H. H. HOLMES.
> Have you written to her Lafayette friends asking them if they have heard from her? If not I should think it well to do so. Let me hear from you at all events.

Emeline's father later received the following letter from Holmes:

CAMPBELL-YATES CO.,
701-703 Sixty-third street, Chicago
April 3, 1893

Mr. Peter Cigrand, Oxford, Ind.
Dear Sir—I received your letter some days ago and called on Dr. Cigrand [Emeline's uncle in Chicago] in regard to same, and was pleased to learn from him of Mrs. Phelps's [sic] whereabouts, for it seemed exceedingly strange until he explained matters to me, that she should have neglected to write you, and inasmuch as she was working for us, I felt, in a measure, responsible for her.

Kindly let me know her address upon your receiving it, as there is a paper pertaining to the Campbell-Yates Company, of which she acted as secretary, which should properly be signed by her. Very truly yours,
H. H. HOLMES.

Holmes lied about calling on Emeline's uncle, Dr. Cigrand, who was a dentist. Her family told the *Indianapolis News* they believed Holmes murdered Emeline on December 7, 1892, the night Holmes said she married Robert E. Phelps and left for England.[23]

Of the two letters her family last received from Emeline, one claimed she was to marry soon and the next one announced she married a bad man and would leave him at the first opportunity.[24]

Emeline's father told *Indianapolis News* that during the ten days his daughter, Philla, visited Emeline at Holmes castle in 1892, she never saw Phelps or Holmes or a photograph of them.

Her families' close inspection of a letter signed by Emeline, three weeks after her supposed marriage, determined it was not her handwriting. A lock of her hair from an old keepsake was a likely match to hair found in the cellar of Holmes' castle. Sometime later, Emeline's trunk arrived at her families' home with her clothing and a bogus letter. It was reported an articulator mounted three skeletons in his dealings with H. H. Holmes, one man and two women.[25]

Dr. and Mrs. Maurice B. Lawrence lived in the Holmes building at the time Emeline lived there. Mrs. Lawrence told an interesting story:

"It would seem impossible and wholly unlike the girl, knowing me as well as she did, not to say anything about going away or getting married, as Holmes claimed she had done," said Mrs. Lawrence. "When she was not busy in the office she used to come into my rooms and sit with me by the hour; so that I became greatly attached to her and she to me, and that made her disappearance, without ever a word to me, very strange."

"Holmes seemed to be very fond of her also and went with her everywhere. He bought her a bicycle and they used to ride together a great deal. Then sometimes they would go to the theater together or to other places of amusement up town," said Mrs. Lawrence.[26]

Fig. 51. Emeline Cigrand illustration from photo just before she was murdered
Source: "Both Under Arrest," *Daily Inter Ocean,* July 27, 1895, p. 2.

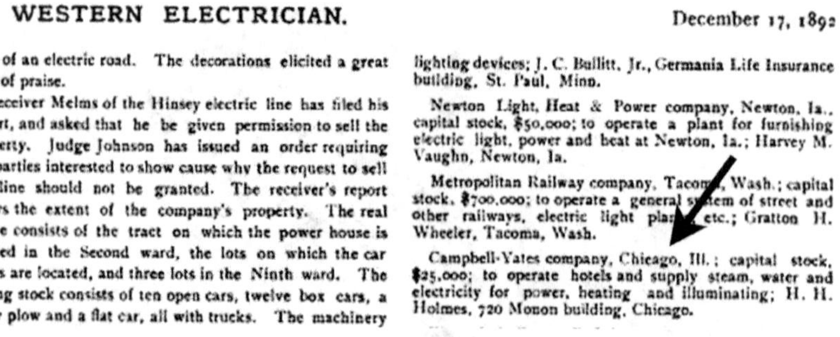

WESTERN ELECTRICIAN.   December 17, 1892

rails of an electric road. The decorations elicited a great deal of praise.

Receiver Melms of the Hinsey electric line has filed his report, and asked that he be given permission to sell the property. Judge Johnson has issued an order requiring the parties interested to show cause why the request to sell the line should not be granted. The receiver's report shows the extent of the company's property. The real estate consists of the tract on which the power house is located in the Second ward, the lots on which the car barns are located, and three lots in the Ninth ward. The rolling stock consists of ten open cars, twelve box cars, a snow plow and a flat car, all with trucks. The machinery

lighting devices; J. C. Bullitt, Jr., Germania Life Insurance building, St. Paul, Minn.

Newton Light, Heat & Power company, Newton, Ia., capital stock, $50,000; to operate a plant for furnishing electric light, power and heat at Newton, Ia.; Harvey M. Vaughn, Newton, Ia.

Metropolitan Railway company, Tacoma, Wash.; capital stock, $700,000; to operate a general system of street and other railways, electric light plant, etc.; Gratton H. Wheeler, Tacoma, Wash.

Campbell-Yates company, Chicago, Ill.; capital stock, $25,000; to operate hotels and supply steam, water and electricity for power, heating and illuminating; H. H. Holmes, 720 Monon building, Chicago.

Fig. 52. Announcement of Campbell-Yates Company in *Western Electrician*

Source: W. A. Kreidler, ed. "New Incorporations [Campbell-Yates Company]," Western Electrician, vol. XI, no. 1-27, (1892): 314.

Three Unsuccessful Attempts for Triple Murder

Then follows an unsuccessful attempt to commit a triple murder for the $90 that my agent for disposing of "stiffs" would have given me for the bodies of the intended victims, who were three young women working in my restaurant upon Milwaukee avenue, Chicago.

That these women lived to tell of their experience to the police last summer is due to my foolishly trying to chloroform all of them at one and the same time.

By their combined strength they overpowered me and ran screaming into the street, clad only in their night robes.

I was arrested the next day, but was not prosecuted.

To this attempt to kill could very justly be added my attempt to take the lives of Mrs. Pitezel and two of her children at a later date, thus making the total number of my victims 33, instead of 27, as it was through no fault of mine that they escaped.[27]

Murder 12: Miss Rosine Van Jassand

My next attempt was carried out with more caution.

The victim was a very beautiful young woman named Rosine Van Jassand, whom I induced to come into my fruit and confectionery store, and, once within my power, I compelled her to live with me there for a time, threatening her with death if she appeared before any of my customers.

A little later I killed her by administering ferro-cyanide of potassium.

The location of this store was such that it would have been hazardous to have sent out a large box containing a body, and I therefore buried her remains in the store basement, and from day to day during the recent investigation at the Castle I expected to hear that excavations had been made there as well.[28]

Fig. 53. Emily Van Tassel
Source: "The Emily Van Tassel Holmes Sensation," *Hopkinsville Kentuckian,* August 27, 1895, p. 3.

Murder 13: Robert Latimer

Robert Latimer, a man who had for some years been in my employ as janitor, was my next victim.

Several years previous, before I had ever taken human life, he had known of certain insurance work I had engaged in, and when, in after years, he sought to extort money from me, his own death and the sale of his body was the recompense meted out to him.

I confined him within the secret room, and slowly starved him to death. Of this room and its secret gas supply and muffled windows and doors, sufficient has already been printed.

Finally, needing its use for another purpose and because his pleadings had become almost unbearable, I ended his life.

The partial excavation in the walls of this room found by the police was caused by Latimer's endeavoring to escape by tearing away the solid brick and mortar with his unaided fingers.

Murder 14: Miss Anna Betts

The fourteenth case is that of Miss Anna Betts, and was caused by my purposely substituting a poisonous drug in a prescription that had been sent to my drug store to be compounded, believing that it was known that I was a physician, I should be called in to witness her death, as she lived very near the store.

This was not the case, however, as the regular physician was in attendance at the time.

The prescription, still on file at the Castle drug store, should be considered by the authorities if they still are inclined to attribute this death to causes that reflect upon Miss Betts' moral character.

Murder 15: Miss Gertrude Conner

The death of Miss Gertrude Conner, of Muscatine, Iowa, though not the next in order of occurrence, is so similar to the last that a description of one suffices for both, save in this case Miss Conner left Chicago immediately, but did not die until she had reached her home at Muscatine.

Perhaps these two cases show more plainly than any others the light regard I had for the lives of my fellow-beings.

Murder 16: Miss Kate Durkee

The sixteenth murder is that of Miss Kate [Durkee], of Omaha, a young woman owning much valuable real estate in Chicago, where I acted as her agent.

This was at the time so graphically described by a local writer —as when I was allowed to hold property under one name, act as notary public under another and carry on a general business under still another title.

I caused Miss Kate [Durkee] to believe that a favorable opportunity had come for her to convert her holdings into cash, and, having accomplished this for her, she came to Chicago and I paid her the money, taking a receipt in full for same, and thus protected myself in the event of an inquiry at a later date.

I asked her to look about my offices and finally to look within the vault, and, having once passed that fatal door, she never came forth alive.

She did not die at once, however, and her anger when first she realized that she was deprived of her liberty, then her office of the entire forty thousand dollars in exchange for same and finally her prayers are something terrible to remember.

It was stated that I had also killed a sister of Miss Kate [Durkee], but I think this report has already been contradicted.[29]

Murder 17: Mr. Warner

The next death was that of a man named Warner, the originator of the Warner Glass Bending Company, and here again a very large sum of money was realized, which prior to this death had been deposited in two Chicago banks, nearly all of which I secured by means of two checks, made out and properly signed by him for a small sum each.

To these I later added the word thousand, and the necessary ciphers, and by passing them through the bank where I had a regular open account I promptly realized the money, save a small amount not covered by the checks in the Park National Bank, northwest corner Dearborn and Washington Streets, in that city.

It will be remembered that the remains of a large kiln made of fire brick was found in the Castle basement. It had been built under Mr. Warner's supervision for the purpose of exhibiting his patents. It was so arranged that in less than a minute after turning on a jet of crude oil atomized with steam the entire kiln would be filled with a colorless flame, so intensely hot iron would be melted therein.

It was into this kiln that I induced Mr. Warner to go with me, under pretense of wishing certain minute explanations of the process, and then stepping outside, as he believed to get some tools, I closed the door and turned on both the oil and steam to their full extent.

In a short time not even the bones of my victim remained. The coat found outside the kiln was the one he took off before going therein.

Fig. 54. Holmes Murdering the Glass Inventor, Mr. Warner
Source: "Holmes Confesses 27 Murders," *Philadelphia Inquirer*, April 12, 1896, p. 8.

Murder 18: Rogers, A Young Englishman

In 1891 I associated myself in business with a young Englishman, whose name I am more than willing to publish to the world, but I am advised it could not be published on my unsupported statement, who by his own admission, had been guilty of all other forms of wrongdoing, save murder, and presumably of that as well.

To manipulate certain real estate securities we held so as to have them secure us a good commercial rating was an easy matter for him and he was equally able to interest certain English capitalists in patents so that for a time it seemed that in the near future our greatest concern would be how to dispose of the money that seemed about to be showered upon us.

By an unforeseen occurrence our rating was destroyed and it became necessary to at once raise a large sum and this was done by my partner enticing to Chicago a wealthy banker named Rogers from a North Wisconsin town in such a manner that he could have left no intelligence with whom his business was to be.

To cause him to go to the Castle and within the secret room under the pretense that our patents were there was easily brought about, more so than to force him to sign checks and drafts for seventy thousand dollars, which we had prepared.

At first he refused to do so, stating that his liberty that we offered him in exchange would be useless to him without his money, that he was too old to again hope to make another fortune; finally by alternately starving him and nauseating him with the gas he was made to sign the securities, all of which were converted into money and by my partner's skill as a forger in such a manner as to leave no trace of their having passed through our hands.

I waited with much curiosity to see what propositions my partner would advance for the disposal of our prisoner, as I well knew he, no more than I, contemplated giving him his liberty.

My partner evidently waited with equal expectancy for me to

suggest what should be done, and I finally made preparation to allow him to leave the building, thus forcing him to suggest that he be killed.

I would only consent to this upon the condition that he should administer the chloroform, and leave me to dispose of the body as my part of the work. In this way I was enabled to keep him in ignorance of my dealings with the medical college agent.

That evening this large sum of money was equally divided between us, and my partner went to the Palmer House, where he was well known, and passed the night at cards with three other men, and at 10 o'clock the next morning came to the office to borrow $100 with which to redeem his overcoat, watch and rings that he had[.]

So much has already been written of my own extravagancies and wrong methods of living that I can add little to what the detectives have already pointed out, save to say that during these years, reckoning only the amount of money which they have discovered that I defrauded others of, and as it is known to them that when I was arrested I had very little money, it is evident that my disbursements were over ten thousand dollars per month.

Murder 19: A Female Boarder

The nineteenth case is that of a woman, whose name has passed from my memory, who came to the Castle restaurant to board.

A tenant of mine at the time immediately became very much infatuated with the woman, who he learned was a widow and wealthy.

This tenant was married, and his wife occasionally came to the restaurant when this boarder was there, which did not tend to decrease a family quarrel that for quite a time had threatened this tenant's family with disruption.

Finally he came to me for advice, and I was very willing to have him in my power in order that I could later use him in my work if need be. I suggested that he live with the woman in the Castle for a time, and later, if his life became unpleasant to him, we would kill her and divide her wealth.

Soon, he suggested it was time to take his companion's life. This was done by my administering chloroform while he controlled her violent struggles.

It was the body of this woman within the long coffin-shaped box that was taken from the Castle late in 1893, of which the police were notified.[30]

Murders 20 and 21: Minnie and Nannie Williams

The Williams sisters come next. In order that these deaths may be more fully understood it is necessary for me to state that what has been said by Miss Minnie R. Williams' Southern relatives regarding her pure and Christian life should be believed; also, that prior to her meeting me in 1893 she was a virtuous woman, thus rendering truthful the statements of Mr. Charles Goldthwaite, of Boston, that he had never known her other than as an intimate friend of his wife, and that in June, 1893, he did not wire her a considerable sum of money to Chicago in response to a demand for some from her; that she was not temporarily insane at a hotel opposite the Pullman Building, Chicago, May 20-23, 1893; was not a little later secluded within the Baptist Hospital at Chicago under the name of Mrs. Williams, and still later at a retreat in Milwaukee; and that she did not kill her sister and threaten to kill a nurse having her in charge at 1220 Wrightwood Avenue, Chicago.

All these statements it gives me a certain amount of satisfaction to retract, thereby undoing so far as I can these additional wrongs I have heaped upon her name.

I first met Miss Minnie R. Williams in New York in 1888, where she knew me as Edward Hatch and later under the same name in Denver, as has been testified by certain young women who recognized my photograph.

Early in 1893 I was again introduced to her as H. H. Holmes in the office of Campbell & Dowd, of Chicago, to whom she had applied for them to secure her a position as a stenographer.

Soon after entering my employ I induced her to give me $2500 in money to transfer to me by deed $50,000 worth of Southern real estate and a little later to live with me as my wife, all this being easily accomplished owing to her innocent and child-like nature, she hardly knowing right from wrong in such matters.

Thereafter I succeeded in securing two checks from her for

$2500 and $1000 each, and I also learned that she had a sister Nannie in Texas who was an heir to some property and induced Miss Minnie Williams to have her come to Chicago upon a visit.

Upon her arrival I met her at the depot and took her to the Castle, telling her Miss Minnie Williams was there.

It was an easy matter to force her to assign to me all she possessed.

After that she was immediately killed in order that no one in or about the Castle should know of her having been there save the man who burned her clothing.

It was the foot-print of Nannie Williams, as later demonstrated by that most astute lawyer and detective, Mr. Copps, of Fort Worth, that was found upon the painted surface of the vault door made during her violent struggles before her death.

It was also easy to give to Miss Minnie Williams a delayed letter, stating that her sister's proposed visit had been given up and also by intercepting later letters and substituting others to keep her from learning that the sister had left the South.

Having secured all the money and property Miss Williams had[,] it was time that she were killed.

Owing to a fire that had occurred in the Castle I was unable to resort to the usual methods in taking her life, and, after some delay, took her to Momence, Ill., [Illinois] about November 15, 1893, registering at a hotel near the postoffice under an assumed name, but as man and wife.[31]

My intention was to quietly kill her in some sure manner, but a freight wreck that occurred upon the outskirts of the town the day following my arrival there, which, out of curiosity, I visited, brought me in contact with a passenger conductor named Peck, who knew me, and I therefore abandoned it, but later returned and took her eight miles east of Momence upon a freight line that is little used, and ended her life with poison and buried her body in the basement of the house spoken of at about the time of the Irvington discovery in 1895.

It was a great wonder that the body was not found at that time if the detectives in reality went to that location.

Nothing would at the present time give so much satisfaction as to know that her body had been properly buried, and I would be willing to give up the few remaining days I have to live, if by so doing this could be accomplished, for, because of her spotless life before she knew me, because of the large amount of money I defrauded her of, because I killed her sister and brother, because not being satisfied with all this, I endeavored after my arrest to blacken her good name my charging her with the death of her sister, and later with the instigation of the murder of the three Pitezel children, endeavoring to have it believed that her motive for so doing was to afford an avenue of escape for herself it ever apprehended for her sister's death, by pointing to her as a wholesale murderess, and, therefore persumably [sic] guilty of the sister's death as well; for all these reasons this is without exception the saddest and most heinous of any of my crimes.

Fig. 55. Minnie Williams
Source: "Holmes Confesses 27 Murders," *Philadelphia Inquirer,* April 12, 1896, p. 9.

Fig. 56. Anna "Nannie" Williams
Source: "Holmes Confesses 27 Murders," *Philadelphia Inquirer,*
April 12, 1896, p. 9.

Murder 22: Unknown Chicago Man

A man who came to Chicago to attend the Chicago Exposition, but whose name I cannot recall, was my next victim.

The Chicago authorities can, if they choose, learn the name by inquiries made of the Hartford Insurance Company, a Mr. Lasher, of the Stock Exchange Building; D. F. Duncombe, Metropolitan Building; all of Chicago; a sash and door manufacturing company opposite the Deering, Illinois, Station, or F. L. Jones, a notary public at Indianapolis, at some one of which places I hope either his name or handwriting may have been preserved, thus affording a clue for identification by his friends.

I determined to use this man in my various business dealings, and did so for a time, until I found he had not the ability I had first thought he possessed, and I therefore decided to kill him.

This was done, but as I had not had any dealings with the "stiff" dealer for some time previous to this murder, I decided to bury the body in the basement of the house that I formerly owned near the corner of Seventy-fourth and Honore Streets, in Chicago, where, by digging deply [sic] in the sandy soil, the body will be found.

Murder 23: Baldwin Williams

After Miss Williams' death I found among her papers an insurance policy made in her favor by her brother, Baldwin Williams, of Leadville, Col. [Colorado].

I therefore went to that city early in 1894, and, having found him, took his life by shooting him, it being believed I had done so in self-defense.

A little later, when the assignment of the policy to which I had forged Miss Williams' name was presented to John M. Maxwell, of Leadville, the administrator of the Williams estate, it was honored and the money paid.

Both in this instance and that of a $1000 check given by Dr. Tolman and checks aggregating $2500 by I. R. Hitt & Co., both of Chicago, inasmuch as the indorsements [sic] are forgeries, the Williams heirs can now recover these amounts, although it will be an undeserved hardship upon those who have once advanced the money upon them.

Murder 24: Benjamin F. Pitezel

Benjamin F. Pitezel comes next.

So much has already been printed (even in South Africa, where the case was recently given considerable prominence in a local issue there) regarding this case that there will be little for me to tell, save the actual manner in which his death was brought about.

It will be understood that from the first hour of our acquaintance, even before I knew he had a family who later afford me additional victims for the gratification of my blood thirstiness, I intended to kill him, and all my subsequent care of him and his, as well as my apparent trust in him by placing in his name large amounts of property, were steps taken to gain his confidence and that of his family so when the time was ripe they would the more readily fall into my hands.

It seems almost incredible now as I look back that I could have expected to have experienced sufficient satisfaction in witnessing their deaths to repay me for even the physical exertion that I had put forth in their behalf during those seven long years, to say nothing of the amount of money I had expended for their welfare, over and above what I could have expected to receive from his comparatively small life insurance.

Yet, so it is, and it furnishes a very striking illustration of the vagaries in which the human mind will, under certain circumstances, indulge; in comparison with which the seeking of buried treasure at the rainbow's end, the delusions of the exponents of perpetual motion or the dreams of the haschisch[32] fiend are sanity itself.

Pitezel left his home for the last time late in July, 1894, a happy, light-hearted man, to whom trouble or discouragements of any kind were almost unknown.

We then journeyed together to New York and later to Philadelphia, where the fatal house upon Callowhill street in which he met his death September 2, 1894, was hired.

Then came my writing to him the discouraging letters, purporting to be from his wife, causing him to again resort to drink.

Then the waiting from day to day until I should be sure of finding him in a drunken stupor at midday.

This was an easy matter, as I was acquainted with his habits and so sure was I of finding him thus incapacitated that when the day came upon which it was convenient for me to kill him, even before I went to his house I packed my trunk and made other arrangements to leave Philadelphia in a hurried flight immediately after his death.

After thus preparing I went to the house, quietly unlocked the door and stole noiselessly within and to the second story room, where I found him insensibly drunk, as I had expected.

But even in this condition the question may be asked had I no fear that he might be only naturally asleep or partially insensible and therefore liable to at any moment come to his senses and defend himself? I answer no, and that even had he done so my great strength would have enabled me to have still overpowered him.

Only one difficulty presented itself. It was necessary for me to kill him in such a manner that no struggle or movement of his body should occur, otherwise his clothing being in any way displaced it would have been impossible to again put them in a normal condition.

I overcame this difficulty by first binding him hand and foot and having done ——[Holmes omitted what he did], I proceeded to burn him alive by saturating his clothing and his face with benzine and igniting it with a match.

So horrible was this torture that in writing of it I have been tempted to attribute his death to some inhumane means—not with a wish to spare myself, but because I fear that it will not be believed that one could be so heartless and depraved, but such a course would be useless, for by exclusion, the authorities have determined for me that his death could only have occurred in this manner, no blows or bruises upon his body and no drug administered, save chloroform, which was not placed in his stomach until at least 30 minutes after his death, and to now make a misstatement of the facts would only serve to draw out additional criticism from them.

The least I can do is to spare my reader a recital of the victim's cries for mercy, his prayers and finally, his plea for a more speedy termination of his sufferings, all of which upon me had no effect.

Finally, when he was dead I removed the straps and ropes that had bound him and extinguished the flames and a little later poured into his stomach one and one half ounces of chloroform.

It has been asked why I did this after I knew that he was dead, what possible use it could have served? My answer to this is that I placed it there so that at the time of the post mortem examination, which I knew would be held, the Coroner's physician would be warranted in reporting that the death was accidental, and due to an explosion of a cleaning fluid, composed of benzine and chloroform, and that the chloroform had at the time of the explosion separated from the benzine and passed into his stomach, and upon receipt of such intelligence I believed the insurance company would at once pay the full amount of the claim.

The chloroform did worse than this, however, and developed a condition of this body that in my limited medical experience I have never seen or read of, and I mention it here as a fact of scientific interest, that I believe is not generally known.

It drove from his entire body tissue, brains and viscera, all evidence of recent intoxication to such an extent that the physicians who examined the body after death were warranted in stating under oath that there was no evidence of, and they did not believe the man was drunk at the time of his death, or within twelve hours thereof.

That they were wrong in making such deductions is proven by

the well-known fact that all other testimony and circumstances at my trial tended to show that he must have been insensible from liquor, and that only in this condition could I have killed him; a fact so strongly brought out that the learned trial judge in his arguments commented upon it at some length.

After his death I gathered together various assignments of patents and deeds to property he had held for me that I had been careful to have him sign some days before, so I should not suffer pecuniary loss.

I also wrote the cipher message found by the insurance company among my papers after my arrest; imitating his handwriting, and after placing the body in such a position that by a cunning arrangement of a window shutter upon the south side of the building the sun would be reflected upon his face the entire day, I left the house without the slightest feeling of remorse for my terrible acts.

For one month and six days thereafter I took no human life, although about three weeks after Pitezel's death I was afforded an opportunity to gratify my feverish lust for blood by going to the graveyard where he had been buried and under pretense of securing certain portions of his body for microscopical examination removed the same with a knife, and the heartless manner in which I did this and the evident gratification it afforded me has been most forcibly told by Mr. Smith upon the witness stand.

As an instance of the infallibility of justice, as a triumph of right over wrong, and of the general safety of condemnation to death upon circumstantial evidence alone this case is destined to long remain prominent as a warning to those viciously inclined that their only safe course is to avoid even the eppearance [sic] of evil.

Two questions that have been often asked I would answer—why did I make no defense at my trial when by so doing I could lose nothing, and possibly could have gained?

I answer that after Detective Geyer's Western investigation, which we could not at that time in any way refute, and in the face of Dr. Leffmann's learned statements to the effect that no one could or had ever been known to lose consciousness by chloroform self-administered, provided they had not first confined their movements.

It would have been but a waste of my counsel's energies, and of my own, to have tried to convince the most impartial juries that it was a case of suicide and not murder.

Is it to be wondered at that I hesitated before placing the defense of suicide before a jury composed of men who had, with three exceptions, stated under oath, before being passed upon by the court as competent, that they had already formed opinions prejudiced to my interests?

The second question is, did Pitezel during his eight years' acquaintance and almost constant association with me, know that I was a multi-murderer, and if he did know was he a party to such crime?

I answer that he neither knew of nor was a party to the taking of any human life, and I earnestly beg that this statement may be believed, both in justice to his memory and on account of the surviving members of his family.

The worst acts he ever participated in were dishonesties regarding properties and unlawful acts of trade, in which he aided me freely.

In support of my statement that he was not cognizant of any of the graver crimes which I have so freely confessed herein I will mention one of many instances already known to the authorities, viz., that for six months previous to his death he had planned openly with his wife that their daughter Alice should spend a year at a school he believed Miss Williams intended to open near Boston, and these plans were of such a nature that Mrs. Pitezel knows he was not deceiving her.

He would not have made these arrangements, and there would

have been no occasion for him to have deceived his own family, if he believed Miss Williams was not alive.

Fig. 57. Benjamin F. Pitezel
Source: "Holmes Confesses 27 Murders," *Philadelphia Inquirer*, April 12, 1896, p. 9.

Fig. 58. Callowhill Street house where Benjamin Pitezel was murdered
Source: "Holmes Confesses 27 Murders," *Philadelphia Inquirer,* April 12, 1896, p. 1.

ROOM WHERE "B. T. PERRY'S" BODY WAS FOUND.

Fig. 59. Room where B. F. Perry's [Pitezel's] body was found
Source: "Crime is His Passion," *New York Herald,* November 25, 1894, p. 1.

Murder 25: Howard Pitezel

The Irvington, Indiana, tragedy is next. Upon the 1st day of October, 1894, I took the three Pitezel children to the Circle House in Indianapolis, where I engaged permanent board for them until such a time as I could kill one or more of them.

Upon the evening of that day I went to St. Louis, where I remained until October 4, busily engaged in settling up the insurance matter with McDonald and Howe, the attorneys.

During this time I also called upon the agent or owner of the Irvington House.

This was my first incautious step and was destined to fasten crime upon me, for later when the detectives learned that I made this call upon the date that they knew the insurance settlement took place, they no longer hesitated in stating that I, and I alone, could have murdered the boy.

Upon October 4, I returned to Indianapolis, and later in the same day went to Franklin, Indiana, which is situated south of Indianapolis, while Irvington is east thereof, Franklin to Irvington representing the hypothenuse of a triangle—Franklin to Indianapolis and Indianapolis to Irvington the two shorter sides— so that one could go from Franklin to Irvington direct without making the longer journey via Indianapolis.

On October 5th the rent of the house was paid and at about 9 A. M. October 6th I called upon Dr. Thompson at Irvington for the keys, he having been a former occupant.

At 5 o'clock upon the same day I called upon Mr. Brown at Irvington to engage him to make some repairs upon the house, and upon his appearing indifferent I became very angry with him and my only wonder is that I did not entice him to the house and kill him also.

This small circumstance aided in bringing the crime home to me when it was made known to the detectives and considered by them in connection with many other complaints of my violent and ungovernable temper that had come to their knowledge.

On October 7 I called at the Irvington drug store and purchased the drugs I needed to kill the boy and the following evening I again went to the same store and bought an additional supply, as I feared I had not obtained a sufficient quantity upon my first visit.

My next step was to secure the furniture for the house. This was done upon October 8, late in the afternoon, at such an hour that made it impossible for the store owner to deliver them, and as I wished to stay at Irvington that night I hired a conveyance and carted the goods to the house myself, keeping the horse there until the next day.

It was also upon the 8th, early in the forenoon, that I went to the repair shop for the long knives I had previously left there to be sharpened.

Early in the afternoon of October 10th I had the boy's trunk and a stove I had bought taken to the depot, and they arrived at the Irvington house at about 6 P. M., at which time Mr. Moreman was the last person who saw the boy alive, for almost immediately I called him into the house and insisted that he go to bed at once, first giving him the fatal dose of medicine.

As soon as he had ceased to breathe I cut his body into pieces that would pass through the door of the stove and by the combined use of gas and corncobs, proceeded to burn it with as little feeling as 'tho it had been inanimate object.

If I could now recall one circumstance a dollar of money to be gained, a disagreeable act or word upon his part, in justification of this horrid crime, it would be a satisfaction to me, but to think that I committed this and other crimes for the pleasure of killing my fellow beings to hear their cries for mercy and pleas to be allowed even sufficient time to pray and prepare for death—all this is now too horrible for even me, hardened criminal that I am, to again live over without a shudder.

Is it to be wondered at that since my arrest my days have been those of self-reproaching torture, and my nights of sleepless fear? Or that even before my death, I have commenced to assume the form and features of the [the rest of the sentence was missing from the confession printed in the *Philadelphia Inquirer*].

After I had finished the cremation of my victim I made the excavation in which the few remaining portions were found at the time the horror was brought to light, which together with the stove and other evidences of my wrong-doings, were brought here to Philadelphia at the time of my trial to mock me in my efforts to save my life.

Then after I had removed the blood and other evidences of the crime, and had burned the contents of the trunk, I went to the office of Powell & Harter, at Indianapolis, for my mail; from there to the hotel for the other two children, whom I took at once to Chicago.

I immediately returned to the Irvington House, and was seen there by Mr. Armstrong, a teamster, or such, in time as to have made it a foolish act for me to have persisted in saying that it was some other person whom he saw.

My identification in Chicago by a woman with whom the children boarded and by the station agent at Milwaukee, and later at Adrian, Mich., [Michigan], all show the uselessness of trying to escape from one's self or from the responsibility of one's wrong acts.

In Detroit I hired a house and made an excavation in the basement, where I left a note in my own handwriting, all of which I hastened to tell the detectives as soon as I was arrested, so that by their going to the house and finding both the excavation and the note they would not be inclined to prosecute a similar search in Toronto or other places.

Fig. 60. Howard Pitezel
Source: "Holmes Confesses 27 Murders," *Philadelphia Inquirer*, April 12, 1896, p. 9.

Fig. 61. The Irvington Cottage Where Howard Pitezel Was Murdered
Source: "Holmes Confesses 27 Murders," *Philadelphia Inquirer,* April 12, 1896, p. 9.

Murders 26 and 27: Alice and Nellie Pitezel

I now, with much reluctance, come to the discussion of the twenty-sixth and twenty-seventh murders. The victims were Alice and Nellie Pitezel, whose deaths will seem to many to be the saddest of all, both on account of the terribly heartless manner in which it was accomplished, and because in one instance, that of Alice, the oldest of these children, her death was the least of the wrongs suffered at my hands.

Here again I am tempted to either pass the matter by without speaking of it, or to altogether deny it, but to what purpose? It is publicly known and was freely commented upon at my trial, and to deny it now would only serve the double purpose of breaking my resolution to hold nothing in reserve, and of causing many who are somewhat familiar with the details of the different cases to disbelieve me in other matters; moreover, the testimony already given by Mrs. Actlia Allcorn, and the opinion of Coroner Ashbridge and a Mr. Perry, who knew the mental condition of the child upon that following day, would, if called for, be sufficient to decide the matter.

These children, after boarding in Detroit for about one week, reached Toronto, October 19, and were taken to the Albion Hotel, where they boarded until they were killed.

Upon October 20 I hired the Vincent street house, having the lease made in the name of H. M. Howard, in order to avert suspicion as much as possible in case an investigation followed.

Between 5 and 6 P. M. the same day I took a large empty trunk to the house and then passed the following day at Niagara Falls.

On the 22d, I bought and had taken to the house the furniture, stove and bedding, and on the 23d, the children went to the house for a few hours.

The 24th was passed in other parts of the city, but upon the 25th, the fatal day of these deaths, they were seen at the house at 1

P. M., and a little later they accompanied me to several clothing stores and finally at 4 P. M., while they were in a restaurant near-by [sic] I entered a large store in which I believed I should meet Mrs. Pitezel, holding in my hands some heavy winter underwear I had bought for the little boy already dead.

Of this meeting Mrs. Pitezel has said:

"I believe my children were at that time in that store with me."

I immediately took them to the Vincent Street house and compelled them through the cover of which I made a small opening.

Here I left them until I could return and at my leisure kill them.

At 5 P. M. I borrowed a spade of a neighbor and at the same time called on Mrs. Pitezell [sic] at her hotel.

I then returned to my hotel and ate my dinner, and at 7:00 P. M. went again to Mrs. Pitezel's hotel, and aided her in leaving Toronto for Ogdensburg, N. Y.

Later than 8:00 P. M. I again returned to the house where the children were imprisoned, and ended their lives by connecting the gas with the trunk, then came the opening of the trunk and the viewing of their little blackened and distorted faces, then the digging of their shallow graves in the basement of the house, the ruthless stripping off of their clothing, and the burial without a particle of covering save the cold earth, which I heaped upon them with fiendish delight.

Consider what an awful act this was!

These little innocent and helpless children, the oldest only being 13 years of age, a puny and sickly child, who to look at one would believe much younger; consider that for eight years before their death I had been almost as much a father as though they had been my own children, thus giving them a right to look to me for care and protection, and in your righteous judgment, let your bitterest curses fall upon me, but again I pray upon me alone!

There is little more to tell. The next day was passed in burning the children's clothing, and in resting from my terrible night's work, and upon the 27th I called an expressman and had the trunk removed from the house, and after giving the keys to a neighbor went away never to return.

Fig. 62. Alice Pitezel
Source: "Holmes Confesses 27 Murders," *Philadelphia Inquirer,*
April 12, 1896, p. 9.

Fig. 63. Nellie Pitezel
Source: "Holmes Confesses 27 Murders," *Philadelphia Inquirer,*
April 12, 1896, p. 9.

Fig. 64. Holmes Murdering Alice and Nellie Pitezel in the Trunk
Source: "Holmes Confesses 27 Murders," *Philadelphia Inquirer,* April 12, 1896, p. 8.

Fig. 65. The Vincent Street House, Toronto Canada, Where Alice and Nellie Pitezel Were Murdered
Source: "Holmes Confesses 27 Murders," *Philadelphia Inquirer,* April 12, 1896, p. 8.

Attempted Murder of Mrs. Pitezel and Two Children

From Toronto I went to Ogdensburg, from there to Burlington, Vermont, where I hired a furnished house for Mrs. Pitezel's use, and a few days prior to my arrest in Boston I wrote her a letter in which I directed her to carry a bottle of dynamite that I had previously left in the basement so arranged, that in taking it to the third story of the house it would fall from her hands, and not only destroy her life, but that of her two remaining children, who I knew would be with her at the time.

This was my last act, and happily did not have a fatal termination.

Fig. 66. Mrs. Pitezel
Source: "Holmes Confesses 27 Murders," *Philadelphia Inquirer*, April 12, 1896, p. 9.

Conclusion of Confession

The eighteen intervening months I have passed in solitary confinement, and in a few days am to be led forth to my death.

It would now seem a very fitting time for me to express regret or remorse in this, which I intend to be my last public utterance for these irreparable shortcomings.

To do so with the expectation of even one person who has read this confession to the end, believing that in my depraved nature there is room for such feelings, is I fear, to expect more than would be granted.

I can at least, and do refrain, from calling forth such a critcism [sic] by openly inviting it.

Fig. 67. Holmes signature from confession to *Philadelphia Inquirer*
Source: "Holmes Confesses 27 Murders," *Philadelphia Inquirer,* April 12, 1896, p. 9.

Fig. 68. Holmes' Castle
Source: "Holmes Confesses 27 Murders," *Philadelphia Inquirer*, April 12, 1896, p. 8.

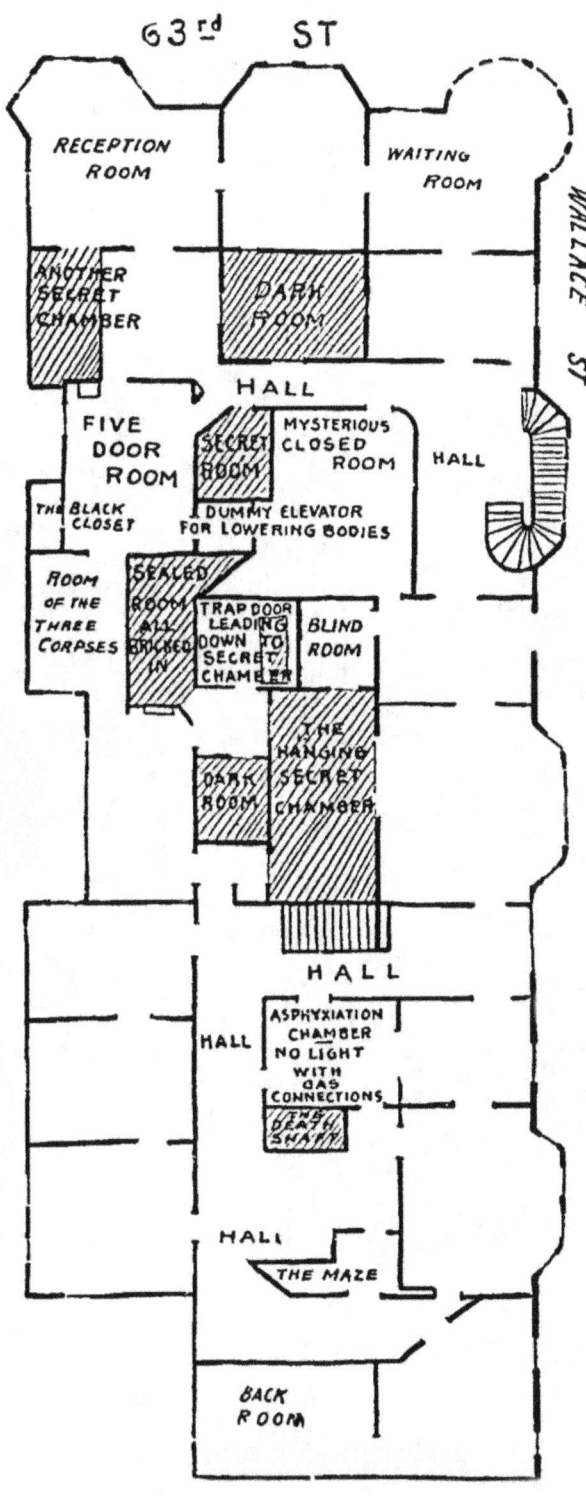

Fig. 69. Plan of the Holmes' Castle
Source: "Holmes Confesses 27 Murders," *Philadelphia Inquirer,*
April 12, 1896, p. 8.

Fig. 70. The Stove and False Safe in the Castle
Source: "Holmes Confesses 27 Murders," *Philadelphia Inquirer,*
April 12, 1896, p. 8.

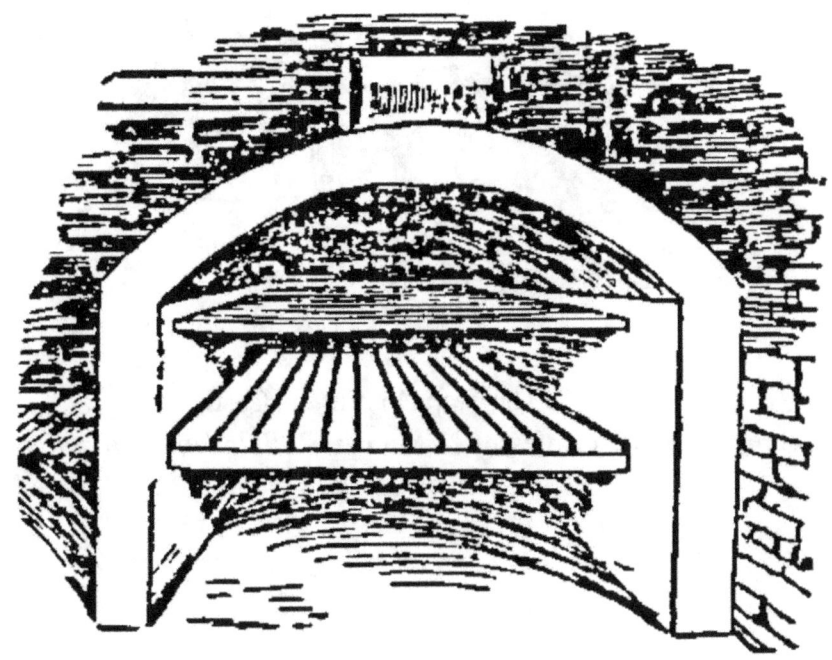

Fig. 71. The Gas Oven in the Castle
Source: "Holmes Confesses 27 Murders," *Philadelphia Inquirer,*
April 12, 1896, p. 8.

Fig. 72. The Trap Door in the Castle
Source: "Holmes Confesses 27 Murders," *Philadelphia Inquirer,* April 12, 1896, p. 8.

Fig. 73. The Gas Tank in the Castle
Source: "Holmes Confesses 27 Murders," *Philadelphia Inquirer*, April 12, 1896, p. 9.

Fig. 74. Articulator of Skeletons (M. G. Chappell)
Source: "Holmes Confesses 27 Murders," *Philadelphia Inquirer,* April 12, 1896, p. 9; and *Daily Inter Ocean,* July 30, 1895.

Fig. 75. Assistant District Attorney Barlow
Source: "Holmes Confesses 27 Murders," *Philadelphia Inquirer,*
April 12, 1896, p. 8.

Fig. 76. District Attorney George S. Graham prosecuted Holmes case
Source: "Holmes Confesses 27 Murders," *Philadelphia Inquirer,* April 12, 1896, p. 9.

Fig. 77. Miss Yoke, Holmes third wife, testified against Holmes during his trial
Source: "Holmes Confesses 27 Murders," *Philadelphia Inquirer,* April 12, 1896, p. 8.

Fig. 78. Pat Quinlan, Holmes janitor at the Castle
Source: "Holmes Confesses 27 Murders," *Philadelphia Inquirer,*
April 12, 1896, p. 9.

Fig. 79. A young Pat Quinlan, Holmes janitor at the Castle
Source: "Hounded to Death by Ghosts of Castle He Built," *Ogden Standard,* July 4, 1914, p. 19.

Fig. 80. President Fouse, Fidelity Mutual Insurance Co

Source: "Holmes Confesses 27 Murders," *Philadelphia Inquirer,* April 12, 1896, p. 8.

Statement from Detective Geyer

Three months after the confession of Holmes was printed in the *Philadelphia Inquirer,* Frank Geyer, the Philadelphia detective assigned to investigate Holmes, was interviewed by a reporter from the *Indianapolis News.*

Geyer said Holmes called on real estate agent, John L. Wright, for the purpose of disposing his wife's interest in the Yoke estate, but failed for lack of time.

Geyer believed that if Holmes had been able to trade the interest in the Yoke estate for a parcel of city property, he would have murdered Georgiana Yoke and her mother, Mrs. Yoke, and disposed of the property for his own benefit.

"You see, Holmes was a long-headed man, and looked some distance into the future. All of his crimes were premeditated, carefully thought out, and executed according to plans already formed. If he murdered Howard Pitzel [sic] in this city, he rented a house first, made his arrangements, dug a place to put the body in, and then took the victim to the already-prepared grave," said Detective Geyer.

The reporter asked Geyer about Hatch.

"He still sticks to it that he gave him [Howard Pitezel] in charge of Hatch. That is all that we can get out of him on that point. Find Hatch, and you will find the boy, he says."

"Who is Hatch?" asked the reporter.

"Hatch was, I believe, mythical. There never was such a person except in the mind of Holmes. I tell you that there has never been such a criminal as Holmes. He is shrewd, calculating, long-headed. Say, a man that wants to kill two girls, takes the clothes off them and burns them one place and then buries the bodies in another, so as to prevent identification—he's nobody's fool. He is the nicest fellow in the world to talk to, as polite as you please and nervy. He smiles all of the time, and can talk on any subject you choose.

There has been an awful lot of rot written about him, but after all there is no doubt that he is the greatest murderer and all-around criminal of the century. He'll be hanged, though. If they don't do it in Toronto or Chicago, or here [Indianapolis], they will do it in Philadelphia. There's no escape for him," said Geyer.[33]

Fig. 81. Detective Geyer
Source: "Holmes Confesses 27 Murders," *Philadelphia Inquirer,* April 12, 1896, p. 9.

Fig. 82. Detective Frank P. Geyer
Source: Frank P. Geyer. *The Holmes-Pitezel case; a history of the greatest crime of the century and of the search for the missing Pitezel children.* Philadelphia, PA: Publishers' Union, 1896.

PART THREE
LIED THEN DIED

Judgment Day - Thursday, May 7, 1896

Holmes slept like a baby his last night on earth. After a second attempt to wake him, Holmes got up and dressed. Keeper John Henry asked Holmes how he felt.

"Are you nervous?" said Keeper Henry.

"Not a bit," said Holmes. He smiled and slid his arms between the prison bars and stretched out his fingers.[34]

"Look at that," said Holmes. His hands were steady as a rock.[35]

At 7 o'clock, Fathers Daily and McPeak arrived in his cell. As a new convert to Catholic religion, Holmes knelt with the priests while they administered Holy Communion.[36]

Holmes ate a last meal of eggs, dry toast, and coffee. He seemed to enjoy it.

A wall of police held back a huge crowd gathered outside the gates of Moyamensing prison. A rope stretched across the entire front of the passageway leading to the convict department. The sheriff, city officials, jurors and newspaper reporters gathered to witness the execution. Gates opened at 9 o'clock and a crowd of onlookers filed in. Sheriff solicitor William Grew called the list of twelve jurymen into the superintendent's office near the scaffold. Two ex-sheriffs, seven physicians, and an undertaker responded. Special Deputies were also assigned and included Detective Frank P. Geyer, Coroner Samuel H. Ashbridge, and President Fouse, of Fidelity Mutual Life Association.[37]

At two minutes after 10 o'clock, Prison Superintendent Perkins and Assistant Superintendent Richardson led Holmes' procession toward the gallows. The solemn parade halted before the scaffold.

The platform stood eight feet above the floor. Witnesses passed around the structure and faced it. Silence followed. The priests began praying from the other side of the scaffold as they escorted Holmes to the gallows. Priests stood on both sides of the condemned man and chanted the psalm Miserere while Holmes fixed his eyes on a crucifix in his hands. He wore a sack coat, gray trousers, and a white shirt. His neck was covered with a handkerchief and he had a thin growth of a beard on his chin.[38]

Holmes stepped forward and the audience grew silent. Holmes spoke for two minutes in a slow, calm manner, enunciating and raising his arms to emphasize important words:[39]

> "Gentlemen, I have very few words to say. In fact, I would make no remarks at this time except that by not speaking I would appear to acquiesce in my execution. I only wish to say that the extent of my wrongdoing in taking human life consisted in the death of two women, they having died at my hands as the result of criminal operations. I wish to state here, so there can be no chance of misunderstanding, that I am not guilty of taking the lives of any of the Pitezel family—the three children and Benjamin, the father, of whose death I was convicted, and for which I am today to be hanged. That is all I have to say."

His voice never quavered. His hands did not tremble. Holmes stopped speaking and stepped back. He turned to his attorney, Mr. Rotan, shook hands, and gave him a hug.

"Goodbye," said Holmes.

Holmes looked at Assistant Superintendent Richardson and said, "Take your time. Don't bungle it."

"Are you ready?"

"Yes, goodbye," Holmes said in a low tone.

He buttoned his coat, nodded to the sheriff, and at the sound of a pistol, the drop fell at 10:12:20. While the priest's chanted prayers, the body shot up and then hung without a tremor.

Deputy Sheriff Saybolt fainted.[40]

Drs. Sharp and Butcher felt for a pulse and after a few minutes, Holmes was dead.

The body hung there until 10:45, then it was lowered and placed on a stretcher. A sort of revolting incident occurred where the knot jammed and efforts to remove it from Holmes neck failed. Finally, they cut the knot.

Holmes was an avid newsreader, especially when it pertained to articles about him. Almost immediately after his execution, a letter carrier walked up to the gates of the prison and delivered a newspaper addressed to H. H. Holmes.[41]

THE MARCH TO THE SCAFFOLD.

Fig. 83. Holmes march to the scaffold
Source: "Holmes Met Death Without a Tremor," *Philadelphia Inquirer,* May 8, 1896, p. 1.

Fig. 84. Holmes makes his final address before his execution
Source: "The Execution of Holmes," *The Times*, May 8, 1896, p. 1.

Fig. 85. Holmes at the scaffold
Source: "H. H. Holmes Was Hanged Today in Moyamensing Prison," *The World*, May 8, 1896, p. 3.

After Holmes' execution, a *Philadelphia Inquirer* reporter interviewed Mrs. Pitezel. She was still dressed in her deep mourning attire from the deaths of her husband and three children. The reporter asked her if she was happy with the justice Holmes received. Mrs. Pitezel choked up with emotion and said, "Yes, and it is a relief for me to know that he did not succeed in escaping the gallows. Still, that does not bring my husband and my poor little children back to me." She began weeping.[42]

"Have you read the newspaper accounts of the execution?" asked the reporter.

"No, I have not," said Mrs. Pitezel.

"Holmes made a last statement upon the gallows in which he solemnly declared that he did not kill Mr. Pitezel or either of your children."

Mrs. Pitezel gathered her composure, dried her eyes with a handkerchief and said, "That is untrue. I know he murdered my little ones and also my husband. And had he not been arrested when he was I feel that he would have killed my only remaining daughter and baby boy and myself. It was for that and nothing else that he was taking us from place to place all over the country."[43]

Mrs. Pitezel remained in Philadelphia while attorney Rotan went over Holmes' papers and materials to see if Holmes left a will. A few days later, Rotan announced there was no will after all and no provision made for Mrs. Pitezel. He did not keep his promise to give Mrs. Pitezel one-third of his property. As the *Trenton Evening Times* put it, Holmes was a scoundrel to the end. Poor Mrs. Pitezel left Philadelphia for good and made her way to her home in Galva, Illinois.[44]

At the age of forty-eight, Mrs. Pitezel [Carrie Alice Canning] married Peter Van Arsdale in Knox, Illinois on December 20, 1905. Carrie died September 30, 1929 at the age of seventy in Kirkland, Washington.[45]

Concrete Burial - Friday, May 8, 1896

Undertaker O'Rourke and his staff prepared Holmes' coffin at their place of business early Thursday morning. According to Holmes' own instructions, they lined his oversized, pine coffin with concrete in the shape of a man. They added soft material to protect his body from the concrete and a rest to comfort his head and neck.[46]

Holmes' crazy concrete idea was to prevent greedy scientists and grave robbers from desecrating his remains. And he had good reason to believe his grave would be desecrated.

Surgeons and scientists from all over the country wrote letters to Philadelphia officials requesting to assist in an autopsy and to possess various parts of Holmes' body. All such requests were denied.[47]

Holmes also received letters from a museum and a New York physician, offering Holmes a good sum of money for his heart, brain, and skull. He feared there would not be enough of his body left for a proper funeral so he spent several hours with attorney Samuel P. Rotan and insisted Rotan use every legal means to prevent an autopsy and they planned his elaborate concrete burial.[48]

After he was declared dead, officials sent for O'Rourke, who arrived at the prison shortly afterwards. O'Rourke and his staff placed Holmes in the coffin, covered his body with the soft cloth, then poured cement on top of the cloth and closed the lid. Not that anyone would be able to see it once buried, a silver cross rested on top of the coffin. Inscribed was his name and the words: "Died May 7, 1896, aged 35 years."[49]

At half past 12 o'clock, the iron doors at the rear of the prison opened and the horse-drawn wagon rolled out. Onlookers pursued the wagon for some distance, pounding on the sides of the vehicle until police escorted it away.[50]

Undertaker O'Rourke, Mr. Mullen, his assistant, and two armed Pinkerton detectives rode in the wagon with Holmes. Newspaper men in carriages followed close behind. The somber caravan drove several miles through the countryside, past Philadelphia farms and gardens. At the county line, they stopped to address a health permit. After a short wait, the horses were off again. They arrived at Holy Cross Cemetery on a hill with a breathtaking view of the valley below. Due to a technicality, Holmes could not be buried because of a problem with the burial permit and Mr. Mullen went by train to resolve it.[51]

Mullen returned around 5 o'clock, and they moved Holmes to a vault near the main entrance. They locked the gate and armed Pinkerton men stood guard. The next day, Friday, May 8, 1896, a crowd of over one hundred watched as they buried Herman Webster Mudgett, alias H. H. Holmes in a double grave purchased for $24.[52]

It was quite the spectacle to see the heavy pine coffin removed from the vault, placed into a furniture car, and driven to the grave site. The coffin was so heavy, a brass handle broke off in the process.[53]

Workers removed the lid so Father McPake could read the burial service and sprinkle the water of blessing upon Holmes' concrete-encased feet. At 4:25 PM, they lowered Holmes ten feet into the grave and poured a mixture of concrete and dirt on top of his coffin.[54]

Holmes was buried at Holy Cross Cemetery in Yeadon, Pennsylvania, Section 15, Range 10, Lot 41, in unmarked graves 3 and 4.

Holmes was not the only criminal buried at the sacred Holy Cross Cemetery. Philadelphia family mob boss, Angelo 'Gentle Don' Bruno, assassinated March 12, 1980, was also buried there.[55]

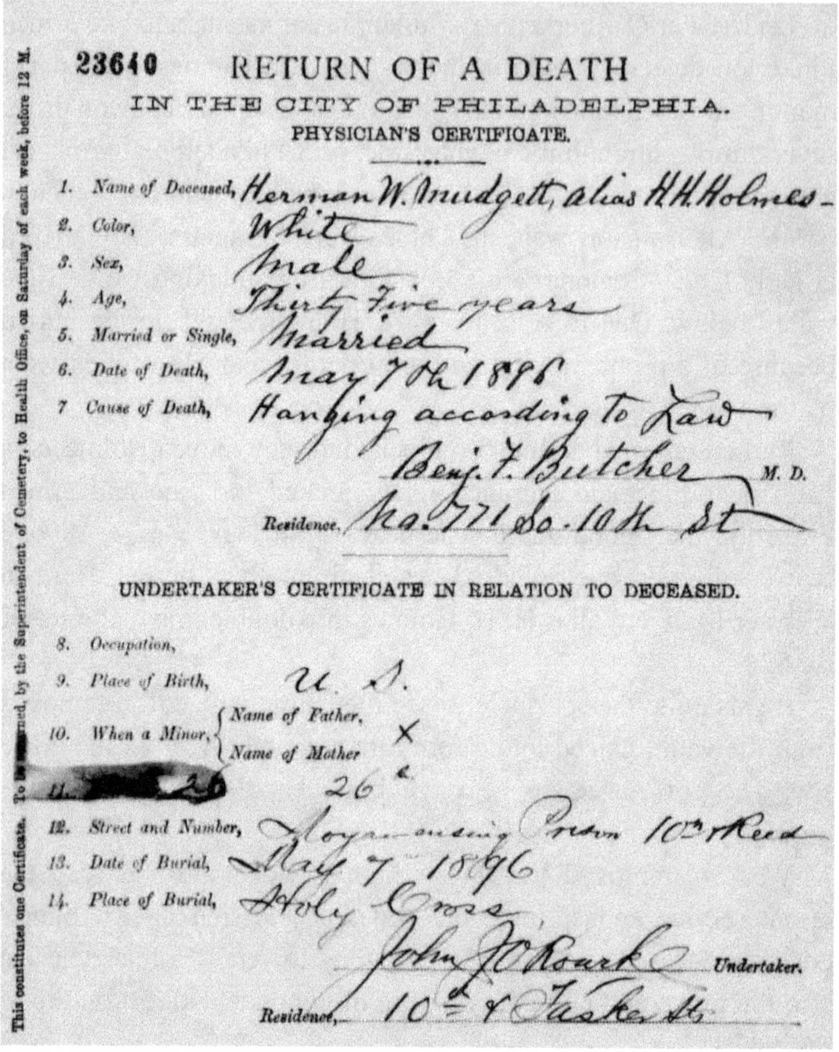

Fig. 86. Holmes' Death Certificate
Source: Philadelphia City Archives, Return of a Death in the City of Philadelphia, Physician's Certificate No. 23640.

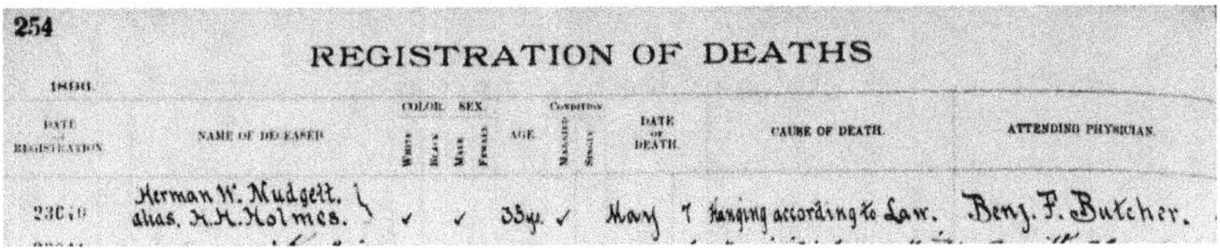

254

REGISTRATION OF DEATHS

1896

DATE OF REGISTRATION	NAME OF DECEASED	COLOR: White	COLOR: Black	SEX: Male	SEX: Female	AGE	CONDITION: Married	CONDITION: Single	DATE OF DEATH	CAUSE OF DEATH	ATTENDING PHYSICIAN
[illegible]	Herman W. Mudgett, alias. H.H. Holmes.	✓		✓		35y.	✓		May 7	Hanging according to Law.	Benj. F. Butcher.

Fig. 87. Registration of Death for Herman Mudgett, *alias* H. H. Holmes

Source: Philadelphia City Archives, Registration of Deaths, 1896, No. 23640.

Holmes' Reincarnation?

A young news reporter, who wished to remained unnamed, had long conversations with Holmes while he was in prison. The reporter retold one odd encounter. "Holmes was a man of very strong ideas and personality, and I think when he took up a matter for thought he never rested until he had finally settled all its pros and cons in his own mind," said the reporter.[56]

"One day just a few weeks before his last day, we were discussing the theory of metempsychosis—the passing of the soul after death into another body. Holmes believed in it firmly."

"I know as well as you do, and everybody else that on the 7th of May I shall be hanged until my body is dead. I feel confident of that as I do of anything. Moreover, I enjoy the same confidence in the fact that my soul will immediately transmigrate to another animal. Do you believe me?" said Holmes to the reporter.

The reporter expressed doubts.

"I will prove it. At 12 o'clock midnight of the 7th I shall in all probability have been dead thirteen or fourteen hours. If you will stand in the middle of City Hall court, just at the stroke of the hour, I will appear to you," said Holmes.

The reporter asked how he shall know it is Holmes.

"Just as the clock ceases to strike, a little yellow dog will run into the court and up to where you are standing. The dog's body will contain my soul. Now it is barely possible that a dog of that sort might happen along just at that time. In order to prove that there is no mistake, you must throw a stone at me. I shall come up to you in spite of it, and after barking three times will lick your hands. If it is not I, the dog will assuredly run when he is hit," said Holmes.

After the execution, the reporter went to City Hall as Holmes told him to do. At the stroke of 12 o'clock, a little yellow dog ran half sideways into the West corridor and came straight for him.

The reporter's body shook with excitement and he made two or three fumbles for a stone to throw. He threw it and hit him in the head. The dog yelped, turned, and ran away.

"And the thought struck me square in the head that no matter how much Holmes amounted to as a man, he certainly wasn't cutting much ice as a ghost," said the reporter.

Illustration Credits

HOLMES' OWN STORY:
Mudgett, Herman W. *Holmes' Own Story*. Philadelphia, PA: Burke & McFetridge Co, 1895.

    Alice Pitezel, 151.
    Benjamin Pitezel, 26.
    Callowhill Street House, 135.
    Emeline Cigrand, 38.
    Holmes Burning Pitezel's Clothing, 124.
    Herman Webster Mudgett Handwritten Statement for Book
    Holmes Castle, 140.
    Howard Pitezel, 171.
    Minnie R. Williams, 258.
    Mrs. Pitezel, 88.
    Nannie Williams, 49.
    Nellie Pitezel, 199.
    Room Where Nannie Williams Was Killed, 51.

CONFESSION:
"Holmes Confesses 27 Murders," *Philadelphia Inquirer*, April 12, 1896.

    Alice Pitezel, 9.
    Articulator of Skeletons, M. G. Chappell, 9.
    Assistant District Attorney Barlow, 8.
    Benjamin F. Pitezel, 9.
    Callowhill Street House, 1.
    Detective Geyer, 9.
    District Attorney George S. Graham, 9.
    Gas Oven, 8.
    Gas Tank, 9.
    Herman Mudgett, *alias* H. H. Holmes, 1.
    Holmes' Castle, 8.
    Holmes Murdering Alice and Nellie Pitezel in the Trunk, 8.
    Holmes Murdering the Glass Inventor, Mr. Warner, 8.
    Holmes Writing His Confession, 1.
    Holmes Signature, 9.
    Howard Pitezel, 9.
    Irvington Cottage Where Howard Pitezel Was Murdered, 9.
    Minnie Williams, 9.
    Miss Yoke, 9.
    Mrs. Julia Connor, 9.
    Mrs. Pitezel, 9.

Nannie Williams, 9.
Nellie Pitezel, 9.
Pat Quinlan, 9.
Pearl Connor, 9.
Philadelphia Inquirer Headline with Holmes' Note, 1.
Philadelphia Inquirer Holmes' Denial Note, 9.
Plan of Holmes' Castle, 8.
President Fouse, 8.
Stove and False Safe, 8.
Trap Door, 8.
Vincent Street House, Toronto [Canada], Where Alice and Nellie Pitezel Were Murdered, 8.

ADDITIONAL CREDITS:

"Both Under Arrest [Miss Emeline Cigrand]," *Daily Inter Ocean*, July 27, 1895, 2.

Calendar of the University of Michigan. Ann Arbor, Michigan: Courier Printing House, 1885, 148.

Cipriani, Frank. "The Murder Castle," *Chicago Tribune,* March 21, 1937, 7.

City of Philadelphia, Department of Records, August 24, 1894 [1316 Callowhill Street House].

"Crime is His Passion [Room Where B. F. Perry Found]," *New York Herald*, November 25, 1894, 1.

"Crime is His Passion [Mrs. Pitezel in Jail]," *New York Herald*, November 25, 1894, 1.

Geyer, Frank P. *The Holmes-Pitezel case; a history of the greatest crime of the century and of the search for the missing Pitezel children* [Detective Frank P. Geyer Photo]. Philadelphia, PA: Publishers' Union, 1896.

Geyer, Frank. P. *The Holmes-Pitezel case; a history of the greatest crime of the century and of the search for the missing Pitezel children* [Alice Pitezel Photo]. Philadelphia, PA: Publishers' Union, 1896, 38.

Geyer, Frank. P. *The Holmes-Pitezel case; a history of the greatest crime of the century and of the search for the missing Pitezel children* [H. H. Holmes Booking Photo]. Philadelphia, PA: Publishers' Union, 1896.

Geyer, Frank. P. *The Holmes-Pitezel case; a history of the greatest crime of the century and of the search for the missing Pitezel children* [Holmes Castle]. Philadelphia, PA: Publishers' Union, 1896, 91.

Geyer, Frank. P. *The Holmes-Pitezel case; a history of the greatest crime of the century and of the search for the missing Pitezel children* [Howard Pitezel Photo]. Philadelphia, PA: Publishers' Union, 1896, 218.

Geyer, Frank. P. *The Holmes-Pitezel case; a history of the greatest crime of the century and of the search for the missing Pitezel children* [Nellie Pitezel Photo]. Philadelphia, PA: Publishers' Union, 1896, 199.

"H. H. Holmes Was Hanged Today in Moyamensing Prison," *The World*, May 8, 1896, p. 3.

"Holmes Great Crimes [Dr. Robert Leacock]," *Philadelphia Inquirer*, April 26, 1896, 26.

"Holmes Met Death Without a Tremor," *Philadelphia Inquirer*, May 8, 1896, 1.

"Hounded to Death by Ghosts of Castle He Built [Young Pat Quinlan]," *Ogden Standard*, July 4, 1914, 19.

Hudson, Sam. *Pennsylvania and Its Public Men*. Philadelphia: unknown publisher, 1909, 75.

"Jeptha D. Howe is Dead," *Kansas City Star*, March 12, 1919, 2.

Kreidler, W. A., ed. "New Incorporations [Campbell-Yates Company]," *Western Electrician*, vol. XI, no. 1-27, (1892): 314.

"Mrs. Pitezel Faces Holmes [O. La Forrest Perry]," *New York Herald*, October 31, 1895, 3.

"Necrology," *The Michigan Alumnus*, Vol. VII, No. 57 [Robert Leacock death announcement], (1900-1901): 175.

Philadelphia City Archives, Registration of Deaths [Herman Mudgett], 1896, No. 23640.

Philadelphia City Archives, Return of a Death in the City of Philadelphia, Physician's Certificate No. 23640 [Herman Mudgett].

"Remains of B.F. Perry," *Philadelphia Public Ledger*, September 4, 1894.

"Say the Checks are Forgeries [Article]," *Daily Inter Ocean*, October 6, 1893, 5.

"Shoemaker's Fate [William A. Shoemaker]," *Philadelphia Inquirer*, March 15, 1896, 1.

Smith, William B. *First Annual Message of William B. Smith, Mayor of Philadelphia with the Accompanying Documents, for the Year 1884* [Philadelphia City Hall]. Philadelphia, PA: Dunlap & Clarke,

Printers, 1885, i.

State of New Hampshire, Office of Registrar of Vital Statistics, Herman Webster Mudgett Birth Certificate.

"Tears Dim Holmes Eyes [Georgiana Yoke]," *Philadelphia Inquirer*, November 1, 1895, 1.

"The Emily Van Tassel Holmes Sensation [Emily Van Tassel]," *Hopkinsville Kentuckian*, August 27, 1895, 3.

The Evanston Rogers Park & Wilmette Directory [ABC Copier]. Evanston: Evanston Press Co, 1892, 419.

"The Execution of Holmes," *The Times*, May 8, 1896, 1.

The Miriam and Ira D. Wallach Division of Art, Prints and Photographs: Photography Collection, The New York Public Library. "Gilmanton Academy, Gilmanton, N.H., circa 1869" *New York Public Library Digital Collections*. Accessed September 21, 2016. http://digitalcollections.nypl.org/items/510d47e1-8c4c-a3d9-e040-e00a18064a99.

The Miriam and Ira D. Wallach Division of Art, Prints and Photographs: Photography Collection, The New York Public Library. "Mercantile Library, Philadelphia, Pa." *New York Public Library Digital Collections*. Accessed October 6, 2016. http://digitalcollections.nypl.org/items/510d47e0-a9f4-a3d9-e040-e00a18064a99

Toronto Public Library, Virtual Reference Library,[Albion Hotel, 1873], public domain, retrieved on October 5, 2016, http://www.virtualreferencelibrary.ca/detail.jsp?Entt=RDMDC-PICTURES-R-2477&R=DC-PICTURES-R-2477&searchPageType=vrl.

United States Patent and Trademark Office. Patent No. US000460181, B. F. Pitezel, Receptacle for Granular Substances [Benjamin Pitezel US Patent]. Patented September 29, 1891.

"Various Types of that Many-Sided Individual, H. H. Holmes," *Chicago Tribune*, November 25, 1894.

Watts, William B. And Eldridge, Benjamin P. *Our Rival, The Rascal* [Boston Chief Inspector Watts]. Boston, Massachusetts: Pemberton Publishing Company, 1897, i.

Wild, J. C. *Panorama and Views of Philadelphia and its Vicinity* [Moyamensing Prison], plate 9, Philadelphia, PA: J.T. Bowen, 1938.

"You Can't Read Character by the Eye [Smiling Marion Hedgepeth],"

The Ogden Standard, June 20, 1914.

MILLER IMAGES:
Benjamin Pitezel, circa 1888.
Marion Hedgepeth Booking Number 11,205.

Bibliography

"Among His Victims," *Chicago Tribune*, April 15, 1896.

"A Shroud of Stone," *Philadelphia Inquirer,* May 8, 1896.

"Angelo Bruno," *Wikipedia,* September 2, 2016, https:// en.wikipedia.org/ wiki/ Angelo_Bruno.

Bisel, George T. *The Trial of Herman W. Mudgett, alias, H. H. Holmes, for the Murder of Benjamin F. Pitezel.* Philadelphia: George T. Bisel, 1897.

Childs, Ward J. *"Crime, Criminals, Law Enforcement and Records (Part IV),"* City of Philadelphia Department of Records, retrieved September 28, 2016 at http://www.phila.gov/phils/docs/otherinfo/ newslet/crime5.htm.

"Confessions of H. H. Holmes, *Boston Herald,* April 12, 1896.

Corbitt, Robert L. *The Holmes Castle; A Story of H.H. Holmes' Mysterious Work.* Chicago, Ill: Corbitt & Morrison, 1895.

"Crimes of One Man," *The San Fransisco Call*, July 28, 1895.

"Deep Under Ground," *Philadelphia Inquirer,* May 9, 1896.

Ellis, Havelock. *The Criminal.* New York: Scribner & Welford, 1890.

"Folk Pardons Bandit Who Betrayed Holmes," *San Jose Mercury News*, July 9, 1906.

Geyer, Frank P. *The Holmes-Pitezel case; a history of the greatest crime of the century and of the search for the missing Pitezel children.* Philadelphia, PA: Publishers' Union, 1896.

"Ghost of H. H. Holmes," *Philadelphia Inquirer,* March 26, 1899.

"Hall Caine Visits Holmes," *Springfield Republican,* November 15, 1895.

"Hanged for Many Crimes," *The San Francisco Call,* May 8, 1896.

"Holmes Alleged Crimes," *New York Tribune,* July 27, 1895.

"Holmes' Confesses 27 Murders," *Philadelphia Inquirer*, April 12, 1896.

"Holmes Final Wish," *Philadelphia Inquirer,* May 5, 1896.

"Holmes History," *Plain Dealer Cleveland,* July 29, 1895.

"Holmes is Cheerful," *Philadelphia Inquirer,* April 11, 1896.

"Holmes Lied Then Died," *Indianapolis Journal,* May 8, 1896.

"Holmes 'Mascot' Found," *Los Angeles Harold,* April 12, 1896.

"Holmes Met Death Without a Tremor," *Philadelphia Inquirer*, May 8, 1896.

"Holmes Mother Loves Him," *Wichita Daily Eagle*, August 9, 1895.

Kirkland, Washington Bureau of Vital Statistics, FHL #2,022,644 [Carrie A. Van Arsdale].

Kirlin, Joseph Louis J. *Catholicity in Philadelphia; From the Earliest Missionaries Down to the Present Time*. Philadelphia, PA: John Jos. McVey, 1909.

Knox, Illinois Marriages, FHL # 1,412,063, Peter Van Arsdale and Carrie A. Pitezelle [sic].

Kreidler, W. A., ed. "*New Incorporations* [Campbell-Yates Company]," Western Electrician, vol. XI, no. 1-27, (1892).

Kress, Wilson C. and Allinson, Edward P. *Pennsylvania Superior Court Reports, Vol. 2, Containing Cases Adjudged in the Superior Court of Pennsylvania*. NY: Banks & Brothers, Law Publishers, 1897.

Larson, Erik. *Devil in the White City; Murder, Magic, and Madness at the Fair that Changed America*. New York: Vintage Books, a Division of Random House, Inc.

"Light on the Crimes," *Daily Inter Ocean*, July 30, 1895.

"Miss Cigrand's Father," *The San Francisco Call*, July 28, 1895.

"More Crimes Added," *Daily Inter Ocean*, July 25, 1895.

Moses, Adolph ed., *National Corporation Reporter*, Index to Vol. 10, (1895).

"Mrs. Pitezel Talks," *Philadelphia Inquirer*, May 8, 1896.

Mudgett, Herman W., M. D. *Holmes' Own Story*. Philadelphia, PA: Burke & McFetridge Co, 1895.

"Necrology," *The Michigan Alumnus*, Vol. VII, No. 57 [Robert Leacock death announcement], (1900-1901).

"New Victim is Emily Van Tassel," *Chicago Tribune*, July 28, 1895.

"Not in the Castle," *Daily Inter Ocean*, July 28, 1895.

Pennsylvania Courts. *District Reports of Cases Decided in All the Judicial Districts of the State of Pennsylvania During the Year 1896*, Vol. V., "Shoemaker's Case," Philadelphia, PA: 1896.

Pinkerton, William A. *Train Robberies, Train Robbers, and the "Holdup" Men* [Marion Hedgepeth]. Jamestown, VA: International Association Chiefs of Police, 1907.

Schechter, Harold. *Depraved; The Definitive True Story of H. H. Holmes, Whose Grotesque Crimes Shattered Turn-of-the Century Chicago*. New York: Pocket Star Books, a Division of Simon & Schuster, Inc., 1994.

"Shrewd to the Last," *Trenton Evening Times*, May 8, 1896.

"Signs a Deed as Notary Public," *Chicago Tribune*, July 25, 1895.

State of Colorado, Division of Vital Statistics, Marriage Record Report No. 16256, January 17, 1894.

"Still Another Victim," *The San Francisco Call*, July 29, 1895.

"Still Another Victim," *Indianapolis Journal*, July 29, 1895.

"Still Find Clews," *Daily Inter Ocean*, August 6, 1895.

Talbot, Eugene M. D., D. D. S. "H. H. Holmes," *The Journal of the American Medical Association*, Vol. XXVII, (1896).

"That Arch-Fiend Holmes," *The Sunday Herald*, August 4, 1895.

"The Confession of H. H. Holmes," *Daily Inter Ocean*, April 12, 1896.

"The Confession of H. H. Holmes [reprinted from the previous day with new info in disclaimer]," *Daily Inter Ocean*, April 13, 1896.

"The Emily Van Tassel Holmes Sensation [Emily Van Tassel]," *Hopkinsville Kentuckian*, August 27, 1895.

"The Holmes Confession," *Philadelphia Inquirer*, April 11, 1896.

"The Holmes Sensation," *Hopkinsville Kentuckian*, August 27, 1895.

"Two Letters From Holmes," *Indianapolis News*, July 29, 1895.

"Two Texas Girls," *The Galveston Daily News*, November 22, 1894.

"What His Confession Cost," *St. Albans Daily Messenger*, April 13, 1896.

Wild, J. C. *Panorama and Views of Philadelphia and its Vicinity*, plate 9, Philadelphia, PA: J.T. Bowen, 1938.

United States District Court, District of Minnesota, Passport Application for Lucy Theodate Holmes, October 15, 1918.

United States Patent and Trademark Office. Patent No. US000460181, B. F. Pitezel, Receptacle for Granular Substances [Benjamin Pitezel US Patent]. Patented September 29, 1891.

"Various Types of that Many-Sided Individual, H. H. Holmes," *Chicago Tribune*, November 25, 1894.

"Victims of a Fiend," *The Chicago Daily Tribune*, July 20, 1895.

Notes

To the Reader
1. Robert L. Corbitt. *The Holmes Castle; A Story of H.H. Holmes' Mysterious Work*. Chicago, Ill: Corbitt & Morrison, 1895.
2. Corbitt, 1895; "Light on the Crimes," *Daily Inter Ocean*, July 30, 1895, 2; and "Still Find Clews," *Daily Inter Ocean*, August 6, 1895, 2.
3. "The Holmes Confession," *Philadelphia Inquirer*, April 11, 1896, 6.
4. "Holmes is Cheerful," *Philadelphia Inquirer*, April 11, 1896, 1.
5. Harold Schechtor. *Depraved: The Definitive True Story of H. H. Holmes, Whose Grotesque Crimes Shattered Turn-of-the Century Chicago*. New York: Pocket Star Books, a Division of Simon & Schuster, Inc., 1994. [$7,500]; "What His Confession Cost," *St. Albans Daily Messenger*, April 13, 1896, 4 [$5,000]; "Holmes Lied then Died," *Indianapolis Journal*, May 8, 1896, 1 [$5,000]; "Hanged for Many Crimes," *The San Francisco Call*, May 8, 1896, 1 [$7,500]; "Holmes Confesses 27 Murders," *Philadelphia Inquirer*, April 12, 1896, 1, 8, 9, and 18; "Confessions of H. H. Holmes," *Boston Herald*, April 12, 1896, 12-13; and "The Confession of H. H. Holmes," *Daily Inter Ocean*, April 12, 1896, 1.
6. "The Confession of H. H. Holmes [reprinted from the previous day with new info in disclaimer]," *Daily Inter Ocean*, April 13, 1896, 1.

Holmes' Preface
7. His true initials were H. W. M., Herman Webster Mudgett.

Holmes' Own Story
8. Holmes was arrested in St. Louis by the Merrill Drug Company, on July 19, 1894, for fraud. During imprisonment in the St. Louis jail, he met Marion C. Hedgepeth, who later snitched on Holmes (whom he knew as Howard). Hedgepeth was said to have snitched because Holmes did not pay him for his help in providing the name of an attorney for Holmes insurance scheme. This ultimately led to Holmes arrest and conviction, a fact of which was a factor in influencing Governor Folk to pardon Marion Hedgepeth in 1906. George T. Bisel. *The Trial of Herman W. Mudgett, alias, H. H. Holmes, for the Murder*

of *Benjamin F. Pitezel*. Philadelphia: George T. Bisel, 1897, 609; and "Folk Pardons Bandit Who Betrayed Holmes," *San Jose Mercury News*, July 9, 1906, 7.

9. H. H. Holmes used his Howard alias while in prison with Hedgepeth.
10. Holmes' note: "The name he had assumed for the purpose of aiding me to organize our company," Herman W. Mudgett, M. D. *Holmes' Own Story*. Philadelphia, PA: Burke & McFetridge Co, 1895, 115.
11. Holmes' note: "Mrs. Pitezel's initials." Mudgett, 128.
12. Holmes' note: "Before going to Denver when he had felt so sure of carrying out the plan, I afterwards learned that he had spoken to one of his family about his sudden disappearance at any time not necessitating them to worry," Mudgett, 131.
13. Holmes' note: "At the time referred to a daily paper had stated that these lawyers were to act as my attorneys, and upon Pitezel's calling upon them, they had given him this card, and also directed him to the attorney they had recommended to me in the same street," Mudgett, 142.
14. Holmes' note: "The claim so persistently advanced that this note was a forgery is untrue; it was still in existence a short time ago, and if the prosecution will produce it the signature can speak for itself," Mudgett, 167.
15. Holmes' note: "In any instance, when not registering under my own name, my handwriting will substantiate my statements," Mudgett, 172.
16. Holmes' note: "At the risk of being tedious, I have entered into a minute description of our stay while in Toronto, especially as it applies to Saturday, the 19th, and Thursday, the 25th of October, as they seem vital dates in the case," Mudgett, 180.
17. Holmes' note: "The tacks used later to replace the portion removed were taken from the carpet in the room, and have been compared with those still there to make good my statement that here was where the mutilation of the trunk occurred," Mudgett, 205.
18. Holmes' note: "In answer to a recent question from the authorities, if, after Hatch had thus changed his appearance, he looked like myself, I answer, No, at least not to a sufficient extent to be mistaken for me by one who knew us both," Mudgett, 230.

The Tale of the Greatest Criminal in History

19. Dr. Eugene S. Talbot, MD, DDS, examined Holmes several times while in prison. In a report published in the *Journal of American Medical Association* (JAMA), Dr. Talbot thoroughly documented Holmes deformities indicating degeneracy. "Holmes, since his confinement, had no doubt lost flesh, which made these deformities appear more prominent. That they had developed as a result of his criminal tendencies is perfectly absurd," wrote Dr. Talbot. He explained that Holmes deformities must have developed with the osseous system, which would be complete by the time Holmes turned twenty-six. Eugene Talbot, MD, DDS, "H. H. Holmes," *The Journal of the American Medical Association*, Vol. XXVII, (1896), 253-257.
20. Hall Caine, a British novelist, visited Holmes in Moyamensing prison while he was in Philadelphia for other business. "Before I went there I hesitated some time, to satisfy myself that it was not morbid curiosity that took me...The interview affected me very much. After we talked a little the tears came to his [Holmes] eyes and his voice choked. That was too much for me, and I broke down and had to leave," said Caine during an interview reported by Springfield Republican. "Hall Caine Visits Holmes," *Springfield Republican*, November 15, 1895, 3.

Murders 3 and 4: Mrs. Julia L. Connor and Daughter, Pearl

21. H. H. Holmes wrote her last name as Connor in both *Holmes' Own Story* and his *Philadelphia Inquirer* confession.

Murder 11: Miss Emeline Cigrand

22. "Two Letters From Holmes," *Indianapolis News*, July 29, 1895, 1; and "Miss Cigrand's Father," *The San Francisco Call*, July 28, 1895, 3.
23. "Two Letters," 1.
24. "Two Letters," 1.
25. "Two Letters," 1.
26. "Holmes History," *Plain Dealer Cleveland*, July 29, 1895, 1.

Three Unsuccessful Attempts for Triple Murder

27. Prior to Holmes' published confession April 1896, when he admitted

to the attempted chloroforming of three women from Wisconsin, the *Los Angeles Herald* printed an article about two Wisconsin girl's who worked as waitresses at a restaurant Holmes ran under the name of H. H. Howard. A few nights after they began working at the restaurant, neighbors were startled by hysterical screams. Several men ran to the restaurant and at the same time, two girls dressed in their nightclothes, ran out of a hallway. After the girls calmed down, they said they were sleeping together and were awakened by a man who put a wet cloth, thought to be saturated with chloroform, over their faces. Neighbors took the girls in and cared for them until police came, but before police could arrest Holmes, he fled. "Holmes 'Mascot' Found," *Los Angeles Harold*, April 12, 1896, 27.

Murder 12: Miss Rosine Van Jassand

28. There was an Emily Van Tassel that matched Holmes' description in his confession, who vanished in 1893. *The Hopkinsville Kentuckian* reported, "To these must be added Miss Emily Van Tassel, who was employed in a candy store on Milwaukee Avenue, Chicago, where a man, supposed to be Holmes, made her acquaintance. After he had visited her a few times, she, too, disappeared, and has been seen no more. "The Holmes Sensation," *Hopkinsville Kentuckian*, August 27, 1895, 3.

Mrs. Van Tassel, Emily's mother, was interviewed by officials in 1895 and said they lived at 641 North Robey Street in Chicago. She told authorities Emily disappeared Wednesday, June 1, 1892. She was sixteen years old and a brunette with short, curly hair. At the time, Emily was employed as a cashier at Frank Wilde's fruit and candy store. Mrs. Van Tassel said Holmes took a fancy to Emily two or three weeks before she disappeared and had treated Emily to ice cream about four times. Mrs. Van Tassel met Holmes at the restaurant one time when he treated Emily to ice cream. On the Sunday before her disappearance, Emily was seen at Sunday school and was in her usual good spirits. Detectives showed Mrs. Van Tassel photos of Holmes and though her daughter introduced a man named Holmes to her, she could not positively identify Holmes three years later. "New Victim is Emily Van Tassel," *Chicago Tribune*, July 28, 1895, 2; and

"Crimes of One Man," *The San Fransisco Call*, July 28, 1895, 3.

Murder 16: Miss Kate Durkee

29. The *Chicago Tribune* reported in 1896, "Miss Kate Durkee of Omaha, whom Holmes says he killed, is very indignant at the allegation, and says she was never killed by Holmes or any one else." — "Among His Victims," *Chicago Tribune*, April 15, 1896.

Murder 19: A Female Boarder

30. *The San Francisco Call* interviewed Albert Phillips of Aurora, Illinois. He was the father of Clarence Phillips, who managed a restaurant in the Holmes building on Sixty-Third Street during the World's Fair. Albert Phillips assisted his son at the restaurant for several months and was confident that Holmes was responsible for the disappearance of a woman named Mrs. Lee who fit Holmes description in his confession. "The revelations in the case of Holmes make clear to me the mysterious disappearance of Mrs. Lee while I was at the restaurant. She went out of sight as completely and mysteriously as though she had fallen off the earth, and my son and I were greatly puzzled over it at the time," said Albert Phillips. "Still Another Victim," *The San Francisco Call*, July 29, 1895, 1.

"Mrs. Lee came to the place while I was there. She was a handsome brunette, tall and stately and well dressed. She often displayed banknotes of large denominations, claimed to be worth $60,000, and said that her husband and two children had died two years before…I studied Holmes well while at the restaurant, and knew him as a sleek, smooth rascal. I had evidence of his crooked business dealings daily…" - "Still Another," 1.

Murders 20 and 21: Minnie and Nannie Williams

31. Holmes took out several polices in the name of Campbell Yates Manufacturing Company to insure the castle, which totaled $60,000. Early in November 1893, the castle caught fire but insurance companies believed it to be incendiary. Investigators tailed Holmes and eventually located him in a hotel at the Plaza near Thirty-Eighth Street. He was living there with Minnie Williams, known by hotel

staff as Mrs. Holmes. Insurance investigators were unable to locate Campbell or Yates and the claims were eventually denied. "Victims of a Fiend," *The Chicago Daily Tribune*, July 20, 1895, 1.

Murder 24: Benjamin F. Pitezel
32. Haschisch is German for purified extract of hemp used as a hallucinogen.

Statement from Detective Geyer
33. "Two Letters From Holmes," *Indianapolis News*, July 29, 1895, 1.

Judgment Day - Thursday, May 7, 1896
34. "Holmes Met Death Without a Tremor," *Philadelphia Inquirer*, May 8, 1896, 1.
35. "Holmes Lied Then Died," *Indianapolis Journal*, May 8, 1896.1; and "Hanged for Many Crimes," *The San Francisco Call*, May 8, 1896.
36. "Holmes Lied," 1; and "Hanged for Many."
37. "Holmes Met," 1; Holmes Lied," 1; and "Hanged for Many."
38. "Holmes Met," 1; "Holmes Lied," 1; and "Hanged for Many."
39. "Holmes Met," 1; "Holmes Lied," 1; and "Hanged for Many."
40. "Holmes Met," 1.
41. "Holmes Lied," 1.

Mrs. Pitezel Interviewed
42. "Mrs. Pitezel Talks," *Philadelphia Inquirer*, May 8, 1896, 1. 43. "Mrs. Pitezel," 1.
44. "Mrs. Pitezel" 1; and "Shrewd to the Last," *Trenton Evening Times*, May 8, 1896, 4.
45. Knox, Illinois Marriages, FHL # 1,412,063, Peter Van Arsdale and Carrie A. Pitezelle [sic]; and Kirkland, Washington Bureau of Vital Statistics, FHL # 2,022,644 [Carrie A. Van Arsdale].

Concrete Burial - Friday, May 8, 1896
46. "A Shroud of Stone," *Philadelphia Inquirer*, May 8, 1896, 1.
47. "Holmes is Cheerful," *Philadelphia Inquirer*, April 11, 1896, 1
48. "Holmes is Cheerful," 1.
49. "A Shroud," 1; "Holmes Final Wish," *Philadelphia Inquirer*, May 5,

1896, 1; "Holmes Lied Then Died," *Indianapolis Journal*, May 8, 1896, 1; and "Deep Under Ground," *Philadelphia Inquirer*, May 9, 1896, 1.
50. "Holmes Lied," 1; and "Hanged for Many Crimes," *The San Francisco Call*, May 8, 1896, 1.
51. "Deep Under," 1.
52. "Deep Under," 1; and "A Shroud," 1.
53. "Deep Under," 1.
54. "Deep Under," 1; "A Shroud," 1; and "Holmes Lied," 1.
55. "Angelo Bruno," *Wikipedia*, September 2, 2016, https://en.wikipedia.org/wiki/Angelo_Bruno.

Holmes' Reincarnation?
56. Source for the entire reincarnation section: "Ghost of H. H. Holmes," *Philadelphia Inquirer*, March 26, 1899, 1.

Index

Page numbers in *italics* refer to photos and illustrations.

A
ABC Copier Company, 35, *38*
accidental death, 50, 54, 75, 99, 101, 238
Adrian, Michigan, 246
agent
   of baggage, 140
   of books, 21, 72
   of company, 81
   Holmes' as, 223
   of Holmes, 87, 88, 130, 178, 181, 217
   of insurance, 101
   of medical college, 227
   Pitezel and, 90-91
   of real estate, 138, 272
   of rental, 244
   of train, 246
alias, see Mudgett, Herman W.: Pitezel, Benjamin; Pitezel, Mrs.; and Williams, Minnie.
Albion Hotel, 137, *138*, 139-40, 249
Allcorn, Mrs. Actlia, 249
American Express Company, 132
ammonia, 63, 96
Ann Arbor, Michigan, 16, *20*, 21
Armstrong, Mr. (Holmes seen by), 246
arrest, 36
   of Hedgepeth, Marion, 78
   of Holmes, H. H., 31, 60, 76-77, 100, 152-54, 158, 217, 301
   of Howe, Jeptha (attorney), *84-85*
   of Pitezel, Benjamin, 68, *69*
      liable to, 75, 93
   of Pitezel, Mrs., 154
      liable to, 131
     Western Union message and, 62
     Yoke, Georgiana threatened with, 175
articulator of skeletons, 214, *264*
Ashbridge, Coroner Samuel H., 120, 249, 276
attempted murder
   of Pitezel, Mrs., 255
   of three girls, 304
attorney, 31, 46, 78, 85, 87, 100, 109, 111, 112-13, 125-26, 130, 162,

164, 169
Cops (or Copps), Mr. (Forth Worth), 179
Howe, Jeptha D., (fraudulent insurance) *84*, 114, 116-19, 121-23, 155, 244
Judge Harvey (Holmes' attorney), 78, 86, 110-11, 125
McDonald, Mr. (Howe's office), 244
Rotan, Samuel P. (Holmes' attorney), *189*, 277, 281, 284
    Shoemaker, William A. (Holmes attorney), 158, *161*
Aurora, Illinois, 179, 305
autopsy, 282

B
bail, 162
Bank of England notes, 88
Barlow, Mr. (Ass't District Attorney), 167, 169, 171, 176, 195, *265*
basement, 131
    Detroit house and, 246
    dynamite in, 255
    fruit and confectionery store and, 218
    Holmes' Castle and, 2, 26, 30, 224
    Honore Street house and, 234
    Pitezel, Alice and Nellie grave in, 250
    Pitezel, Mrs. house in, 150
    Williams, Minnie R. in, 230
Belknap, Myrta Z., (Holmes second wife), 3, 38-39
Belknap, Lucy T., (Myrta's mother), 107
benzine, 96, 98, 237-38
Bertillon system, 197
Betts, Miss Anna (victim fourteen), 221
bill of sale, 76
blistered hands, 15
body, 61, *102*, 227
    articulator and, 203, 208, 220
    buried and, 50, 174, 230-31, 234, 272, 282
    burned and, 104, 218
    in coffin, 228
    decomposed and, 22
    discovery of, 105, 117, 207, *243*
    dismembered/mutilated and, 168, 245
    examination of, 119, 238-39
    exhumation of, 118
    Holmes questioned about, 171
    identification of Pitezel, 113, 118-19, 168
    moved and, 55, 57-59, 104, 174, 199, 237

substitution and, 54-55, 59, 65, 72, 75-76, 79-80, 99-100, 114, 164
    in trunk, 174, 250
    in vault, 210
    boarder, 31
    wealthy female (victim nineteen), 228, 305
Boston, Massachusetts, 39, 46, 150-51, 153, 156, 229, 240
    Holmes' arrest in, 154, 158, 255
Bristol Hotel, 121
Brown, Mr. (Irvington house), 244
Bruno, Angelo "Gentle Don," 283
buried, 112, 145-46, 218
    Holmes, H. H. and, 282-84
    Perry, B. F. and, 113
    Pitezel, Benjamin F. and, 120, 239
    Pitezel, Howard and, 171, 174
    package and, 26
    Williams, Minnie R. and, 230-31
Burlington, Vermont, 16, 150-51, 153, 174, 176-77, 185, 255
burial permit, 283
burn, burned, burning, 15, 26, 41, 52, *94,* 101, 104, 146, 171, 230, 237, 245-46, 250, 272
business venture, 15, 21, 25, 31-32, 68, 74, 87, 90, 141, 226
Butcher, Dr. (at execution), 277

C
Caine, Hall (British novelist), 197
    broke down after prison visit, 303
Callowhill Street, 1316, Philadelphia, 90, 92-93, *94, 102-3,* 105, 168, 236, *242*
Campbell & Dowd office, 229
Campbell, William, 36
Campbell-Yates Co., 180, 182, *216,* 306
    Holmes' letter to Cigrand, Peter from, 212-13
Canada, 4, 131, *138,* 146, 183, *202,* 210, *254*
castle. *See* Holmes' Castle
Chamber of Commerce, Chicago, 65
Chandler (bought Holmes' Castle), 107
Chappell, M. G., 264. *See also* articulator of skeletons
checks, 183, 186, 224, 229-30
    forced to sign and, 226
    forgeries/fraud and, 69, 235
    gas machine and, 30
    worthless and, 68

Chicago, Illinois, 2, 21, 23-25, 29, 31, 35-36, 41, 53-54, 69, 71, 75, 86-87, 99, 121-22, 130, 180, 182, 222, 273
    medical college in, 54, 203
    Pitezel girls and, 126-27, 129, 246
    safe and vault company in, 180
    warehouse in, 109
    witness who saw Holmes in, 184, 246
    World Columbian Exposition in, 2, 46

Chicago Tribune, 305-06
chloroform, 2, 86, 97
    attempted attack with, 217, 304
    for Hedgepeth use of, 104
    Pitezel, Benjamin and, 96, 98, 104, 238, 240
    wealthy banker and, 227
    wealthy boarder and, 228

Cigrand, Dr. (Emeline's uncle), 213
Cigrand, Emeline (victim eleven), 37, 181-82, 211, *215*
    hair lock of, 214
    Holmes offered to marry, 211
    trunk of, 214

Cigrand, Peter, 212-13
Cincinnati, Ohio, 112-13, 120-21, 125-26, 172, 184
    Pitezel children argue in, 173

cipher, 96, 99, 169, 224, 239
Circle House, 122, 244
City Hall, Philadelphia, 99, 154, 158, *160*, 166-67, 171, 286
cleaning fluid, 95
coffin, 228
    broken handle and, 283
    concrete encased, 282-83

Cole, Charles (victim six), 183, 208
Colonel Bosbyshell, 113
Columbus, Mississippi, 76
conductor, 63-64, 144, 230
confession, *see* Holmes, H. H.
Conner, Miss Gertrude (victim fifteen), 35-36, 222
Connor, Julius L., 31, 35-36
Connor, Mrs. Julia L. (victim three), 2, 31, 204-205, 303
Connor, Pearl (victim four), 204, 206, 303
conspiracy charge, 155, 167
Cook, unborn baby (victim nine), 210
Cook, Frank, 210
Cook, Mrs. Sarah (victim eight), 174, 210
Cooke, Mr. (letter to), 174

Cops (or Copps), Mr. (Fort Worth attorney), 179, 230
Corbitt, Robert, 2
Coroner, 98, 119-20, 249, 276
    jury and, 100
      office and, 99, 118, 120
      physician and, 98, 238
Crawford, Thomas (detective), chained to Holmes, 154
creditors, 73
cremated, 26, 42, 171, 245
cries for mercy, 203, 238, 245
criminologist, 196-97
customs officer, 144-45

D

Daily, Father, 276-77
Daily Inter Ocean, 5, 107
Dartmouth College, New Hampshire, 16
Dearborn Street, Chicago, 32, 36, 224
death certificate, 3, 284
death warrant, 195
death watch, 85
Deering, Illinois station, 234
degenerate, 2, 197
Denison, Texas, 74
depraved, 237, 257
depressed (morose), 36, 75
Detroit, Michigan, 23, 69-70, 126, 133, 137, 171-73, 177
    Pitezel girls in, 130
    Pitezel, Mrs. in, 131
    spade bought in, 173
    trunk from, 140
      shovel in, 145
Devil in the White City, The (Larson), 2
disinterred, 117-18, 120
District Attorney, *see* Graham, George
doctor, 2, 23, 119, 168
    child yelled in pharmacy for, 24
    examined Holmes and, 197, 302
    Gilmanton village of, 11
draft (s), 42, 68, 124, 186, 226
Drexel & Company, 88
drugstore, 23-25, 31, 63, 76, 180, 221, 245
Duncombe, D. F., 234
Dunkee, Mary, 183

Dunkee, Miss Kate, *see* Durkee, Miss Kate
Durkee, Miss Kate (victim sixteen), 183, 223, 305
Dwight, Illinois, 211
dynamite, 255

E
Elverson, James Jr., 4-5, 195
encumbrance, 71, 74
engineer killed, 64
Englewood, Illinois, 50, 52, 107, 183, 210
Englewood Jewelry Company, 31, 180, 303
Englewood Post Office, 107
English's Hotel, 122
estate
    of Williams family, 46, 235
    of Yoke, 272
examination, 54, 97, 118-20, 168, 238-39
executed document, 46, 73, 125
excavation, 131, 170, 218, 220, 246
explosion, 79, 98, 181, 238

F
F. W. Devoe and Company, New York, 183
faked death, 4, 54
Fallon, Thomas, 25
falsifier, *see* liar
Ferro-cyanide of potassium, 218
Fidelity Mutual Insurance Association, 65-66, 79, 81, 113, 116-18,
    120, 153, *157*, 165, 167, 175-76, 196, 238-39, 244, *270*, 276
Fidelity Warehouse, Chicago, 24, 26, 109
fire, 93-94, 108, 180-81, 230, 301
fleas, eaten by, 75
Folk, Governor Joseph W., 296
foreclosure, 107
forgery, 181, 302
Fouse, Levi G. (Fidelity Mutual President), 116-19, 176, *270*, 276
Frank Wilde's fruit and candy store, 181, 218, 304-5
fraud, 21, 24, 30, 72-73, 101, 110, 113, 123, 153, 168, 227, 231, 301
funeral, 41, 282-83

G
gallows, 85, 276, 280-81
Galva, Illinois, 125-26, 281
Geyer, Detective Frank P., 169-70, 196, 240, 272, *273-74*, 276

Gilmanton Academy, New Hampshire, 11, *18*
Gilmanton village, New Hampshire, 12-14
    doctor in, 11
    farmer in, 15
    wagon maker in, 12
Gilmanton, New Hampshire, 3
Gilmer House, 76
Globe Democrat and Chronicle, 79, 105
gold watch, 13
Goldthwaite, Charles, 229
Governor Joseph W. Folk, 301
Graham, District Attorney George S., 167, 169, 175-79, 199, *266*
Grand Rapids, Michigan, 57, 62, 64, 199
Grand Rapids Station, 58, 63
grave, 250, 272, 282-83
    robbers, Holmes concern of, 282
graveyard, grave yard, grave-yard, 21, 120, 239
Grew, Sheriff Solicitor William, 276
gruesome relics, 85
gun barrel, 60, *see also* pistol

H

hallucinogen, 306
Hamilton, Ontario Canada, 140, 144, 146, 179, 183, 210
handcuffs, handcuffed, 60, 77, 170, 178
handwriting, 117, 182, 214, 234, 239, 246, 302
Haracamp, Miss Mary (victim ten), 210
Hartford, Connecticut, 132
Hartford Insurance Company, 234
haschisch, 236, 306
Hatch, Edward (*alias,* alter ego of Holmes), 4, 122, 129, 132, 139, 145-46, 169, 171-74, 178-79, 185, 302
    presents to children, 173
    Holmes, H. H., admits Hatch is *alias,* 229
    mythical person and, 176-77, 179, 229, 272-73
    shovel and, 131, 133, 145
    took charge of Pitezel children and, 4, 121, 126-27, 130, 133, 137, 139, 141, 142-44
    Williams, Minnie R. and, 46, 52-53, 70, 120, 126, 133, 137, 140, 141, 142, 172, 184
Hearst, William Randolph, 4-5, 195
hemp extract, 306
Hedgepeth, Marion C., (notorious criminal, jailhouse snitch) 77, *82, 83,* 104

letter of, 78-81
pardon of, 301
Henry, John (keeper at prison), 276
Hitt, Issac. R. & Company, 43, 235
Holmes' Castle, 2, *106-7*, 203-4, 208, 210, 213-14, 218, 226, 228, 230, *258-60*, 306
    basement in, 2, 26, 30, 218, 224
    blood in, 2
    carbolic acid, bottle in, 2
    death in, 105, 179, 183, 199, 203, 208-11, 223-24, 226
    drug store in, 221
    false safe in, *260*
    fire at, 108, 180-81, 230, 306
    gas oven in, *261*
    gas tank in, *263*
    hair in stove pipe at, 2, 214
    human ribs at, 2
    jewelry store in, 31, 180, 303
    pearl buttons at, 2
    restaurant in, 42, 209, 217, 228, 304
    secret room in, 226
    stove in, 2, 42, 52, *260*
    trap door in, 2, *262*
    vault in, 2, 179-80, 209-11, 223, 230
Holmes, H. H. *9-10*
    aliases, see Mudgett, Herman W., *alias*
    arrest of, 31, 56-57, 60, 62, 73, 76-77, 86-87, 100, 110, 124-26, 131, 152-54, 158, 162, 164, 172, 174, 187, 197, 217, 227, 231, 239, 245-46, 255, 281, 296, 299, 301
    birth of, 11, 17-18, 166
    bought drug store and, 25, 76, *see also* drugstore
    burial of, 282-85
    childhood and adolescence of, 11-16
    confession of, 3-5, 191, *192, 194,* 195-96, 257, 272, 304-05
    conviction of, 301
    daughter (Holmes, Lucy Theodate), 3
    death, execution of, 276-280
    diploma of, 21
    doctor examination of, 197, 302
    druggist exam of, 25
    education and training of, 16, 21, 165
    employment of, 16, 21-22, 23-24, 25, 31, 79, 223
    father and use of rod, 11
    first business venture of, 15

first dishonest act of, 21
  forged William's name and, 235
  friends, 8, 13-14, 16, 20, 22-24, 53-55, 65-66, 88-89, 101, 185, 199
    sarcasm by Holmes about, 58-59, 62-64
  last meal of, 276
  letters by, 15, 32, 42, 139, 148, 151, 162, 164, 166, 212-13, 237, 25
  long-headed and, 272
  handwritten statement by, 7, 191-92
  medical degree of, *20*, 21
  medical symptoms since arrest, 197, 302
  mother of, 14, 148-49, 167
  ran into Mrs. Pitezel at store, 142-43, 250
  reincarnation of, 286-87
  religious beliefs of, 276
  sense of humor of, 154, 181
  son, (Mudgett, Robert Lovering), 3, 5
  speech delivered by, 277
  substitute body in place of, 54
  temper, anger of, 124, 175
  thumb screws applied to, 154
  wander through swamps, Pitezel and, 75
  weight loss of, 164, 302
  wives of
    Belknap, Myrta Z., 3
    Lovering, Clara, A., 3
    Yoke, Georgiana, *see* Yoke, Georgiana
  see also Mudgett, Herman W.
Holmes, Lucy Theodate (Holmes' daughter), 3
Holy Communion, 276
Holy Cross Cemetery, 283
Honore Street house, 234
horses, 22, 74, 245
    stolen (encumbered) horses and, 74
    arrested/charged with stealing, 153
Howard, H. H., 304, *see also* Mudgett, Herman: *alias*
Howard, H. M., 78-80, *see also* Mudgett, Herman: *alias*
Howe, Jeptha (Mrs. Pitezel's attorney), 79-81, *84*, 85, 169, 244
human remains, 23, 171, 174-75, 203, 218, *see also* body
humiliation, 162, 164

I
ice in bathtub, 59

identification marks, of Pitezel, 117-19, *see also* Pitezel, Benjamin
Imperial Hotel, Canada, 146
imprisonment, 13, 73, 77, 86, 155, 168, 301, *see also* arrest
Indianapolis, Indiana, 105, 112, 120-22, 126, 130, 172, 174, 177, 184, 234, 244, 246
Indianapolis News, 212-13, 272
inmate, 5, 74
Inspector Watts, *see* Watts, William
insurance, 22-24, 35, 53, 65-66, 72, 74-76, 78-79, 81, 84, 87-89, 92, 99-101, 110, 112-13, 116-18, 120-21, 123-26, 153, 165-68, 175-76, 181, 186, 199, 203, 220, 235-36, 238-39, 244, 296, 301
    agent and, 101
Inter Ocean, Chicago, 5, 107
intoxication, *see* Pitezel, Benjamin: intoxication
iron cage, 77
Irvington Cottage, *248*
Irvington drug store, 245
Irvington, Indiana, 230, 244-46

J
jail, 76-77, *163*, 301
Jones, F. L., 234
Judd, John L., 181
Judge Hare, 167
Judge Harvey, 78, 86, 110-11, 125
jurors, jury, 100, 167-68, 240, 276

K
Kansas, 29, 75
Kirk, Arthur S., 182
Kirk & Company, 182
Kirkland, Washington, 281
Knox, Illinois, 281

L
Lafayette, Indiana, 182, 212
lameness, 12
lancet, 119
Larson, Erik, 2
Lasher, Mr., of Stock Exchange Building, 234
Latimer, Robert (victim thirteen), 183, 220
laudanum, 199
Lawrence, Dr. and Mrs. Maurice B., 214
Lawrence Street, 1609, Denver, 181

Leacock, Dr. Robert Charles (victim one), *20*, 199, *201-2*
Leadville, Colorado, 41, 235
Lee, Mrs. (possible victim), 181, 306
Leffmann, Dr., Philadelphia, (statement about chloroform), 240
Les Miserables, 85
liens, 73
Linden, Superintendent Robert J., Philadelphia Police, 122, 124, 154, 176, 178
Link Belt Engineering Company, 90
Lizzie (domestic, victim seven), 183, 209
loan, 25, 29, 71, 73-74, 76, 107, 112, 131
London, England, 70, 141, 144, 169, 181
Los Angeles Herald, *304*
Lovering, Clara (Holmes' legal wife), 3
Lowell, Massachusetts, 151, 153
Lyman, Benton T., *see* Pitezel, Benjamin: *alias* Lyman, Benton

M

Mascot (Holmes' friend), 71, 73-74
Maxwell, John M., 235
McDonald, Mr. (attorney), 244
McPeak, Father, 276
medicine, 11, 50
    fatal dose and, 24, 245
Mercantile Library, Philadelphia, 93, *95*
Merrill Drug Company, 301
metempsychosis, *see* reincarnation
Michigan, 20-21, 35, 57, 64, *202*, 212
Michigan Ave, 6342 South, 81
Michigan, Lake, 51
Milwaukee Avenue candy store, 304
Milwaukee, Wisconsin, 52-53, 184, 217, 227, 246
missing children, 4, 169, *see also* Pitezel, Alice; Howard; and Nellie
Mississippi River, 75
Mobile, Alabama, 76
Momence, Illinois, 230
Mooers Forks, New York, 22
Moon, R. O. (Holmes' attorney), 167
moral degenerate, *see* degenerate
Moreman, Mr. (last to see Howard Pitezel alive), 245
morose, *see* depressed
motive, 4, 31, 40, 42, 164-65, 171-72, 180, 185-87, 196, 231
Moyamensing Prison, 158, *159*, 169, 178, 187, 276, *280*, 303
Mudgett, Herman W., *7, 9*, 11, *17*, *20*, 31, *193*, 283, *285-86*, 300

(note: *aliases* listed below are not a complete list, but are aliases listed within this book):
   alias Hatch, Edward. *See* Hatch, Edward
   alias Holmes, H. H. (primary alias) *See* Holmes, H. H.
   alias Howard, H. H., 299
   alias Howard, H. M., 78-80, 249
Mudgett, Robert Lovering (Holmes' son), 3, 5
Mullen, Mr. (undertaker assistant), 283
Murder Castle, *see* Holmes' Castle
mutilation, 100, 302

N

National Typewriter Exchange, Chicago, 181, 211
neglected, negligence, 31, 63, 76, 126, 213
New Baltimore, Michigan, 199
New England, 40-41,
New England Village, 11
New York, 21-25, 41, 43, 87-90, 120-21, 124, 150, 177, 183, 229, 236, 282
New York Morning Journal, 4-5
newspaper in-fighting, 5
Niagara Falls, 140-43, 146-47, 249
nitroglycerine, *see* dynamite
Norristown Asylum, Philadelphia, 24
notary public, 223, 234

O

odor, 26, 42, 58, 63, 95-96, 171
Ogdensburg, New York, 145, 250, 255
Olive Street, 520, Philadelphia, 79
O'Rourke, Undertaker, 276, 282-83

P

Palmer House, 140-41, 143-46, 227
patent 72, 87, 89-90, 92, 98, 187, 224, 226, 239
   see also Pitezel, Benjamin: patent
Pennsylvania Railroad, 90
Perkins, Superintendent (Moyamensing Prison), 5, 276
Perkinsville, Alabama, 76
Perry, B. F, *see* Pitezel, Benjamin: *alias;* Perry, B. F.; and buried: Perry, B. F.
Perry, Ophir La Forrest, 118, 153, *157*, 176, 196, 249
pharmacy, *see* drugstore
Phelps, Robert E., 213

Philadelphia City Hall, 99, 154, 158, *160*, 166-67, 171, 286
Philadelphia Inquirer, 2, 4-5, 196, 257, 272, 303
    Holmes' handwritten denial, *192*
    Holmes' handwritten statement *191*
Philadelphia Police Department, 124
Phillips, Albert (father of Phillips, Clarence), 305-6
Phillips, Clarence (managed restaurant at Holmes' Castle), 305
photographic identification, 4, 183-85
Pinkerton detective, 153, *156*, 283
pistol, shot into air, 61
Pitezel, Alice (victim twenty-six), 4, 112-14, *115-16*, 118, 120-21,
    130, 133, 137, *138*, 142-44, 173-74, 240, *251, 253*
    death of, 249-51
    identified papa's teeth and, 120
    sickly and, 250
Pitezel, Benjamin F. (victim twenty-four), 2-4, 8, *27-28*, 30, 32, *34*,
    36, 52-53, 65-66, 68-71, 73-76, 79-80, 84, 87, 89-90, *94*,
    96-97, 100, 102, 105, 109-114, 117-18, 126, 153-55, 164,
    167-68, 186, 236-40, *241-43, 241-43*, 297
    alias Lyman, Benton T. of, 70-71, 74, 154
    alias B. F. Perry of, 89-90, 105, 112-13, 243
    arrest of, 68, *69*
        liable to arrest of, 75
    attempted suicide and, 76, 99
    death of, 29, 96-101, *102-3*, 105, 110-12, 164, 167-68, 236-41
    description of, 113
    employment, work of, 29-30, 32, 36, 65, 68, 70, 73, 87, 117-18
    expiration of insurance of, 89
    identification marks on body of, 117-19
    identification of, 113, 118-19, 168
    insurance of, *see* insurance
    intoxication of, 22, 36, 39, 71, 74, 90, 237-38
    Holmes sold rights, title, interest to, 76
    married another woman and, 71
    patent of, 32, *33-34*
    Sellers, Col. (nickname) and, 72
    sick and, 76
    wander through swamps, Holmes and, 75
Pitezel, Jeanette 'Dessie,' 106, 144, *163*
Pitezel, Horton, 4, 144, *163*, 281
Pitezel, Howard (victim twenty-five), 4, 121, 126-27, *128-29*, 130,
    137, 142, 144, 173, *247-48*, 272
    death of, 244-46
Pitezel, Mrs. Carrie Alice, 4, *67*, 81, 84, 89, 99, 105-6, 109-12, 114,

121, 126, 131-33, 136, 139-42, 144, 151, 164, 172, 174, *256*
   arrested and, 154, *163*
   attempted murder of, 217, 255
   court and, 168
   death of, 281
   Holmes disclosed location of, 153
   Holmes broken promise to, 281
   Holmes wished to provide bail for, 162, 165, 167
   insurance settlement and, 84, 125
   Philadelphia Inquirer interview of, 280-81
   ran into Holmes at store, 142-43, 250
   remarriage of, 281
   use as alibi by Holmes, 177
   visited parents and, 122
   Yoke, Georgiana seen for first time by, 154
Pitezel, Nellie (victim twenty-seven), 4, 121, 133, *134-35*, 137, *138*, 144, 173, *252*
   death of, 249-51, *253-54*
   post mortem exam of, 238
post office, postoffice, post-office, 89, 93, 107, 137, 139-40, 142, 150-51, 230
   Dead Letter Office, 181
Powell & Harter office, 246
Presbyterian Hospital, Chicago, 43
priests, 276-77
prison, 4-5, 8, 13, 71, 74, 77-78, 85-86, 155, 158, *159*, 162, *163*, 164-65, 169, 171, 175-76, 178, 181, 188, 191, 276, *278*, *280*, 282, 286, 297-98
   mail delivery and, 150
   see also Moyamensing Prison
psalm Miserere, 276

Q
Quinlan, Cora, 181
Quinlan, Patrick (janitor at Holmes' castle), 35, 50, *268-70*
   paid attention to Lizzie and, 209

R
reincarnation, 286-87
reward, 16
Richard (Holmes' neighbor), 14
Richardson, Assistant Superintendent, 276-77
Robey Street, 641 North, Chicago, 304
Rodgers, Mr. (witness), 145

Rodgers, Mr. (victim five), 207
Rogers, Mr. (victim eighteen), 226-27
Rose, William H., 107-8
Rotan, Samuel P. (Holmes' attorney), 166, *189*, 277, 281-82
Russell, Dr. (victim two), 203

S
Sanforth, Mr. (Chicago lawyer), 25
Saybolt, Deputy Sheriff, 277
scaffold, 276, *277*, *280*
Secret Service, 57, 63
    Holmes showed dead body to, 61
    Holmes fired weapon and, 61
    points weapon at Holmes and, 60
self defense, 235
Sharp, Dr. (at execution), 277
sharpen, long knives, 245
skeleton, 11, 214
Shoemaker, William A. (Holmes' attorney), 158, *161*, 166-67
shooting, 235
shovel, 131, 133, 145
Smith, Mr. (witness), 118, 239
solitary confinement, 158, 257
South America, 73
Southern Lumber Company, 74
spade, 145-46, 173, 250
St. Joseph, Michigan, 179
St. Louis, Missouri, 29, 71, 73-74, 76, 78, 89, 91-93, 100, 105, 112, 114, 120-22, 124-26, 131, 244, 301
steamboat landing, 177
stiff dealer, 217, 234
Stubbin's Hotel, 121
subpoena, 168
suffocation, 179, 209
Superintendent Linden, *see* Linden, Superintendent Robert J.

T
Talbot, Dr. Eugene S. (Holmes' doctor in prison), 302
Taylor, Dr. Reverend, 210
teacher, teaching, 14-16, 22, 41, 112, 148
telegram, 46, 58, 80, 121, 139
    Holmes wrote to himself and, 143
    Yoke, Georgiana requested by, 174
Terre Haute, Indiana, 68, *69*, 70, 75

testimony, 120, 168, 185, 239, 249
    Holmes and trivial case, 31
    Toronto inquest and, 138, 145
Thompson, Dr., Irvington, Indianapolis, 244
Thompson's (restaurant), 182
Tolman, Dr., Chicago, 235
Tombigbee River, 75
Toronto depot, 140
Toronto, Canada, 96, 133, 137, *138*, 140-43, 145-46, 151, 173-74, 177, 179, 249-50, *253-54*, 273, 302
    children found dead in, 170
torture, 2, 211, 237, 246
train crash, 41
trial, 8, 78, 162, 166-68, 195-96, 199, 207, 209, 239, 246, 249, *267*
Trilby, by George du Maurier, 166
trunk, 57, 65, 129, 131-33, 140, 144-46, 150, 152, 173, 237, 302
    body and, 58, 62-64, 174
    Cigrand, Emeline and, 214
    lead pipe and, 59
    Pitezel girls and, 126, 249-51, *253*
    Pitezel, Howard and, 245-46
    water-proof and, 55
    threatened expressman and, 56
    Williams, Minnie and, 179
    Williams, Nannie and, 51-52

U

unknown Chicago man (victim twenty-two), 234
University of Michigan, *20*, 22
University of Vermont, 16
unsuccessful triple murder
    Los Angeles Herald article about, 304

V

Van Arsdale, Peter (Pitezel, Mrs. second husband), 281
Van Jassand, Rosine, *see* Van Tassel, Emily
Van Tassand, Rosine, *see* Van Tassel, Emily
Van Tassel, Emily (victim twelve), 218, 304
Van Tassel, Mrs. (Emily's mom), 304
vaporous fumes, 98
Vincent Street house, 138, 145, 147, 249-50, *254*

W

Walker house, 133, 136-37, 139-40, 146

Warner Glass Bending Company, 32, 224
Warner, Mr. (victim seventeen), 224, *225*
Washington Life Company, 66
Watts, William B (Pinkerton agency), 152-53, *156*
Williams, Baldwin (victim twenty-third), 235
    estate of, 46, 235
Williams, Minnie R. (victim twenty-one), 2, 8, 36, 42-44, 46-47, 49-53, 68, 70, 88, 112, 120-22, 126, 130, 133, *136*, 137, 140-45, 162, 164, 166, 169, 171-74, 177, 179-81, 184-86, 229-31, *232*, 235, 240-41, 301
    accused sister of stealing husband (Holmes) and 49
    alias Adele Covell, 41
    as Mrs. Holmes, 306
    cipher and, 169
    death of, 229-231, 241
    estate of her brother, 46, 235
    first met Holmes and, 36
    Hatch, Edward and, 46, 52, 126, 133, 137, 141, 172, 177, 184
    Holmes claim, advertisement to, 166
    Holmes claim, letters to, 162
    illness of, 43, 47
    laughed at Holmes by, 179
    massage establishment and, 140
    office duties, 42
    Pitezel girls and, 141-45, 164, 184
    Pitezel, Howard and, 130, 172-73
    screamed to Holmes and, 47
    threatened Holmes and, 171
    Wilmette property accounting, 186
Williams, Nannie (victim twenty), 41, 44, *45*, 47, *48*, 49, 185, *233*
    death of, 47, 49-51, 229-231
    footprint of, 230
    trunk of, 52, 179
Wilmette, Illinois, 43, 70, 107, 186
World's Fair, 42, *see also* Chicago, Illinois, World Columbian Exposition
Wright, John L. (real estate agent), 272
Wrightwood Ave., 1220, Chicago, 44, 229

Y

Yeadon, Pennsylvania, 283
Yoke, Georgianna (Holmes third wife), 4, 69, 89, 90-91, 100, 105, 162, *188*, 122, 130, 133, 136-37, 140-42, 144-45, 151, 153, 166, 174, 177-78, *267*

    brought flowers to Holmes and, 166
    brought by District Attorney to see Holmes and, 17
    estate of, 272
    Holmes disclosed why arrested to, 152
    illness and, 154, 158
    letter to Holmes from, 165
    met Pitezel, Mrs. and children for first time, 154
    subpoena to appear and, 168
    visited Holmes in prison and, 154, 156, 162-63
Yoke, Mrs. (Georgiana's mom), 272
Ypsilanti, Michigan, 132

Other Books by This Author

On the web:
jdcrighton.com
Twitter: @jdcrighton
Instagram: @jdcrighton
FB: jdcrightonauthor
Pinterest: jdcrighton

Email:
jd@jdcrighton.com

www.ingramcontent.com/pod-product-compliance
Lightning Source LLC
Chambersburg PA
CBHW071558080526
44588CB00010B/942